LAW AGAINST GENOCIDE

Cosmopolitan Trials

David Hirsh

Patricia Chinkumolina.

London • Sydney • Portland, Oregon

First published in Great Britain 2003 by
The GlassHouse Press, The Glass House,
Wharton Street, London WC1X 9PX, United Kingdom
Telephone: + 44 (0)20 7278 8000   Facsimile: + 44 (0)20 7278 8080
Email: info@cavendishpublishing.com
Website: www.cavendishpublishing.com

Published in the United States by The GlassHouse Press, Cavendish Publishing
c/o International Specialized Book Services,
5824 NE Hassalo Street, Portland,
Oregon 97213-3644, USA

Published in Australia by The GlassHouse Press
c/o Cavendish Publishing (Australia) Pty Ltd
3/303 Barrenjoey Road, Newport, NSW 2106, Australia

© Hirsh, D 2003

The GlassHouse Press is an imprint of Cavendish Publishing Limited

British Library Cataloguing in Publication Data
Hirsh, David
Law against genocide: cosmopolitan trials
1 Genocide
I Title
341.7'78

Library of Congress Cataloguing in Publication Data
Data available

ISBN 1-904385-04-4

1 3 5 7 9 10 8 6 4 2

Printed and bound in Great Britain

This book is dedicated to my children

Dora Poulot Hirsh
and
Edouard Hans Solomon Hirsh

Acknowledgments

Thank you to the people at the *Sociological Review*. They gave me their fellowship of 2001–02 at Keele University, which supported me financially while I wrote this book. The only thing they asked in return was that I use the time to develop myself as a writer and to produce this work. Amazing that such a thing still exists: academic funding for its own sake.

Thank you to Robert Fine, to whom I owe a considerable debt, both personal and academic, for the help, inspiration, advice and support that he has given me over many years. He ought to be more generally recognised as one of the most profound contemporary social theorists. Everything good in this book has something to do with Robert. Chapter Two was written jointly with him.

Thank you to Beverley Brown at GlassHouse. How much nicer to be found by a publisher than to find a publisher. Her help and advice were much appreciated, and made this a better book; also to Sanjeevi Perera, for her detailed editing.

Thank you to Alison Diduck for reading an early draft and giving me the confidence to finish it.

Thank you to Stephan Feuchtwang who, as well as teaching me at City University, has subsequently been interested in my work and ideas, and has taken time to discuss and clarify them with me.

Thank you to David Seymour for his encouragement, help and friendship; Max Seymour too.

Thank you to Margaret Archer, Jim Beckford and Peter Wagner who taught me at Warwick University, and to John Cowley who taught me at City University. Thanks are also due to Gillian Rose who taught me at Warwick while she was dying of cancer.

Thank you to Adam Keller and Beate Zilversmidt, who star in Chapter One, for inspiration. It is not easy to fight for a cosmopolitan politics in Tel Aviv. They produce *The Other Israel*, available from POB 2542, Holon 58125, Israel (otherisr@actcom.co.il).

Thank you to my mum and dad, Mirjam and Julian, and to my sisters, Deborah and Judy, for their support and for making me who I am.

Thank you to Fella, Fischel, Rushka and Yidl, members of my family who survived the Holocaust and told their stories.

Thank you, above all, to Alexandra, my wife, for her warmth, energy and love. She has worked very hard so that I could write this book.

David Hirsh
March 2003

Contents

Abbreviations

BNP	British National Party
FLN	Front de Libération Nationale (National Liberation Front)
HV	Army of the Republic of Croatia
HVO	Army of the Bosnian Croats
ICJ	International Court of Justice
ICC	International Criminal Court
ICTR	The International Criminal Tribunal for the Prosecution of Persons Responsible for Genocide and Other Serious Violations of International Humanitarian Law Committed in the Territory of Rwanda and Rwandan Citizens Responsible for Genocide and Other Such Violations Committed in the Territory of Neighbouring States, between 1 January 1994 and 31 December 1999
ICTY	The Ad Hoc International Criminal Tribunal for the Prosecution of Persons Responsible for Serious Violations of International Humanitarian Law Committed in the Territory of the former Yugoslavia since 1991
IMTFE	International Military Tribunal for the Far East
JNA	Yugoslav National Army
KGB	Committee for State Security ((post-war) name of NKVD)
KLA	Kosovo Liberation Army
NA	National Alliance
NATO	North Atlantic Treaty Organisation
NKVD	People's Commissariat for Internal Affairs
RSHA	Head Office for Reich Security
SA	Sturm Abteilung (stormtroopers founded in 1922; an elite formation of the Nazi party later to be eclipsed by the SS)
SDA	Muslim Party of Democratic Action
SDS	Political party of the Bosnian Serbs
SS	Schutzstaffel (protection squad; Hitler's bodyguards, Nazi party police and later the most 'racially pure' elite guard of the Third Reich)
TO	Bosnian Territorial Defence
UN	United Nations
UNHCR	United Nations High Commission for Refugees
UNPROFOR	United Nations Protection Force
WVHA	Head Office for Administration and Economy

Abbreviated cases

Demjanjuk case	*Ivan (John) Demjanjuk v State of Israel*, Criminal Appeal 347/88 (special issue) at 395396, summarised in English in (1994) 24 Israel Yearbook of Human Rights 323
Eichmann case	*Attorney General of the Government of Israel v Eichmann* (1961) 36 ILR 5
Irving v Lipstadt/Irving case	*Irving v Penguin Books Limited, Deborah E Lipstadt* [2000] EWCH QB 115
Prosecutor v Blaskic/Blaskic case	*Prosecutor v Blaskic*, Case No IT-95-14-PT, ICTY, Judgment, 3 March 2000, www.un.org/icty/blaskic/trialc1/judgement/index.htm
Prosecutor v Kordic and Cerkez	*Prosecutor v Kordic and Cerkez*, Case No IT-95-14/2, ICTY, Judgment, 26 February 2001, www.un.org/icty/kordic/trialc/judgement/index.htm
Prosecutor v Kristic	*Prosecutor v Kristic*, Case No IT-98-33, ICTY, Judgment, 2 August 2001, www.un.org/icty/krstic/TrialC1/judgement/index.htm
Prosecutor v Kunarac, Kovac and Vukovic	*Prosecutor v Kunarac, Kovac and Vukovic*, Case No IT-96-23, ICTY, Judgment, 22 February 2001, www.un.org/icty/foca/trialc2/judgement/index.htm
Prosecutor v Tadic/Tadic case	*Prosecutor v Dusko Tadic*, Case No IT-94-1, ICTY, Appeals Chamber, 2 October 1995, www.un.org/icty/tadic/appeal/decision-e/51002.htm
	Prosecutor v Dusko Tadic, Case No IT-94-1, ICTY, Judgment, 7 May 1997, www.un.org/icty/tadic/trialc2/judgement/index.htm
Sawoniuk case	*R v Sawoniuk* (2000) Cr App R 220
Zundel case	*Zundel* case [1992] 2 SCR 731

Introduction

On 28 January 2000, I was at the Royal Courts of Justice in the Strand, in London. Outside the building was a large, angry, noisy demonstration consisting mainly of Chileans, displaying hundreds of photographs of individuals who had been murdered by the Pinochet regime. Augusto Pinochet was attending an appeal by the Kingdom of Belgium against the British Home Secretary's decision that, due to his poor health, the General was unfit to stand trial for crimes against humanity. Upstairs in the same building, judges were hearing the unsuccessful appeal of Andrei Sawoniuk against his conviction for the murder of Jews in Belorus during the Holocaust. And in Court 73 there was a gathering of Jews, historians, Nazis and journalists watching the *Irving v Lipstadt* libel trial. In the *Pinochet* case the court confirmed the principle of universal jurisdiction for crimes against humanity and torture. In the *Sawoniuk* case the court upheld the conviction of a man for crimes committed as part of a genocide in another country. In the *Irving* case the court produced a long, closely argued judgment that placed the propaganda of David Irving outside what may be properly referred to as historiography. On that sunny winter's day in London, it felt as though something interesting was happening.

On the same day, there were crimes against humanity trials being routinely heard by international courts in The Hague, in relation to ethnic cleansing in the former Yugoslavia, and in Arusha, in relation to the genocide in Rwanda. In recent years there have been trials, and campaigns for trials, in many countries that were occupied by the Nazis; also in Cambodia in relation to the genocide there; in South East Asia in relation to the organised mass rape of the so called 'comfort women' by Japanese soldiers during the Second World War;[1] and in East Timor in relation to the mass killings carried out by the Indonesian regime. In the summer of 1998, 120 states agreed in Rome to set up an International Criminal Court, extending the ad hoc tribunals for the former Yugoslavia and Rwanda into a permanent institution. Slobodan Milosevic, the man who many held would never face justice at The Hague, is on trial.

There is much darkness in the world; genocide, racist ethnic cleansing, torture, industrialised humiliation and the mass production of terror are commonplace. Those who perpetrate such cruelties – the ideological, the greedy, the enraged victims of some previous injustice, the stupidly loyal, the sadists – move stealthily in their self-created dusk. On reflection, perhaps the bright winter sunshine in London did not really work as a metaphor for the business that was going on in the court. The image of enduring brilliant light

---

1   When the Japanese Prime Minister offered a letter of apology and monetary reparations to some 500 survivors of the 200,000 'comfort women', only six of them accepted the offer. 'Some of the women – from Korea, Taiwan, China, the Philippines, and Indonesia – found more gratification when the US Justice Department placed the names of 16 Japanese individuals involved in enslaving the women for sex on a "watch list" of suspected war criminals barred from entering the United States. Some argued that only prosecutions by the Japanese Government would adequately express governmental contrition and redress the abuse. Others supported treatment of the "comfort women" in school textbooks as a kind of reparation through memory.' Minow, 1998, p 105.

penetrating all the shadows of totalitarianism was surely illusory. But there have been flashes and sparks that have momentarily lit up the landscape. This book focuses on those. It seeks to sketch some of the scenes that are briefly illuminated by cosmopolitan criminal law, and to assess the significance and trajectory of the fragments of cosmopolitan criminal law that find a fleeting and tentative existence. Sparks and flashes are unreliable, unpredictable and dangerous, but they create bright light nevertheless. The existence of these fragments of light is the starting point of this work.

The term 'cosmopolitan' – deriving from the Greek *cosmos* (world) – was first used in this context by Immanuel Kant,[2] who picked up a thread of classical Greek thought[3] when he set out his theory of cosmopolitan right in 1795. He argued that the relationships between democratic republics must be regulated by a framework which provides for the peaceful settlement of disputes between states. But he went further, arguing that cosmopolitan law must set minimum standards for the treatment of individuals, both citizens and 'foreigners'.

Contemporary social theory is rediscovering and radicalising the concept of cosmopolitanism and recognising cosmopolitan law as one of its key actualisations. James Bohman and Matthius Lutz-Bachmann[4] argue that Kant's framework for a universal community of all peoples is given new urgency by the current development of globalisation. Steven Vertovec and Robin Cohen[5] chart the possibilities of peaceful human co-existence using the framework of a cosmopolitanism which focuses on human commonality. Ulrich Beck[6] sees the development of a cosmopolitan politics as a necessary response to globalisation. For David Held,[7] a democratic response to globalisation requires a cosmopolitan law that can regulate the unbounded growth of capital and other power structures. For Mary Kaldor,[8] a cosmopolitan approach is necessary because the nature of war is changing profoundly. Outdated categories of sovereignty, national interest and international law do not provide an adequate framework either to make sense of current conflicts or to challenge their worst excesses. Robert Fine says that:

> ... cosmopolitan social theory may be viewed as a multi-disciplinary attempt to reconstruct the core concepts of the human sciences – society, political community, democracy, culture, sovereignty, etc – in such a way as no longer to presuppose the givenness or centrality of the nation state in their designation.[9]

For Jürgen Habermas too the concept of cosmopolitanism and the development of cosmopolitan law are key to contemporary responses to totalitarianism and globalisation.[10]

Cosmopolitan criminal law is a new form of law which is evolving out of international humanitarian and human rights law that regulates not only the conduct of states, but also the conduct of non-state organisations and

2 Kant, 1991.
3 Nussbaum, 1997.
4 Bohman and Lutz-Bachmann, 1997.
5 Vertovec and Cohen, 2002.
6 Beck, 1999.
7 Held, 1995, 2002.
8 Kaldor, 1999.
9 Fine, 2002a.
10 Habermas, 2001.

individuals. It is new because its authority does not originate in state sovereignty but in a set of supra-national principles, practices and institutions. It is concerned with a specific set of crimes that are so huge that they transcend national boundaries both spatially and conceptually: genocide, ethnic cleansing and crimes against humanity.

Following the end of the Second World War, the four victorious powers organised trials at Nuremberg under the authority of international law to hold the Nazi leadership to account for their crimes. Within a year the energy and idealism of the process was spent. The Cold War that followed it lasted for half a century; half a century in which talk of cosmopolitan criminal law seemed to be little more than utopian dreaming. After 1989 there was widespread re-emergence of such talk, culminating in the creation of new institutions of enforcement, two ad hoc tribunals for Yugoslavia and Rwanda and the treaty for the International Criminal Court (ICC). These events can be understood in two contrasting ways. Nuremberg, it could be argued, was the start of the process of the actualisation of cosmopolitan criminal law, and the 50-year Cold War was simply a brief intermission before the process resumed; it has been gaining momentum ever since. Alternatively, Nuremberg could be seen as a fundamentally flawed display of victor's justice, the Cold War as the usual business of international relations between murderous and ruthless powers, and the re-emergence since 1989 as no more than a short-lived fantasy before lawless power again eclipses any hope of global authority. The American response to the attacks on New York and Washington in September 2001, similarly, can be understood either as an aberration from the path of progress or as a return to reality.

Neither of these approaches is adequate; or, at least, we have no way of knowing which will turn out to appear the more correct. We do not know whether the 12 years that have followed the Cold War will be followed by a long period of darkness or by a period in which the sparks and flashes of law become more enduring, regular and predictable, transforming into something that can sustainedly illuminate the dark shadows of mass murder and terror.

In this book, I try to restrict myself to looking at the flashes, and to theorising their potentialities. I am not committed to a framework that understands cosmopolitan criminal law as part of an inevitable civilising process, nor to one that understands it as simply a cover for the great powers to carry on their usual business of domination. I start with the social phenomena of crimes against humanity themselves and with the institutions of law that designate them as such.

The existence of some isolated successes for cosmopolitan criminal law is problematic for those who hold the view that such law is nothing other than a legal fiction or a form of imperialist domination. If there are gaps and spaces that law can fill and enlarge, if law is able to attain some independence from the powerful, then an understanding of law that sees it simply as a subterfuge that lends legitimacy to illegitimate power is unsustainable. If I can show in this book that it is possible for cosmopolitan criminal law to operate effectively at least in some instances, then opposition to law will have to focus more sharply. Criticism will have to relate to the actual functioning of the legal system. The argument that cosmopolitan criminal law is utopian in its concept, and that it therefore must be wholly compromised in its actuality, will no longer be credible.

By May 1994, at least 200,000 people, nearly all Tutsi, had been killed in Rwanda, but the US Government instructed its officials to refuse to call this a genocide.[11] This was because, even though a legal duty to act in defence of those being killed does not flow directly from such a characterisation, a refusal to use the term makes it easier not to act. The moral power of the term 'genocide', which stems partly from its legal existence, is considerable. Why, if the basis of international relations is power, does the US Government find itself playing these word games in order to help it to deny the undeniable? Clearly, there are factors at work other than naked power. This is a small example of how the powerful find themselves having to take notice of moral and legal duties. It is a small crack in the monolith of power; but cracks signify possibilities.

There is a large and comprehensive body of international humanitarian law. There are treaties, conventions, charters; there is customary international law and precedent. One key question that I am trying to answer in this book is to what extent that body of law has attained a genuine existence outside UN libraries and international law journals. It is clear enough that it does not exist as a settled system of criminal law that routinely tracks down and puts on trial those responsible for crimes against humanity, independently of where they commit their crimes or at whose behest. It is also clear enough that international criminal law is bogged down by power politics and the veto of the permanent members of the UN Security Council. International humanitarian law does not exist as a finished set of institutions and principles. But to what extent does it exist in an embryonic and incomplete form? This is the key question that I aim to answer in this work. If cosmopolitan criminal trials are being carried out, if they are based on due process and human rights, if they bring some justice to at least some perpetrators and some victims, then what is the significance of the development of these possibilities?

A number of important legal precedents have established the fact that the greatest violations of international humanitarian law – genocide, ethnic cleansing and torture – are subject to universal jurisdiction. Nuremberg, Tokyo, the ad hoc tribunals, the *Pinochet* judgment: all have clearly established that such crimes may be tried by international courts or by the national courts of any state. A state may no longer argue that the principle of national sovereignty disbars foreign courts from trying its nationals for such crimes or trying those suspected of committing such crimes within its territory. The right of national sovereignty is not absolute, but is related to other rights. Crimes against humanity are the concern of humanity as a whole, irrespective of where and under what jurisdiction they were committed. The principle of individual legal responsibility for such crimes, no matter whether they were carried out at the behest of states, by the leaders of states, or with the blessing of the legal system of states, is also clearly established.

I do not attempt to privilege the development of cosmopolitan criminal law as the most important antidote to totalitarianism, but as one weapon that is levelled against it alongside others. Law does not put an end to the actions that are designated as criminal. Laws against genocide, on their own, cannot stop genocide any more than laws against burglary have stopped burglary. Law is just one weapon. It is a complement to, not a substitute for, political action, education and organisation against those social formations that seek to commit

---

11 Cohen, 2001, p 162.

genocide or ethnic cleansing. There is no necessary contradiction between local people-based action and global institution-based action against totalitarianism; they can enhance each other. My aim is to discuss a number of theoretical and practical issues that relate to cosmopolitan criminal law and to trace possible trajectories for its development.

In the first chapter, I begin by making a distinction between international law and cosmopolitan law. International law is the system of regulation that governs the relationships between states, while cosmopolitan law is a development of this into a new entity. Cosmopolitan law is the emerging body of law that aims to protect the human rights of individuals and groups, primarily from serious threats that may be posed to them by their 'own' states, by invading states, or by other state-like social formations. A fundamental contradiction examined in this chapter is between the conflicting principles of absolute state sovereignty and human rights. This contradiction has usually been resolved in favour of state sovereignty, but the emergence of cosmopolitan law seeks to tip the balance in favour of human rights.

Cosmopolitan law is one response to the inadequacy of nationalism and its actualisation in the nation state. Hannah Arendt's work tracing the origins of totalitarianism makes a compelling case to suggest that the nation state is structurally unreliable in guaranteeing even the most basic human rights to all those who live within its territory. She argues that it was the totalitarian movements themselves that first exploited cracks in the guarantees of nationalism, and that it was they who first broke out of the bounds of national parochialism. What is required in a response to totalitarianism is a recognition that the old institutional and ideological structures of the nation state that were supposed to guarantee rights were prone to failure under stress.

Many contemporary theorists have responded to this problem with theories of cosmopolitanism. These theories typically contain two strands. They identify senses in which cosmopolitanism is emerging to replace the model of international relations which was based on state sovereignty. But as well as mapping its emergence, they also argue for its value as a paradigm which can address the central problems of our epoch. Whilst this book is informed by these theorists of cosmopolitanism, it is more limited in its ambition: it focuses on cosmopolitan law. The development of this law is understood not as a historical narrative of progress but as one which is based on human agency. It is based on the urgent and actual struggle to find methods of fighting against totalitarianism which do not replicate that which is being fought against. The development of this law is rooted in the cosmopolitan principle that human beings are on a fundamental level of equal worth. This is an approach which understands the necessity of operating in the world as it is rather than the world as we would like it to be. Some cosmopolitan theorists are too ready to divine a trajectory of development which automatically changes the world as it is into the world as it might be. Some critics, on the other hand, are so horrified by the world as it is that they see anything that exists as being necessarily wholly compromised by the corruption of the existing world. Cosmopolitan law is neither an emerging civilising process nor a moralistic gloss thinly covering imperialist domination;[12] it is one strategy for fighting against regimes and individuals who engage in genocide and ethnic cleansing.

---

12 See Chomsky, 1999; Chandler, 2002.

Chapters Two and Three focus on the two constitutive innovations of cosmopolitan law that were made by the Nuremberg process, which put leading Nazis on trial following their military defeat. The first was the establishment of individual responsibility for crimes committed by people even when they are acting on behalf of, or in leadership of, a state, and even when their acts appear legal according to existing authority. The other was the use of the new offence of crimes against humanity, which means that such crimes are recognised as the business of humanity as a whole, and that they are therefore subject to universal jurisdiction.[13] Both had arguably been present as principles in international law before, but at Nuremberg an institution of enforcement was built which gave those principles a worldly actuality.

Chapter Two asks whether the legal insistence on individual responsibility is justified. Do individuals actually make a decision to commit a crime against humanity for which it is just to hold them criminally accountable? Zygmunt Bauman[14] provides an important sociological account of how such decisions are made. In his account, the structures of modernity replace moral choice with short term instrumental rationality. Perpetrators are bound so tightly within those structures that it is only possible for a very few 'special' human beings to step outside the existing social world to act morally. The vast majority are condemned to play their role as perpetrators and bystanders, and do not possess the ability to make ethical choices for which they may be held responsible. If Bauman is right, then the insistence on individual responsibility is little more than a legal fiction that reproduces the same immoral rationality that was responsible for the crimes in the first place. We[15] argue that the social universe of modernity is not one that counterposes morality to rationality, and that the structure is very rarely so all-powerful as to eliminate any role for agency. We examine Bauman's argument by looking at how particular perpetrators and groups of perpetrators actually came to be killers. We argue that the evidence supports the thesis that perpetrators make choices about what they do, and that they could act otherwise. We conclude that the legal assignation of individual responsibility for perpetrators of crimes against humanity is justified.

Chapter Three looks at the Nuremberg tribunals more closely, and at the way that the charge of crimes against humanity developed there. I examine some of the responses to the formulation and use of the crimes against humanity charge at Nuremberg. While the Nuremberg process was seriously flawed in many ways, the aspect that I stress is that it indelibly set the two central precedents: that of individual criminal responsibility, and that of the universal jurisdiction over crimes against humanity. If we were to accept that the tribunal found defendants guilty of crimes that did not exist at the time of their commission, or that the prosecuting states were guilty of similar crimes to those they judged, then we could question the justice of the particular convictions at Nuremberg; but, following Nuremberg, no *génocidaires* can claim that they were unaware that genocide was an international crime; no

---

13 The Nuremberg process was 'the first formal recognition of a universal jurisdiction over certain heinous crimes'. Goldstone, 2000, p 75. Richard Goldstone notes that piracy and brigandage had been recognised as crimes of universal jurisdiction, but that they were never authoritatively defined.

14 Bauman, 1993.

15 Chapter Two was written jointly by David Hirsh and Robert Fine.

future *génocidaires* will be able to say 'we were only obeying orders'. Following the tribunals, the innovations at Nuremberg became clearly established precedents in cosmopolitan law.

Chapter Three goes on to discuss the codification of the crime of genocide in the Genocide Convention of 1948, and some of the ways in which social scientists have looked at genocide since then, with the emergence of 'genocide studies'. The genocide studies scholars attempt to discover ever more accurate definitions for key terms, ever more intricate traits common to genocides, ever more numerous statistical correlations. In this way they attempt to understand the social phenomena that they investigate. But they do not pay much attention to the ways in which those phenomena are understood by the structures and norms of society itself, that is to say, by developments in cosmopolitan law. It is, I argue, more fruitful to focus on the structures that develop organically within society than to attempt, as some social scientists do, to impose an abstract understanding based only on their own critique.

In Chapter Four, I explore the ways in which the three goals of peace, justice and security have been pursued in the former Yugoslavia by the international community. In the war in Bosnia, security and justice were subordinated to a vain quest for peace and the avoidance of conflict. The overriding wish to avoid any disruption of the peace enabled the practice of ethnic cleansing to be carried out with little hindrance. In Kosovo, the international community focused on preventing and reversing the ethnic cleansing, yet with such a blunt use of force that peace, security and justice all suffered. The priority given by the intervening powers to avoiding putting their own soldiers at risk had not changed since Bosnia, but the policy that flowed from it took a very different form. The establishment of the International Criminal Tribunal for the former Yugoslavia (ICTY) focuses on justice, yet it was established under the UN Security Council's powers to pursue peace and security. I explore the process by which the ICTY came to be set up and how it developed from a token institution, with no prisoners and a tiny budget, into one capable of putting Milosevic himself on trial.

In Chapter Five, I focus on the trials of a Croatian General, Tihomir Blaskic, and a small-time Bosnian Serb political activist, Dusko Tadic. It is through these two case studies that I investigate the actual working of a cosmopolitan criminal court. The most striking thing about the ICTY is that it exists. There is a courthouse in The Hague, protected by UN security personnel, displaying UN flags and symbols, that is carrying out the routine business of putting people on trial for crimes against humanity and genocide. Political, philosophical and legal discourse about the possibility of cosmopolitan law are confronted by this institution which quietly came into being during the debate. There are a number of factors which make it more difficult and complicated to organise fair trials here under cosmopolitan law than to organise domestic criminal trials, while all of the difficulties usually associated with criminal trials are also still present. These narratives are presented in order to highlight some of the problems and the ways in which the court seeks to overcome them. But these descriptions of the business of ethnic cleansing, and the day-to-day functioning of the court which relates to it, are also presented in order to concretise the often rather elevated theoretical discussion of such social processes.

As I write, Slobodan Milosevic is in the dock at the ICTY, claiming that ethnic cleansing against the Bosniaks and the Kosovars was just the beginning of the 'war against terror'; claiming that the other side – that is, every other side, NATO, Croatia, Kosovo, Bosnia – was worse than he was; using the time allocated for his cross-examination of witnesses to make speeches. Judge May regularly cuts him short, explaining, as to a rather stupid child who will not listen and who does not understand that he, Milosevic, is not in charge, that it is not a valid legal defence of himself to make allegations against others; that the legal process will take precedence; that the court is not impressed with his clever debating tricks. In such ways, those on trial are stripped of their aura of satanic greatness.[16] Ethnic cleansing itself is deconstructed by the ICTY into crime; endless particular episodes are presented whose sum adds up to a huge crime but whose parts are shown to consist in straightforward acts of routine brutality. A village is terrorised by a tank and a group of soldiers; a bus-load of men are taken away; five people are shot here, two people are beaten to death there; a group of women are taken off to a rape camp. In its detail it is simply a series of brutal crimes. In its everyday functioning, the ICTY is simply a court. The extraordinariness of the scale of the crime and of the nature of the court are always present, but so too is their ordinariness.

Chapters Six and Seven centre on two trials concerning the Holocaust that took place in London in 1999 and 2000. They were at the same time cosmopolitan and national trials; held under English law, but concerning the Holocaust that occurred elsewhere. While they had some striking similarities, they were also very different. One was a criminal trial of a *génocidaire*, Andrei Sawoniuk; the other was a libel trial brought by David Irving, a Holocaust denier, seeking to suppress an American writer's work about Holocaust denial. Both cases addressed the Holocaust with the hindsight of more than 50 years, one relying on eye witness accounts of particular incidents of brutality and murder, the other remaining mainly on the terrain of the interpretation of documentary evidence.

Many of the complexities of the Sawoniuk trial were ones which will arise typically in cosmopolitan trials. In an ordinary murder investigation, the police will normally have control of the crime scene, usually very soon after the crime is committed. This is unlikely to be the case in a cosmopolitan trial relating to crimes against humanity, genocide or ethnic cleansing. In a cosmopolitan trial, potential witnesses are likely to be either implicated in the crime or victims of it. The political or national loyalties of witnesses may be important. There will often be problems concerned with the translation of different languages. Local authorities may often be partisan to one side or the other. In this case, great difficulties were added by the long time interval between the crime and the trial.

One issue that was central in the Sawoniuk trial was the question of the admissibility of certain types of evidence. Some strong and arguably illuminating documentary evidence was prevented from going before the jury. The court required direct eye witness testimony. The narratives offered by the witnesses, particularly those presented by the Jewish survivor who gave evidence, Ben-Zion Blustein, were acted upon and changed by the rules and

---

16 An observation made by Karl Jaspers (Jaspers, 2000) in relation to the Nazis on trial at Nuremberg.

requirements of a criminal trial. Witness testimony given in the form of Holocaust memoir was acted upon by the rules and norms of the legal processes, particularly by the process of cross-examination and the sifting out of evidence that was deemed inadmissible: the trial process always strove to transform memoir into evidence. Blustein resisted the court and tried to retain control over his own testimony. The court had difficulty in bounding the extraordinary events and stories which were given to it within the normal rules of criminal evidence. The jury was swayed both by evidence which the court wished it to hear and also by influences which the court wished to suppress. The trial was a struggle between witnesses, the defendant, the lawyers and the judge for control over the information which the jury would use to come to its verdict.

While cosmopolitan criminal trials are intended to bring criminals to justice and to deter future crimes, Chapter Seven, which looks at the defamation case of *Irving v Lipstadt*, focuses on another important aspect of such trials. One of the strongest, most pervasive and widespread forms of collective memory is that which creates and recreates myths of nationhood. Most of the evidence that is presented to crimes against humanity trials is strongly coloured by national social memories; the subject matter of such evidence is the most extreme ethnic and national conflict. I argue that the cosmopolitan legal process is like a machine whose data is input in a form heavily coloured by national myth, yet whose output aims to be free from national particularity. The institutions of cosmopolitan law, as well as the body of law, rules and precedent on which they are based, are the mechanisms by which such cosmopolitan judgments may be arrived at. Crimes against humanity trials aim to produce authoritative narratives of the crimes, narratives given a particular form of authority by the legal processes and norms by which they are created. I argue that this is a part of the process of the evolution of a global collective memory that can play a role in undermining myths of nationhood, particularly those that have played their part in causing ethnic cleansing and genocide. The *Irving v Lipstadt* libel case is discussed as an example of the ways in which battles over narrative can be hosted by a trial process. Irving's 'revisionist' narrative clashed with the academic cosmopolitan discourse of Lipstadt. The court necessarily took on some of the characteristics of a cosmopolitan court and produced a legally authoritative narrative in the form of its 349-page judgment.[17] In Chapter Seven, I discuss the status and possibilities of such narratives.

The particular shape of this book, though not the fundamental arguments that it contains, is a little arbitrary. It is not a comprehensive survey of developments in cosmopolitan criminal law, nor is it an account of all crimes against humanity trials. It does not necessarily focus on the most important cases, nor on the most interesting cases. The empirical heart of this work is the observation of four trials; the *Blaskic* and *Tadic* cases in The Hague and the *Sawoniuk* and *Irving* cases in London. These trials were within my reach, geographically and temporally.

The trials at The Hague represent a sample of the early work of the Hague Tribunal. This tribunal is, along with its sister tribunal in Arusha, among the most interesting and important developments in cosmopolitan criminal legal

---

17 *Irving v Lipstadt* judgment.

history, and I was fortunate to be able to observe some of its operation. Two of the cases taking place there while I was carrying out my research were the *Tadic* and *Blaskic* cases. The *Tadic* case was the first ever to undergo a full trial process by a UN court; and I chose the *Blaskic* case because of its contrast to that case. Tadic was a small-time Bosnian Serb political leader; Blaskic was a General in the Croatian army.

The selection of the *Sawoniuk* and *Irving* cases was more opportunistic on my part. Yet their appearance at the right time for this work was not only a matter of good fortune, since cosmopolitan law is, at the moment, enjoying a limited but real renaissance. The *Sawoniuk* case was the trial of a man who had become a British citizen after the Second World War, for crimes committed in Belorus during that war as part of the Nazi genocide of the Jews. The case exemplified many of the complexities and difficulties associated with cosmopolitan criminal trials, such as the fact that the jurisdiction in which the trial was taking place was different from that in which the crimes were committed. It illustrated very clearly some of the difficulties involved in assigning different kinds of standards and rules that render evidence admissible or inadmissible, and it illustrated some of the ways in which different nationalistic narratives are worked upon by a court to produce a judgment. The *Irving* case was a libel trial in which David Irving sued Deborah Lipstadt for calling him a Holocaust denier and a falsifier of history who had neo-Nazi links. This case shows a contrasting way in which events that may be characterised as crimes against humanity can be examined in a court of law. As well as focusing on the ways in which a trial process can judge between opposing narratives of such events and produce its own legally authoritative narrative, this case also sheds light upon the ways in which the acceptance of certain forms of evidence rather than others can skew the truth that the court or the historian or the witness produces.

The central aim of the empirical investigation was to observe the actual working of these trials. Much has been written and spoken about international law by media commentators and politicians, and the law journals are full of articles by lawyers about the theory of international law. I wanted to observe the social phenomena of cosmopolitan trials as they actually happened. I wanted to look more at how they happened than at how they were supposed, theoretically, to happen. I wanted to come to a judgment not only about whether they could be characterised as fair trials, but also about the substance and character of cosmopolitan trials.

In the case of the ICTY, live sound (delayed by half an hour) from the three courtrooms is broadcast over the internet; full transcripts are available on the official website of all public proceedings; and the judgments that the tribunal produces are of the highest quality: detailed, well written and authoritative. The huge availability of this material is a methodological problem in itself: each day, each courtroom produces something like an 80-page transcript. This is simply an enormous amount of data for a researcher to handle. I still found that being in the building and in the courtrooms themselves gave me an incomparably fuller picture of the institutions and their proceedings. To be able to watch the lawyers, the judges, the witnesses and the defendants, day after day, and to be able to see the trial unfold, proved to be an absolutely invaluable part of my work. This work of observation was important in enriching the mountains of documentary data available.

One methodological problem in particular stands out in relation to the use of trials in the study of the events that they examine. People, of course, consciously present themselves in a trial in which they are involved in a particular light. Defendants want to be found not guilty: if that is not possible, they want sympathy, and they want the least possible condemnation; they want to tell their story. Every side in a trial presents a one-sided case. An observer must take care to understand that everything that is said in a trial is said for a particular reason, and that nothing is straightforward. It is always necessary to be conscious of the social setting in which the evidence is being presented.

Criminal courts offer one great advantage to the researcher: they are open to the public. However, those processes of the criminal justice system that are conducted in public are not necessarily the most important. What happens in jury rooms, and in private conversations between defendants, lawyers and judges, can be more telling than what happens in public. These places are much harder for the researcher to penetrate. Many decisions, such as whether there will be a trial at all, or whether the defendant will plead guilty or not guilty, are made outside court. Also, decisions about the shape that the trial will take, what is agreed upon, what is at issue between the prosecution and the defence, and what exactly the jury will be asked to judge, are made, formally and informally, away from the public courtroom. This process of pre-trial shaping, the off-the-record decision making, often skews sociological research of criminal justice systems when it is carried out by observing public proceedings.[18] In the cases that I followed, it was difficult to get access to sources of information outside the public proceedings. Presence in person at the Sawoniuk trial, the only jury trial that I attended, enabled me to observe legal argument that was not held in the presence of the jury and that was not reported in the press.

My trial observations were all carried out from the public galleries. At the Old Bailey, where I observed the Sawoniuk trial, the public gallery is organised in a particularly cold and rule-bound way. There are guards to enforce the rules about standing up and sitting down at the correct moments of proceedings; the guards file observers in and out of the public gallery at the beginning and the end of a session, while between sessions observers have to wait in a bare corridor. The guards make sure that no one has a secret drink or sandwich, and that everyone sits up respectably straight. The system here is designed to cope with friends and family of defendants queuing up outside the courtrooms next to friends and family of the victims of rapes and murders, as well as sociological researchers, trainee lawyers, homeless people looking for somewhere warm to sit, and those who are simply curious. At one important session of the Sawoniuk trial, I found myself locked out of proceedings because a group of schoolchildren had taken all the places. Perhaps a researcher would get a slightly different view of proceedings from the press gallery; whether it would actually be closer, or would only appear to be closer, I am not sure. The press gallery is fully contained within the building, rather than in a balcony only accessible from outside, as the public gallery is. By contrast, the public gallery in the Royal Courts of Justice for the *Irving* case was less regimented and was much more a part of the courtroom; it

---

18 See Baldwin, 2000, p 246.

did, on the other hand, contain a small collection of Nazi sympathisers, as well as Holocaust survivors, well known historians and students. In The Hague, the public gallery is very close to the court, but is separated from it by soundproof and bulletproof glass, giving an impression of intimacy mixed with remoteness. Usually at The Hague, the public gallery was almost empty, apart from one or two journalists and a few officials from the Bosnian or Croatian embassies. As well as being clear about who the observer is and what is being observed, the researcher is also conscious of the place from where the observations are made.

The strength, for a researcher, of choosing a small number of detailed case studies is that it is possible to achieve more depth. I could have attempted a comprehensive survey of all crimes against humanity trials, obtaining information from law reports, press reports, transcripts and other secondary and mediated sources. My aim was different. It was to attempt to get a feel for the cases; to understand the defendants and their crimes; to see exactly how the volumes, treaties and precedents of international law are given life by particular cosmopolitan institutions and particular lawyers and judges. I did not only want to see that trials take place; I also wanted to see how they take place, how unexpected events are dealt with by the process, and how the rules of the institutions of law are worked upon by the individual agents at work in the process – defendants, lawyers, judges, the press, the public. An immediate relationship between the phenomenon and the researcher requires attendance in court. The researcher makes sense of their own observations first, before being subjected to the opinions of others and the shape given to events by the media.

I did not observe these trials innocently. I did not go to any great lengths to attempt to create some sort of scientific distance from events, that is, to hide my particularity as an observer and as a social agent behind a façade of artificial objectivity. In fact, I observed the trials with all the prejudices that the experience of my life gives me. Observation is not only created by that which is being observed; it is also created by the observer. It is necessary to keep in mind the social context of the observation as well as that of the object. It is necessary to retain some picture of who is observing, and of the interaction between the observer and the observed. The difference between the information that is available when you are an observer in court and that which is available even from a complete transcript lies in the impressions of people and events that are filtered through one's own personal experience, and also impressions of structures, people and events outside the formal proceedings of the institution. I will give three examples to illustrate what I mean.

There was an incident, which I describe in Chapter Four, when I was at the ICTY and was approached by the chief security officer and interviewed by him. I was, at the time, outside the building, sitting on the grass in the sunshine at lunchtime. He approached me in order to ask me why I had been trying to engage members of staff in conversation, what I was observing, and why. I was surprised by the extent and the manner of the security. The incident added, in a small way, to my impression of the institution as a whole. It bolstered a feeling I had that the institution took itself seriously but in a civilised sort of way. It was interesting that he chose an informal interview outside his 'territory' rather than in his (perhaps rather intimidating) office. It was interesting that he had a Northern Irish accent, which I happened to recognise; other researchers may have recognised other things that I failed to notice at all.

When I saw, in court, a video of David Irving addressing an American Nazi meeting, it immediately became clear to me that Irving was sympathetic to those at the meeting. It was clear to me because he was addressing the meeting as a 'comrade', as one of them. I have been to many meetings that have been addressed by 'comrades'. I recognised it in the case of David Irving because I had seen it, or something similar, often before. Again, something from my own particular experience gave me a certain insight that I would not have had from transcripts or from reports. It was not hard fact that it gave me, it was not evidence, just an impression. But it was one that felt valuable to me.

When I first saw Ben-Zion Blustein giving evidence against Sawoniuk, I was struck by his similarity to other Holocaust survivors whom I had seen and met. In the text, I say that Blustein struck me as a 'typical' Holocaust survivor. I am aware that this statement is rather unscientific, unsociological, perhaps even offensive. It was, however, an impression, of the kind that I have just been describing, which seemed to me to be valuable, and which was gained only by the methodology of bringing my experience of life to bear. Clearly, I do not rely on my impressions as incontrovertible facts. I nevertheless value them for the detail and depth they add to the picture that I am trying to sketch.

In his book about research methodology, Bob Burgess[19] describes how one researcher illustrated her unstructured interviews with wives of clergymen by drawing on her own experience of being married, at the time, to a clergyman. The same researcher, similarly, brought to bear her experience of having taken her own child to pre-school playgroups when she interviewed young mothers attending playgroups. Experience, empathy and recognition must be considered important skills for researchers. A methodology that disqualifies such sources of enrichment will produce rather bland research.

I do not write shorthand. When I take notes of trials, I simply do my best to write down as much as I can. Sometimes my notes of what is said are a little confused. Sometimes it is confused in court; sometimes the translation is a little confusing; usually my notes are confusing because I did not write down everything accurately. Sometimes two questions, for example in a cross-examination, are elided into one, so there will be an answer to a question that I did not have time to write down. When I quote from my own notes using quotation marks, this indicates that I am absolutely sure about the accuracy of what is quoted. When there are no quotation marks, then I am sure of the sense of what was said, but not necessarily the exact words.

It is difficult to know what is the best name to use for the set of events that is often known as 'the Holocaust'. The term 'the Holocaust' emerged only in the 1960s, and it accompanied a certain re-emergence of talking and writing about the genocide. It is an unsatisfactory name primarily because of its original meaning, as a burnt offering in ancient religious rituals. It therefore carries with it a sense of holiness, and it endows the genocide with a sense of meaning that was in fact absent. A burnt offering is given in order to please or placate; the genocide was not offered voluntarily, nor did it result in anything positive. The phrase also implies a profound uniqueness, with which I am uncomfortable; it is not *a* Holocaust but *the* Holocaust. However, having made

---

19 Burgess, 1993.

an argument for not using this name for the event, I in fact use it often, simply because it seems to me that this is its usual name. I do not wish to argue about names. I use other names too. 'Shoah' is a Hebrew word that translates as 'violent wind or storm'; this, also, has attained a status as a common name for the event. 'The Nazi genocide of the Jews' is more inoffensive, yet it just sounds technical and clumsy, like a euphemism. I just want to say that when I use different names it is with some awareness that all of the names are unsatisfactory. I do not wish to choose between the unsatisfactory names, and I use whichever seems to fit in a particular context.

The term 'ethnic cleansing' is often seen in quotation marks because it is a term invented by those who carried out the act in Bosnia. The quotation marks seem necessary because we do not agree that the process involves any kind of genuine cleansing. Yet the term is attractive because of its shocking simplicity. Contained within the term is simultaneously an admission of guilt by those who use it and a defiant defence of the indefensible. I do not use it in quotation marks since it seems to me to be a term that describes very clearly its referent. Perhaps it is similar to the term 'final solution', which Hannah Arendt often used; it is a term invented by the perpetrators straightforwardly to describe the process, yet perhaps we can subvert it, somehow, by using it ourselves.

Chapter One
Cosmopolitan law

Classically, international law is the system that protects the right of sovereign states to be free from external aggression, and sets out a framework by which the relationships between states may be regulated. Following the experience of Nazism, a need was felt to extend the scope of international law so that it could protect the rights not only of states but of individuals, and also so that it could hold individuals criminally responsible for the actions of states. It was recognised that states could not always be relied upon to guarantee the most basic rights of their citizens, and neither could they be relied upon to hold those individuals committing the greatest crimes to account. Some crimes are so huge and some rights so fundamental that they become the business not just of the citizens of particular states but of humanity as a whole.

In this way, a new form of law began to emerge out of international law, a form of law that has a logic that transcends international law and is in some respects in contradiction to it. It seeks to limit state sovereignty, and lays down minimum standards for the treatment of human beings by states. It claims the right to put individuals on trial for certain crimes even against the will of their state and the state in whose territory and in whose name the crime was committed. In this chapter I argue that, even though this new form of law can be understood simply as a development in international law, it is more appropriately recognised as cosmopolitan law. Cosmopolitan law represents a break from international law because it does not put the rights of states above the rights of people. Its emergence is tentative and incomplete; it emerges into a world dominated by forms of power that threaten to extinguish it or to strip it of its radical content. But cosmopolitan law exists as an empirical fact, in institutions such as the International Criminal Tribunal for the former Yugoslavia (ICTY) as well as in treaties, conventions and charters that give ammunition and courage to those struggling against state tyranny.

A cosmopolitan law to limit the rights of states

It is a straightforward proposition that the Holocaust must never be allowed to happen again. What is it, that 'Holocaust' that is never to be repeated? One possibility is that we mean that Jews should never again be subjected to a campaign of genocidal antisemitism against which they do not have the means to defend themselves. If the Holocaust is understood as a crime against the Jewish people, then a response based on Jewish national self-determination may logically follow. The Holocaust was possible because Jews, unlike many other ethnic groups, were not organised into a nation state of their own and so did not have the capacity to defend themselves against attack. Future genocidal attacks against Jews will be unsuccessful because Jews have won for themselves national sovereignty in the state of Israel; even if all Jews do not live there, they have the right to do so as citizens. The Sharon regime in Israel is committed to a strong form of the politics of nationalism. It values the rights of Jews above the rights of others; it claims absolute sovereignty within its territory; and it reserves the right to act as a power outside its territory in any way that it believes furthers its own national interests.

There was another parallel response to the Nazi genocide. That response, which began to emerge at Nuremberg, understood the Holocaust not primarily as a crime against Jews but as a crime against humanity as a whole. The Holocaust was not understood as a campaign of genocidal antisemitism but as a campaign of genocidal racism. That which must never happen again was any genocide against any collectivity. This approach was based on a particular notion of humanity; it was one that understood human beings to be of equal value in at least a very basic and minimal sense.[1] Human beings are bearers of fundamental rights. The most basic right, perhaps, is the right to one's identity as a human being. Those who commit genocide must first challenge the universality of that right. The Nuremberg trials began to give a material real-world existence to the concept of human rights. They established the principle that nobody, no state, no head of state, no soldier acting under apparently legal orders, has the right to violate the most fundamental of human rights. Those who had done so were tried as criminals. The trials were not held under the authority of any sovereign power or national legal system, but under the authority of international law.

An Israeli Colonel was interviewed on Israeli television during the current intifada. He said:

> We have entered Taumon in order to catch terrorists. The terrorists managed to escape before our arrival, but we are going to give the townspeople hell, to teach them not to harbour terrorists.[2]

Gush Shalom, an Israeli peace group, wrote a letter to this Colonel pointing out that collective punishment is a violation of the Geneva Conventions, and citing reports that 20 inhabitants of Taumon had already been wounded by soldiers under his command, among them a 70-year-old imam of the local mosque. The Colonel was warned that the evidence might in future be presented to an Israeli or international court empowered to deal with war crimes and violations of international law. The army responded by issuing a new directive, forbidding soldiers and officers to give their full names when interviewed by the media. The reason explicitly given was 'to prevent the possibility of their being prosecuted at the Hague War Crimes Tribunal'. Prime Minister Sharon responded by instructing the Attorney General to look into ways of prosecuting the Gush Shalom activists. Several other ministers who spoke used the word 'treason', and so did nationalist Knesset Members and newspaper columnists. An activist was asked on Israeli television: 'And would you really inform upon a fellow Israeli, a fellow Jew, to a foreign court? Are you that depraved?'[3]

The two responses to the Holocaust, one of Jewish self-determination, the other of cosmopolitan law, thus appear to be turning on each other. The nationalists see an external threat to Jews; they see foreigners under the banner of a new world order claiming to have the right to imprison and punish Jews

---

1 '[O]ur species is one, and each of the individuals who compose it is entitled to equal moral consideration. Human rights is the language that systematically embodies this intuition ...' Ignatieff, 2001, pp 3–4.
2 Keller, 2002.
3 Keller, 2002.

against the legitimate sovereign will of the Jewish state. Those who argue for the extension of a cosmopolitan criminal legal system see a Jewish army and a Jewish state committing, or perhaps preparing to commit, war crimes or crimes against humanity.

But it is not a surprise to see the principles of human rights and those of national self-determination come into such severe conflict. It was precisely the fact that individual Nazis were convicted of crimes under international law – crimes that were not considered as such under their own system of rules – that represented the novelty of the Nuremberg process.

Human rights are instruments that seek to limit the scope of state sovereignty. They affirm that there are certain things that independent states do not have the right to do. States may agree to enforce human rights; they may incorporate this or that human rights principle or charter into their own systems of law. But state national sovereignty is not the source of human rights. It is a fundamental strand of the cosmopolitan argument that the incorporation and enforcement of human rights is not something that states may choose to do but is something that they are obligated to respect.

In the 18th century, the concept of the Rights of Man gave focus and legitimacy to struggles against traditional political systems, which held that some human beings were created with rights to rule over the others, who were created with only the right to obey. The concept of rights was at the heart of the post-revolutionary states in France and America. It was held to be self-evident that all men were created equal; the new society was to be based on liberty, equality and fraternity. These truths were then embedded into national constitutions and imprinted on the coinage. These rights were guaranteed to citizens by national states. As Hannah Arendt put it:

> ... man had hardly appeared as a completely emancipated, completely isolated being who carried his dignity within himself without reference to some larger encompassing order, when he disappeared again into a member of a people.[4]

From the beginning, rights were tied to a national state that could guarantee and enforce them. The Rights of Man were tied to rights of citizenship. The classical conception of the nation state that emerged from the French Revolution was an inclusive one: the nation was defined by the state and citizenship was enjoyed by all inhabitants of the territory. Yet there was always the danger that this relationship between the state and the nation could be reversed: an ethnically defined 'nation' could take control of the state and exclude those whom it defined as not belonging.

But a larger concept of rights, specifically human rights, was to re-emerge in the 20th century. Following the Holocaust and other horrors, it was, as Phil Allot puts it, 'this time ... installed not merely in the constitutions of national societies but in the constitution of international society itself'.[5] The Nuremberg process, and the wave of human rights conventions and declarations which were generally accepted after the war by states, by international law and by the new United Nations (UN), solidified human rights as a clear and agreed principle of the international community.

The two principles, however, by which people seek to protect their collective and individual existence and freedom – national self-determination and

---

4   Arendt, 1975, p 291.
5   Allot, 2001, p 286.

human rights – continue to develop apparently harmoniously in parallel. They have an intertwined existence in national and international law, in political rhetoric, in institutions and in popular consciousness. There are whole industries of diplomacy, international relations and international law that map the subtle detail of the co-existence of national sovereignty and human rights. The UN is founded upon both principles simultaneously; its charter reaffirms the principle of national self-determination[6] and its major foundational project after the Second World War was one of the codification of international humanitarian and human rights law.[7]

But these two principles conflict in the extreme case when genocide or ethnic cleansing is on the agenda. The principle of national sovereignty is one that protects the state from outside intervention on the basis that the sovereign is the ultimate source of authority. The principle of human rights is one that asserts that people have rights by virtue of their humanity, not only by virtue of their citizenship, and so their most fundamental rights are underwritten by international authority. Genocide and ethnic cleansing are necessarily carried out by social formations that hold something approximating to state power. The conflict, then, is about where ultimate authority lies. If it lies in national sovereignty, then states have unlimited rights to act as they see fit within their own territory; if it lies outside, then this raises the possibilities both of external intervention to prevent ethnic cleansing or genocide and of international courts having jurisdiction within sovereign states to bring the perpetrators of such acts to justice.

Historically, the development of international humanitarian law and of international human rights law has been distinct. Humanitarian law aimed at setting limits to what was legitimate in war. This body of law was concerned with the treatment of civilians, prisoners of war and the wounded, and with the types of weapons and tactics that were to be considered legitimate. International human rights law, first codified in the Universal Declaration of Human Rights (1948), was concerned with defending human beings against the arbitrary actions of their states. Humanitarian law originally related to armed conflict, while the law of human rights related particularly to peacetime since it allowed governments to derogate in the event of war or other national emergency.

While international humanitarian law and international human rights law remain distinct specialisms in legal practice, the theoretical basis for such a distinction is thin, particularly in relation to genocide and crimes against humanity. Hersh Lauterpacht argues that the body of humanitarian law upon which the Nuremberg tribunal was based was itself derived from a notion of human rights in international law, and that genocide is both a violation of the individual human rights of those killed and a violation of international humanitarian law.[8] After Nuremberg the link between crimes against

---

6 Eg 'All members shall refrain … from the use of force against the … political independence of any state …' (UN Charter, Article 2(4)); 'Nothing contained in the present Charter shall authorize the United Nations to intervene in matters which are essentially within the domestic jurisdiction of any state …' (Article 2(7)); see fuller discussion below.

7 Eg Universal Declaration of Human Rights (1948); Convention on the Prevention and Punishment of the Crime of Genocide (1948); Geneva Convention for the Amelioration of the Condition of the Wounded and Sick in Armed Forces in the Field (1949). Hoog and Steinmetz, 1993.

8 Lauterpacht, 1950, pp 36–37.

humanity and war was decisively broken; the prosecution of genocide, also, requires no link to armed conflict.[9] In the post-Second World War period, there was much cross-pollination between humanitarian and human rights law.[10] Jean Pictet envisages the possibility of bringing the two forms of law together under the common name of 'humane law'.[11] While humanitarian law and human rights law do have different histories, principles and purposes,[12] it is clear that they often share the same objectives and goals; they also share a common theoretical grounding in the discourse of human rights.

In 1982, at a time when the post-war innovations in international law appeared to have been permanently frozen out in the context of the bipolar power struggle of the Cold War, Leo Kuper wrote that:

> [T]he sovereign territorial state claims, as an integral part of its sovereignty, the right to commit genocide, or engage in genocidal massacres, against people under its rule, and ... the UN, for all practical purposes, defends this right.[13]

Twenty years later this expression of exasperation is not quite as true as it was when it was written. The legacy of the post-war innovations has been defrosted and re-examined following the end of the Cold War. It has been built upon by social theorists,[14] international lawyers[15] and both legal and state practice. A current has been emerging out of international law that vigorously challenges the sovereign right to commit genocide. This current is developing into a new form of law that a number of theorists have referred to as 'cosmopolitan' law.

David Held, for example, sees a progression from the model of classical sovereignty, the law of states, through a model of liberal international sovereignty, in which the liberal concern for limited government is extended into the international sphere, to the model of cosmopolitan sovereignty, the law of peoples.[16]

For Mary Kaldor, the Yugoslavian wars of the 1990s typify the changing nature of warfare. She argues that in 'new wars' the classic distinctions between internal and external, war and peace, aggression and repression are breaking down. War is no longer controlled by sovereign states wielding legitimate monopolies of violence; rather it is fought out between ethnically

---

9 'The prohibition of genocide, derived from the concept of wartime crimes against humanity and later enlarged to prohibit similar peacetime behaviour, can perhaps be seen as an example of the intersection of human rights and humanitarian law.' Provost, 2002, p 6.

10 The Universal Declaration of Human Rights was drafted in the aftermath of the Nuremberg process. It, in turn, influenced the Geneva Conventions of 1949 and its additional protocols of 1977 which set down standards for the treatment of prisoners of war and wounded soldiers. The progressive rejection of military necessity as a valid justification for disregarding humanitarian law over the course of the last century can also be linked to the development of individual human rights: Provost, 2002, p 6.

11 'Humane law comprises the totality of the international legal provisions which ensure for the human person respect and fulfilment.' Pictet, 1985, p 3. Pictet, however, does not argue for such a merger between the two forms of law.

12 Humanitarian law allows lawful killing, even on a large scale, of the enemy, in some circumstances even including civilians; it authorizes various measures of deprivation of freedom which are not recognised by human rights law: Meron, 1997, p 100.

13 Kuper, 1982, p 161.

14 Eg Habermas, 2001; Kaldor, 1999; Held, 1995; Archibugi and Held, 1995; Bohman and Lutz-Bachmann, 1997; Fine, 2002a.

15 Eg Bassiouni, 1999; Higgins, 1999.

16 Held, 2002.

defined social formations that mix the characteristics of nationalist struggles, organised crime and local warlord-based power. For her, the distinction between human rights law and humanitarian law is becoming meaningless because of the degradation of the formal distinction between war and peace:

> The violations of international norms with which both bodies of law are concerned are, in fact, those which form the core of the new mode of warfare ... A war crime is at one and the same time a massive violation of human rights. A number of writers have suggested that humanitarian law should be combined with human rights law to form 'humane' or 'cosmopolitan' law.[17]

Thus both Held and Kaldor attach their theories of cosmopolitan law to a particular narrative of development that seems to give its emergence some sort of historical inevitability. While this evolutionism is problematic, the central insight is that a new body of law has emerged out of international law that is sufficiently different from its classical form to make its recognition as a new form appropriate. This is not an argument about names: it is an argument for the recognition of the centrality of the development that is being made and struggled for. Neither is it a celebration of the historical forces of progress that are remaking the world. While proponents of cosmopolitan theory do point to significant structural changes that are occurring in global relations, often grouped under the heading of globalisation, the recognition of cosmopolitan law is fundamentally an observation of human agency at work. It is the recognition of a movement for a form of law that does not replicate that which is being fought against. The current emergence of cosmopolitan law may turn out to have been just a fleeting one; it is a movement that may be reversed and politically defeated. But human rights have an unusual quality: once they have been asserted, they exist for all time. Once Nazis and ethnic cleansers have been put on trial under cosmopolitan law, that precedent remains.

Sometimes cosmopolitanism looks like a hopelessly radical and utopian project. It begins by asking how to prevent future genocide and it ends up challenging every power structure, institution and principle: nationalism and the nation state; the huge imbalances of power between strong states and weak ones; the agonising gulf between rich and poor; the rule of global capital. Yet sometimes cosmopolitanism looks like a hopelessly conservative project. It is only necessary to make some fine adjustments to international institutions, to take further reforms that are already being made because structural changes in the world demand them; the rules of the UN Security Council must be democratised, the US State Department must learn a few lessons from the experiences of Somalia and of Srebrenica; the International Criminal Court (ICC) must start hearing cases; problems of global inequality and poverty must be addressed by agreements on social issues that can be woven into agreements on free trade and all will be well. Sometimes those who argue for cosmopolitanism appear to be both utopian and conservative at the same time. The emergence of cosmopolitan criminal law is neither. It is, as Robert Fine put it, an expression of 'worldliness as the practical wisdom of those who by hook and crook know how to construct a touch of humanity in the most forbidding circumstances'.[18] It is one instrument that can make a contribution to the fight against the most horrific forms of tyranny.

---

17 Kaldor, 1999, p 116.
18 Fine, 2001, p 162.

The project of bringing into existence a legal cosmopolitan authority that is competent to judge individuals who violate the most fundamental principles of international law is a limited and achievable project. It claims no more and no less than ordinary criminal law. It functions in a world characterised by huge inequalities of power and wealth. It will not eradicate the crimes it condemns. It will be unjust in the same sense that any other criminal law is unjust. It does not promise a new world. But on the other hand it will challenge those men in suits and in military uniforms who are used to being above the law. General Pinochet never anticipated spending a couple of years of his retirement fighting for his liberty in a British court. Slobodan Milosevic never thought that he would have to defend his actions in an international tribunal against the threat of life imprisonment. The present American, Israeli, Russian and Chinese regimes know very well that the currently constituted ICC can never threaten them, yet they feel threatened by it. They understand that cosmopolitan criminal law has a life of its own, that it is not just a tool of the powerful. The powerful seem to understand that it is in their interests to block its development at an early stage.

National sovereignty

Traditional natural law theory held that states were bound by moral considerations when deciding whether to wage war. Augustine wrote about war in terms of justice. He argued that states had a right and, in some circumstances, a duty to take up arms in the cause of justice. Aquinas stressed the point that a just war must be authorised by due authorities, that is, that it must be a concern of the public at large, as distinct from a private quarrel. Neutrality within the framework of traditional natural law could be a dereliction of duty: if a state stood by and watched another being unjustly conquered, it was morally in the wrong.[19] The rise of the modern state and its associated modern sovereignty put an end to the medieval recognition of the (aristocratic) individual as a bearer of international rights and obligations, except in cases where it was in the interests of states to hold individuals to account for crimes such as piracy.[20]

The rise of the modern state also coincided with the generalisation of private property that freed property owners from traditional obligations and duties. Relations between individuals, all of whom were now potential property owners, came to be understood as based on equality.[21] In a parallel shift, states rejected their moral duties and obligations to each other, and instead openly followed their own self-interests, creating the doctrine of the sovereign equality of nation states. Nation states, like citizens, and like property owners, were now all equal before the law. Right replaced duty and ethics.

In the positivist era, argues Stephen Neff, the:

---

19 Neff, 1993, p 162.
20 'Before this gradual change in Europe ... [individuals] once used to enjoy rights which are still now regarded as genuine international rights – mainly, the right to wage war. Several decades were necessary to gradually deprive individuals, ie the nobility in most cases, of their international rights and to subject them to the exclusive domestic jurisdiction and authority of states.' Zoller, 1990, pp 99–100.
21 Fine, 1984.

... duty to come to the rescue of victim states was firmly rejected in favour of a right of each state to follow its own national interest as it saw fit – even if it meant standing stonily aloof while neighbouring countries fell prey to aggression.[22]

Ethical considerations had, in the real world, often been thin cover for the material interests of those clerical authorities who assumed the right to make ethical judgments. Such considerations were replaced by the freedom for individuals and states to pursue their own interests in an enlightened way and within a minimum legal framework.

The signing of the Treaty of Westphalia (1648) is seen by many, both cosmopolitan[23] and more orthodox international relations[24] theorists, as the historical event around which this shift hinged. It is represented as the moment when territorial sovereignty in Europe was entrenched and when the only limit to the pursuit of state interest became state power. Some who still cling to the principle of absolute state sovereignty see Westphalia as the birth of the freedom of nations; some cosmopolitan theorists see it as the moment when ethics disappeared from the discourse of global politics, a historic fall that must be remedied; some European integrationists see it as a specifically European settlement. Yet even if the significance of Westphalia is overemphasised by those who wish to use it as a pivotal moment in their particular narrative of history, it has come to represent the shift towards a new set of principles.

The Thirty Years War (1618–48), which was ended by the Treaty of Westphalia, was a complex set of conflicts, involving wars both between estates within the Holy Roman Empire and with external states, particularly France and Sweden. In fact, the distinction between 'states' and 'estates', *Staate* and *Stände*, or *l'état* and *les états*, was not yet clearly drawn. Indeed, the drawing of these distinctions, the battle for sovereignty, or freedom from domination by the empire or other states, was one of the aims of the war for many of the participants. Some, like the Dutch 'States General', were successful, gaining recognition of sovereignty in 1648, while others, such as the Estates of Bohemia and the Protestant cities and noblemen of France, were forced to accept the reduced status of subjects.[25] The war was exceptionally long, bloody and destructive.[26] The bloodshed was ended by a settlement that provided a framework for national and religious freedom from the Catholic Church.

The key elements of the model of Westphalia, encapsulating the principles of relations between sovereign states, are as follows:

(a) The world consists of, and is divided by, sovereign states which recognise no superior authority.

---

22 Neff, 1993, p 160.
23 Eg Held, 1995.
24 Stanley Hoffman, in his foreword to Hedley Bull's *The Anarchical Society*, remarks that it is now a cliché to call the system of sovereign states the Westphalian system: Hoffman, 1995.
25 Asch, 1997, p 4.
26 As was reported by Edmund Calamay to the English in 1641, in a manner eerily reminiscent of 21st century war reporting: 'Germany ... is now become a Golgotha, a place of dead mens skuls; and an Aceldama, a field of blood. Some nations are chastised with the sword, others with famine, others with the man-destroying plage. But poor Germany hath been sorely whipped with all these three iron whips at the same time and that for above twenty years space.' Quoted in Asch, 1997, p 1.

(b)   The processes of law making, the settlement of disputes and law enforcement are largely in the hands of individual states.

(c)   International law is orientated to the establishment of minimal rules of co-existence; the creation of enduring relationships among states and peoples is an aim, but only to the extent that it allows national political objectives to be met.

(d)   Responsibility for cross-border wrongful acts is a 'private matter' concerning only those affected.

(e)   All states are regarded as equal before the law: legal rules do not take account of asymmetries of power.

(f)   Differences between states are ultimately settled by force; the principle of effective power holds sway. Virtually no legal fetters exist to curb the resort to force; international legal standards afford minimal protection.

(g)   The minimisation of impediments to state freedom is the 'collective' priority.[27]

This model covers a period from the Peace of Westphalia in 1648 up to 1945, and many of the assumptions underpinning it are still held to be operative in international relations today: it is a remarkably stable and enduring set of principles. It is presented by cosmopolitan and international relations theorists as an order that recognises, codifies and legitimises a situation of inter-state anarchy, while at the same time remaining fundamentally unchanged for three and a half centuries. But this period was also clearly one of immense and profound change:

> [E]vents as momentous as the political revolutions of the late 18th century and their conjunction of nation and state, the collapse of the mainland European empires after the First World War and formation of a raft of newly independent nation states out of their fragments, the rise of totalitarian regimes with global ambitions in the interwar period, the collapse of overseas empires after the Second World War and the formation of another raft of new post-colonial nation-states – these events are presented within the cosmopolitan paradigm as having modified, extended and generalised the Westphalian model but essentially as punctuation marks in a continuous Westphalian narrative.[28]

This is not simply an order based entirely on an anarchic relationship between powers. International law, treaty and agreements have had a real and developing existence within it. But international law was created by agreements between states, and its first principle was always to uphold state sovereignty. When sovereign states have clashed, the classical international order has had little to say other than that this was a 'private' matter between them; when sovereign states have turned against their own citizens, it has had even less to say.

In the 19th century international law grew within a legal positivist framework as the system that governed the relationships between states. Sovereign states agreed to follow particular rules established explicitly through treaty and were not bound by any to which they did not agree. Subsequently, this rigid positivistic approach was augmented by other sources of international law, particularly customary international law and a recognition that 'general principles' could be cited as sources of international

---

27 Held, 1995, p 78.
28 Fine, 2002a.

law;[29] but the central principle of classical sovereignty, that a state would not be subject to outside interference in its affairs, remained central.

Following the First World War, and the collapse of the Ottoman and Austro-Hungarian empires, the system of independent nation states was greatly expanded by the victorious powers in Europe. Anthony Giddens[30] argues that the external influence of the international system of states played an important role in the generalisation of the sovereign nation state model. The international system of nation states required the universalisation of national sovereignty, exercised through the rapid proliferation of surveillance within territories and reflexive monitoring between states. Developments as mundane as international postal services required the existence of national postal organisations that had full reach within their territories. Sovereign control of the means of mass violence and the industrialisation and totalisation of war strengthened the detailed control of territory and information that national states were developing. Territorial definitions and the sovereignty of borders, policed according to international agreements, similarly increased the necessity for internal surveillance by states. The influence of the international system of nation states and the requirement for international co-operation were, according to Giddens, centrally important in the consolidation and generalisation of the doctrine, the reality and the myth of national sovereignty. However, Arendt highlights the increasing problem of the nation state's inability to guarantee a framework of rights for all. She focuses on this same post-First World War period when the nation state form was being hurriedly replicated.[31] The form became a pattern to be copied everywhere in order to fill the vacuum left by the breakup of the multinational empires. The great powers wanted to impose the nation state form from above, through the peace treaties and the League of Nations; powerful national groups seized on it in order to win state power for themselves; and the requirements of the international system also fuelled the process.

Arendt argues that the result was that, in large parts of Europe, exclusive ethnic nationalism subverted the classical model of the all-inclusive civic state. The nation state form became the universal form but the content, which had classically guaranteed rights to all citizens, was new. In these new nation states in central and eastern Europe, it was the pre-existing 'nation', defined ethnically, that took state power, rather than the state as a set of civic institutions defining a community of equal citizens as a nation. There was an all-out struggle between nationalities and minorities for some kind of favourable political settlement: Slovaks against Czechs, Croats against Serbs, Ukrainians against Poles, everyone against Jews.[32] Rights became increasingly dependent on national independence, which could only be won at the expense of the exclusion of others. Hence the settlements that the victorious powers tried to impose through the League of Nations in fact encouraged and accelerated the process of competition between national and ethnic groups for independence and hegemony. Everyone became convinced that '[t]rue freedom, true emancipation, and true popular sovereignty could be attained

---

29 Bassiouni, 1999, p 104.
30 Giddens, 1985.
31 Arendt, 1975.
32 Fine, 1994.

only with full national emancipation, that people without their own national government were deprived of human rights'.[33] The appeal to human rights became increasingly one only resorted to if all other rights were out of reach. The Rights of Man had been dependent on common citizenship, a situation to which the nation state could no longer even formally approximate.

The Nazis further subverted the classical model of citizenship, declaring that citizenship of the Reich was dependent upon possession of the correct 'blood'. Arendt quotes the official SS newspaper (*Schwarze Korps*) in 1938: 'If the world is not yet convinced that the Jews are the scum of the earth, it soon will be when unidentifiable beggars, without nationality, without money, and without passports cross their frontiers.'[34] The plight of this 'scum' is 'not that they are not equal before the law, but that no law exists for them; not that they are oppressed but that nobody wants even to oppress them'.[35]

The nation state could not guarantee the rights of its citizens, and the unbounded, perpetually destructive ideological madness of Nazism certainly could not. The logic of cosmopolitan law is to tie the idea of universal human rights to a legal structure that can give those rights some concrete reality independently of the state. The appeal to human rights had become a sign of absolute desperation: cosmopolitan law is one strategy that aims to give the appeal to human rights some muscle. If the movement for cosmopolitan law could begin to offer the *de facto* stateless some kind of protection, this would also undercut the force of the politics of nationalism, which scorns as utopian every politics that does not involve the carving out of nation states and the exclusion as aliens of those who do not fit.

However, the foundation of the UN, which followed the Second World War, did little to undermine the centrality of the doctrine of absolute national sovereignty. Article 2(4) of the UN Charter (1945) states that:

> All Members shall refrain in their international relations from the threat or use of force against the territorial integrity or political independence of any state, or in any other manner inconsistent with the Purposes of the United Nations.[36]

It is clear that the prohibition of the use of force by one state against another was a principle that needed restating and emphasising in the post-war world. Invasion and occupation of a sovereign state was already, and was more clearly now, perhaps the most serious and clear contravention of international law.

But there is an assumption that lies behind this principle: there must be some sense in which the state is seen to represent the people who live within the territory of that state. This is why invasion and occupation is undesirable. The principle of self-determination holds that the people of a territory have the right to determine their own destiny, free from external intervention. So what kind of relationship is assumed to exist between the state and the people who live within its territory?

There are clear and agreed precedents and principles laid down in international law concerning the recognition of states and governments by other states, governments and international bodies. Emphatically, it is not a

---

33 Arendt, 1975, p 272.
34 Arendt, 1975, p 269.
35 Arendt, 1975, p 296.
36 UN Charter, Chapter 1, Article 2(4).

democratic representative structure that bestows international legitimacy on a government or a state. At the heart of the criteria for international recognition is a *realpolitik* acceptance that a regime that *de facto* holds state power and controls a territory will in the end be recognised internationally. There is no requirement for a state or a government to represent its citizens. But if the prohibition of the use of force by states against other states is to contain a democratic content, if it is, as it appears to be, a principle that is good for the people who live in a state, then there must be some assumption of representation. It is not an assumption of democracy, just an assumption that there is some sense in which those who hold state power represent the people who live in their state. But the problem with this assumption of representation, however tenuous the actual representation may be seen to be, comes where groups of people are actively excluded from citizenship by those in state power. For example, in what sense were the Kosovars represented by 'their' Yugoslavian state in 1999? In what sense were Kurds in Halebja represented by 'their' Iraqi state in 1989? In these situations, where the state is actively killing and ethnically cleansing people who live within its own territory, the assumption behind the principle prohibiting the use of force against a sovereign territory can be seen to break down. There is, as Arendt argues, a crucial difference between the right of a *nation* to self-determination and the right of a *state* to self-determination. When the state is the property of a nation, or a ruling clique, when there is not even the most tenuous representative link between the citizens as a whole and the state, then the state's right to freedom from external intervention can in fact constitute a right to commit genocide or ethnic cleansing.

Article 2(7) of the UN Charter emphasises the inviolability of the sovereign state, extending its legal protection against intervention by other states to the UN itself:

> Nothing contained in the present Charter shall authorise the United Nations to intervene in matters which are essentially within the domestic jurisdiction of any state or shall require the Members to submit such matters to settlement under the present Charter; but this principle shall not prejudice the application of enforcement measures under Chapter VII.[37]

Yet Chapter VII appears to offer little hope for people to expect protection against 'their own states'. Article 32 in that chapter states that:

> The Security Council shall determine the existence of any threat to the peace, breach of the peace, or act of aggression and shall make recommendations, or decide what measures shall be taken ... to maintain or restore international peace and security.[38]

Chapter VII seems to offer some possibility that the Security Council may authorise the use of force against a sovereign state, but the charter is careful to emphasise that this may only be done 'to maintain or restore international peace and security'. So if other sovereign states are at risk there is the possibility of intervention; emphatically not, if the only risk is to the internal population of the state.

It must be emphasised that, while these passages from the UN Charter do make a *prima facie* case against the legality of humanitarian intervention, as do other principles of international law, they are open to interpretation and are

---

37 UN Charter, Chapter 1, Article 2(7).
38 UN Charter, Chapter 7, Article 32.

sometimes balanced by opposite principles. It is not my case that these passages from the charter represent the final word on what international law 'says' about these issues, but rather that they indicate the centrality of the principle of absolute state sovereignty both in classical international law and in the foundation of the UN. As will be seen later, the statement of the Security Council's responsibility to ensure international peace and security was in fact used to legitimate the foundation of the ad hoc tribunals for the former Yugoslavia and for Rwanda. There is much work being done by international lawyers and by international institutions to strengthen the weight assigned to humanitarian law as against the rights of states.

The dominant current within international relations, which emerged in the post-war period as an academic discipline, developed along the lines of the Westphalian model. It is based upon the principles that the only source of legitimate authority is the sovereign state and that state action is to be understood as the pursuit of national interest defined in terms of power. International outcomes reflect the struggle for power. International order is based on power counteracting power, forming a balance of power equilibrium. Mainstream international relations theory has been sceptical of the chances of reform of international organisations to create more stable or just outcomes. It held that Western liberal democracies did not wage aggressive war, and that therefore the liberal conscience need not be troubled too much by its apparent endorsement of the legitimacy of war or the threat of war as the central mechanism by which disputes are settled.

Throughout the 20th century there has been a sizeable current on the left as well as on the right that has accepted the *realpolitik* of absolute national sovereignty. Under the slogan 'bourgeois democracy for nations', Lenin argued for the principle of national sovereignty against imperialist domination. After Lenin, the internationalism of some of the left dissolved into a greater Russian nationalism, which constituted support for Russia as the universal nation,[39] the nation whose interests coincided with the interests of the international working class. There has been an acceptance amongst sections of the left that international relations and also human rights were simply matters of power. Power politics was often preferred to bourgeois liberal projects of regulation and law which, the argument goes, made grand promises but in fact entrenched a system of increasing inequality and tyranny. The Western attack on Yugoslavia in 1999 was opposed by many on the left on the basis that it was an infringement of Yugoslavian sovereignty.[40]

The re-emergence of cosmopolitanism

The word 'cosmopolitan' is loaded with negative connotations. The Stalinists and the Nazis used 'cosmopolitan' as a term of antisemitic abuse, constructing Jews as the rootless and the exotic, who prefer opaque and conspiratorial blood links with others of their own kind to the honest community of compatriots or fellow workers. Perhaps the force of the myth of the rootless cosmopolitan originates in the idea that the loyalty of cosmopolitans is primarily to themselves: they are never ready to die or to kill for their country

---

39 Fine, 2001.
40 Coates, 1999.

or for their comrades since they belong nowhere. Cosmopolitans are never 'authentic' since they have no genuine home, no genuine links to the soil and no genuine culture. Roger Scruton defines 'cosmopolitan' as follows:

> The belief in, and the pursuit of a style of life which ... [shows] acquaintance with, and an ability to incorporate the manners, habits, languages, and social customs of cities throughout the world ... In this sense, the cosmopolitan is often seen as a kind of parasite, who depends upon the quotidian lives of others to create the various local flavours and identities in which he dabbles.[41]

A strain of contemporary cosmopolitans have economic freedom that comes from relative wealth, and they have rights guaranteed by their Western passports. They can celebrate 'genuine' cultures wherever they like and can feel the ecstasy of 'authentic' mysticism, always, of course, with their Visa cards sewn into the lining of their jackets. There is even a nation of cosmopolitans where people from all over the world came together to build a society without solidarity or community; one whose central values embody the right of individuality, the right to pursue happiness and the right to exploit others. This nation is called America and is, naturally, run by Jews. The ugly myth of the rootless cosmopolitan has infinite variations. It keys into one of modernity's darkest apparent requirements: to construct some human beings as undeserving of inclusion in the civilised community.

The myth of the rootless cosmopolitan may be bolstered by the power of the state to prove it true by making people actually rootless and rightless. Bogus asylum seekers, economic migrants, illegal immigrants: they are not only the latest victims of a variant of the myth, but are also victims of a concerted effort by states to keep them outside the community of citizenship legally as well as ideologically. Although this sense of the word 'cosmopolitan' is distinct from the sense in which the word is generally used in this book, there is a connection with the project to endow all people with rights regardless of their status as citizens. The project of cosmopolitan law is aimed at bolstering the position of those who are defined as non-citizens by their state: both those who manage to leave, exposing themselves to the dangers of the search for a new citizenship, and those who are unable to leave, but remain at the mercy of the state that stripped them of their citizenship rights.

The aftermath of the Second World War and the Nazi genocide of the Jews saw one of the foundational acts of cosmopolitan law: the creation of a tribunal that was able to bring together the power to call witnesses and punish criminals and the authority of international law. The Nuremberg trials established the precedent of international criminal tribunals, and for the first time explicitly recognised and prosecuted the new offence of crimes against humanity. The Genocide Convention was agreed in 1948 and codified the crime of genocide. Both of these crimes were subject to universal jurisdiction, meaning that any state had the right to arrest and try suspects irrespective of where the crimes were committed. This brief but vigorous bloom of cosmopolitan law, however, was short-lived, and quickly withered under the freeze of the Cold War. Yet immediately at the end of the Cold War it re-emerged. There was no continuous path of historical progress between Nuremberg and the ad hoc tribunals for Yugoslavia and Rwanda: the two significant successes for cosmopolitan law were separated by decades in

---

41 Scruton, 1982, p 99.

which it struggled for any kind of recognition. But, even across that separation, the ad hoc tribunals were able to build from a foundation that had previously been established. In the United States, President Harry S Truman had requested the Senate's advice on, and consent to, the ratification of the Genocide Convention in 1949, but it was not until February 1989 that ratification was completed and became binding upon the US.[42] The Senate spent 40 years debating the issue, asserting the primacy of US sovereignty and the US Constitution over international law and the International Court of Justice, and putting forward possible 'reservations' and 'understandings' that would accompany and clarify ratification. The US was reluctant to allow its sovereignty to be limited, even in the case of genocide. Passed immediately before the start of the Cold War, the Genocide Convention was only finally ratified by the US at its very death.

The end of the Cold War saw the concept of 'cosmopolitanism' rescued from its service as a totalitarian term of abuse by a wave of social theorists and philosophers, who began to use it as a resource with which to come to terms with a rapidly changing world. Many of them picked up the thread of cosmopolitan argument from Immanuel Kant who had in turn rediscovered the concept from the Greek Stoics and Cynics,[43] and had set out a theory of cosmopolitan law in his 1795 essay, 'Perpetual peace'. He saw that the creation of democratic republics both required and made possible a supra-national structure that could prevent war and that could protect the rights of the traveller in a foreign country. David Held writes:

> Cosmopolitan law, thus understood, transcends the particular claims of nations and states and extends to all in the 'universal community'. It connotes a right and duty which must be accepted if people are to learn to tolerate one another's company and to co-exist peacefully.[44]

Central to Kant's conception of cosmopolitan law was a democratic, universal content. Cosmopolitan law could only be a framework that enshrined the principles of mutual recognition and tolerance. Kant's vision was of an international confederation of democratic republics: an international order that not only regulated the relationships between the republics but also set down minimum standards of human rights, not just for citizens of states, but also simply for citizens of the cosmopolis. Kant specifically attacked the 'depravity' of the Westphalian international order in which 'each state sees its own majesty … precisely in not having to submit to any external legal constraint' and in which the glory of a state's ruler 'consists in his power to order thousands of people to immolate themselves for a cause which does not truly concern them, while he need not himself incur any danger whatsoever'.[45]

Held[46] is typical of this new wave of cosmopolitan thinkers who have forcefully argued for a new way of thinking about international relations that puts human rights above state rights and that argues for a new set of supra-national institutions able to provide a democratic authoritative framework capable of addressing pressing global problems. He presents cosmopolitanism

---

42 LeBlanc, 1991, p 2.
43 Nussbaum, 1997.
44 Held, 1995, p 228.
45 Kant, 1991, p 103.
46 Held, 1995.

as a set of ideas and practices that are replacing the Westphalian system, both because that outdated system is no longer capable of creating a stable framework for a changed world, and also because cosmopolitanism is a better, more open and more democratic paradigm. The rapid growth of aspects of life that transcend national borders raises problems of democratic accountability. The world is changing in such a way that it is increasingly diverging, both theoretically and structurally, from existing politics that aim to keep democratic accountability over it. People are increasingly finding that the key networks of power that influence their lives have escaped from their control, and that the powerful have liberated themselves from outdated political arrangements that are increasingly ineffective. Held reworks the concept of sovereignty, arguing for a layered theory in which sovereignty is sited on different levels: local, regional, national, global. What is necessary, he argues, to bind the disparate sites of power and sovereignty into a democratic framework is an agreed set of minimum principles, a system of cosmopolitan democratic law.

He sees the first step in this journey as the reform of the United Nations. This process could begin with the UN taking measures to implement, extend and enforce the UN Rights Conventions. The UN could increase its role in the settlement and prevention of inter-state conflict by requiring states to submit to compulsory jurisdiction in the case of disputes falling within the ambit covered by international law and UN resolutions. The institution of an international criminal court could play a central role in policing serious violations of human rights. The General Assembly could play a more legislative role if a consensus (or near consensus) in that forum were recognised as a legitimate source of international law. The veto arrangements in the Security Council could be modified.

A key question is the degree to which a cosmopolitan global order is becoming a reality or whether, on the other hand, Held's principles of cosmopolitan democracy constitute little more than a utopian yearning. It is not clear whether these kinds of solutions are indeed emerging out of the existing situation or whether, on the contrary, the voices calling for cosmopolitan democratic reform are drowned out by the demands of international capital and great power politics. Indeed, perhaps those liberal voices are simply being incorporated by the great powers as a democratic cover for the usual business of pursuing 'national' interest with all the force that can be mustered.

This book does not focus on cosmopolitanism in general, but on a single manifestation of its narrative: cosmopolitan criminal law. Cosmopolitanism is open to the charge that it may turn out to herald the appearance of a new grand narrative of emancipation to be followed, perhaps, by a new disillusionment with its inability to deliver.[47] Cosmopolitan law, in contrast, is a set of particular ideas that has achieved a limited but real institutional existence. The project for cosmopolitan law has had successes and failures.

The Nuremberg and Tokyo tribunals, as well as many national successor trials, established the principle of individual criminal responsibility for international crimes and the offence of crimes against humanity. They tried and punished many of those guilty of crimes during the Second World War. Many conventions have enshrined rights and prohibitions of their violation in

---

47 Fine, 2002a.

international law.[48] The tribunals in The Hague and at Arusha are currently, routinely, applying international humanitarian law and punishing some of those who are guilty of its contravention. The indictment of Slobodan Milosevic by the tribunal, at a moment during the Kosovo conflict in 1999 when perhaps NATO would have preferred it to remain diplomatically silent, is a small demonstration of the fact that the tribunals do possess some degree of autonomy in relation to the great powers that allowed them to come into existence. The Spanish courts established the principle that a former head of state like General Pinochet may be arrested anywhere in the world and held accountable for his crimes, and this principle was endorsed by English law. The ICC is now formally a reality, although it faces significant opposition from the United States.

On the other hand, there are compelling reasons to be sceptical. Nuremberg was, in many ways, a fundamentally flawed process of victor's justice: the four powers made every effort to limit and control the universal principles that they had allowed the process to enshrine as precedent. Following the post-war trials and the consolidation of much international humanitarian law on paper, history since the war has repeatedly demonstrated that power politics overrides paper law. Even in the former Yugoslavia, where perhaps the most progress has been made, some of the key criminals are still enjoying their freedom; the legal processes are slow, underfunded and badly publicised. The success of cosmopolitan law here, where it has been most successful, is still questionable. And in the former Yugoslavia it happens that the implementation of this law is in the interests of at least some great powers, and not against the interests of the others.

Cosmopolitan law: an emergent property of international law

The British Prime Minister Lord Salisbury reported to Parliament in 1887 that:

> ... international law has not any existence in the sense in which the term 'law' is usually understood. It depends generally upon the prejudices of writers of textbooks. It can be enforced by no tribunal, and therefore to apply to it the phrase 'law' is to some extent misleading.[49]

Whether or not this was true in 1887, it is not true now. There is an enormous number of manifestations of international law that function routinely and form a framework for a world in which people, capital and information move more or less freely. There are binding and enforceable international laws that, for example, prevent airliners from crashing into each other and ensure that letters sent from one country to another have a good chance of arriving. There are international laws and agreements regulating trade, telecommunications, copyright, and numerous other spheres of social life.[50]

---

48 Eg Convention on the Prevention and Punishment of the Crime of Genocide (1948); Geneva Convention for the Amelioration of the Condition of the Wounded and Sick in Armed Forces in the Field (1949); Convention Concerning the Abolition of Forced Labour (1957); Convention against Torture and Other Cruel, Inhumane or Degrading Treatment or Punishment (1984). Hoog and Steinmetz, 1993.

49 Koskenniemi, 2001, p 34.

50 The fact that they operate routinely does not mean that they are not controversial; the rules of international trade, for example, and their institutional expression, the World Trade Organisation, are subject to much criticism.

Article 38(1) of the Statute of the International Court of Justice (1945) sets out a generally accepted statement of the sources of international law:

(a) international conventions ... establishing rules expressly recognised by the contesting states;
(b) international custom as evidence of a general practice accepted as law;
(c) the general principles of law as recognised by civilised nations;
(d) subject to the provisions of Article 59, judicial decisions and the teachings of the most highly qualified publicists of the various nations, as subsidiary means of determination of the rules of law.[51]

The first does not pose any problem for a narrow positivist conception of law that understands state sovereignty as the only source of legitimate authority. The others build a framework of obligation to which states may become subject.

Customary international law is a combination of two elements: state practice and *opinio juris*. The actions concerned must amount to a settled practice, and the states involved must carry them out as though they believe that this practice is required by a rule of law. Customary law binds all states with the exception of those who persistently object; failure to protest against an emerging practice in circumstances where a reaction would be expected contributes to the formation of a new custom. Rules originating in treaties between specific states may pass into the general corpus of international law and become accepted as such by *opinio juris*, so as to become binding even for countries that were not parties to the original treaty. Equally, treaties may be taken as declaratory of customary law that is already in force. Similarly, UN resolutions or declarations may be understood either as recognising existing international law or as signalling an intent to create a new one; but it is state practice combined with *opinio juris* that actually defines the law.[52] UN resolutions or conventions only become law when it can be shown that states in fact treat them as law. The 'general principles' (Article 38(1)c) source is one that allows courts to make use of fundamental principles that are common to different legal systems. The 'highly qualified publicist' (Article 38(1)c) source allows courts to take into account legal argument of respected legal scholars.

Yet Salisbury's denial seems to be more than a view that, empirically, international law did not exist; it also suggests that he was quite happy for it not to exist. Martti Koskenniemi comments that 'an empire is never an advocate of an international law that can seem only an obstacle to its ambitions'.[53] On the one hand, a strong state may be happy to operate in the world as nothing but a power pursuing its own interest. But on the other hand, a strong state, particularly a hegemonic state, may be in a position to wield an overwhelming control over the content and functioning of international law. In that case, it has an interest in bolstering an international legal framework that it can influence both directly, through pressure, and indirectly, through using it to project its own world view and values.[54] It would appear that the strong win either way.

---

51 Cited in Higgins, 1999, p 18.
52 Kontou, 1994, pp 3–6.
53 Koskenniemi, 2001, p 34.
54 Perhaps the current regime in the USA has resolved this paradox by insisting that others follow international law while at the same time insisting that it is not itself bound by it. Examples of this are its treatment of prisoners of war from Afghanistan in Cuba and its refusal to join the ICC while at the same time supporting the ICTY and the International Criminal Tribunal for Rwanda (ICTR).

This paradox is reflected in the debate about the degree of formalism or dynamism that is desirable in international law. In the period following the collapse of the League of Nations and the lawlessness of the First World War, international law was widely discredited. One response to this was to retain a traditionally formalistic and rule-orientated understanding of international law, which aimed to free it from charges of partiality, but at the cost of characterising international law as largely irrelevant in areas of vital national interest. A natural law version of this position recognises that international law is often ignored in areas of vital national interest but that it nevertheless represents an authoritative normative statement of what is right.

Rosalyn Higgins[55] argues strongly against understanding international law simply as a body of rules that are themselves taken to be distillations of accumulated past decisions. The role of lawyers and judges in that conception is to find the correct rule for the new situation and apply it impartially. If the role of the authorised decision maker is other than to apply rules, or if there is a large element of discretion in the application of rules, then their decisions could become contaminated from other spheres of life. The rules view seeks to avoid questions of policy and values in order to avoid charges of partiality.

However, since no application of rules can ever be simply objective and mechanical, judgment necessarily involves some kind of application of values and policy decisions. Hence there is a danger that the rule-based approach can only seek to disguise such questions as neutral and technical ones. Higgins argues that questions of policy and values must, rather, be brought into the open and dealt with systematically. This means that all the factors are properly considered and weighed, instead of the decision maker unconsciously narrowing or selecting what he will take into account in order to reach a decision that he has instinctively predetermined is desirable.[56] International humanitarian and human rights law are explicitly based on a set of clearly defined values.

Higgins argues that the legal formalist and natural law positions counterpose authority to power. They banish 'power to the outer darkness (that is to say, to the province of international relations)' and they assume that authority can exist in the total absence of supporting control, or power.[57] But for Higgins, the authority that characterises law exists not in a vacuum, but exactly where it intersects with power. Of course, there will be particular circumstances when power overrides authority. On such occasions we will not have decision making that we can term lawful. But that is not to say that law is about authority only, and not about power; nor that power is to be regarded by definition as hostile to law. Power is an integral element of law.[58]

The tribunals at Nuremberg and Tokyo brought together a body of international humanitarian law with institutions empowered to prosecute. The Yugoslavia and Rwanda tribunals are building on, broadening and solidifying this precedent, and the ICC is coming into being. In an Austinian sense, these events are crucial because they begin to constitute a missing element of law, that is, enforcement. In Higgins' terms, they are crucial because they reunite

---

55 Higgins, 1999.
56 Higgins, 1999, p 5.
57 Higgins, 1999, p 4.
58 Higgins, 1999, p 4.

authority and power. It is noticeable, however, that the Nuremberg and Tokyo tribunals brought together a great deal of power, that of occupying armies and American political will, with a somewhat hastily and inadequately constructed authoritative framework. In contrast, in the cases of the ICTR, the ICTY and the ICC, the authority is more solidly constructed out of the legal precedents already set by those post-war tribunals and the codification that followed them, and also by their more genuinely international basis, but the power that underwrites the contemporary tribunals is less reliable and less committed. A more complete unity of authority and power is yet to be embodied in a cosmopolitan tribunal.

Higgins argues that her understanding of international law allows for a wider and more open debate as to the identification and articulation of the values to be promoted, and that it allows space for claims and counterclaims, state practice, decisions by a variety of authorised decision makers, and the use of past decisions and rules to develop appropriate decisions for new situations. However, referring back to Lord Salisbury's dilemma, there is clearly huge scope in Higgins' conception of a dynamic and open process of law for powerful states to influence decision making in their own interests. They can influence the appointment of judges who will make decisions; they can imbue processes and institutions with their own systems of value; they can exert pressure on subordinate states and institutions. Koskenniemi argues that anti-formalistic approaches to international law have had an agenda of justifying American dominance in the world. On the other hand, he also recognises that 'formal rules are just as capable of co-existing with injustice as informal principles'.[59] It is apparent that no legal-philosophical 'fix' is possible. A clear system of rules provides transparency insofar as it makes decisions predictable but not insofar as its values are covered behind a veil of impartiality. The worth of a dynamic system of decision making based on a set of core values depends greatly on what the core values are and who is in control of them. The debate between formalism and dynamism must therefore be one of emphasis rather than one of absolutes. What is most important is that in relation to crimes against humanity, genocide and ethnic cleansing, there has emerged a significant body of international humanitarian law, and there is still the possibility for further development.

Cosmopolitan law as a project not a future

Much contemporary cosmopolitan theory is presented as a narrative, sometimes very schematically and sometimes with more sophistication. It begins with a nostalgia for a pre-modern idea of natural law that imposed ethical restrictions on anyone powerful enough to wage war. It understands modernity as the epoch of absolute state sovereignty and of inter-state anarchy. And it understands the period following the Second World War as one in which the rupture between ethics and power is gradually being bridged. There is a growth of structural changes that bypass the system of independent states both from below and from above, creating significant networks of power that are no longer subject to state authority. Armed groups mix organised crime and political or ethnic power struggles to undermine the classical authority of

---

59 Koskenniemi, 2001, p 496.

the civic state from below, as in Yugoslavia, reflecting a fundamental change in the nature of armed conflict.[60] The capitalist market organises on a global level that is ungovernable by individual states and necessitates a supra-national authority that can extend a democratic authoritative framework to the new situation. Cosmopolitanism is both 'happening', as the historical response to globalisation, and is also normatively desirable, as the solution to the most striking problems of our time.[61]

If, however, the quest for this historical narrative is abandoned, then a different picture is allowed to emerge. Typically of contemporary cosmopolitan theorists, Mary Kaldor's notion of cosmopolitanism understands it as a response to specifically contemporary problems and as an analysis that supersedes those that were appropriate to the world as it used to be but not to the world as it is now:

> [I]n the context of globalisation, ideological and/or territorial cleavages of an earlier era have increasingly been supplanted by an emerging political cleavage between what I call cosmopolitanism, based on inclusive universalist multicultural values, and the politics of particularist identities.[62]

But if the cleavage between the universalist values of cosmopolitanism and the politics of more particularist identities is understood not as a product specifically of the postmodern 'now', which supplants previous political cleavages, but is instead understood as a thread that runs throughout the time frame of the narrative, then we develop a clearer and less apocalyptic picture. Cosmopolitanism is not a historical stage that arrives after and as a result of the increasing perception of the deficiencies of the old order. The idea of cosmopolitan law does not follow nationalism, but runs parallel to it. The narrative is more appropriately understood both as one of intertwined development and one of acute competition. Immanuel Kant did not develop his theory of cosmopolitan law after and as a result of the generalisation of absolute state sovereignty. The Genocide Convention (1948) was passed simultaneously with the foundation of the UN as a conference of independent states. The Nuremberg trials did not take place as a response to the failures of Israeli nationalism or against its interests or sensibilities. The tribunals for Rwanda and Yugoslavia did not come into existence because the Security Council became convinced that absolute state sovereignty was no longer a principle worth defending. Many of the events that we can understand as landmarks in the development of cosmopolitan law took place within, and not in opposition to, the existing order of power and law. Part of what is at stake, therefore, in the argument for the recognition of cosmopolitan law, is the degree to which its principles and institutions are able to be brought to life as independent entities. Can they attain sufficient authority, independence and power to threaten some of the interests that brought them into being? If they can, cosmopolitan law attains an existence not just as a set of ideas but as a new form of law.

---

60 Kaldor, 1999.

61 The new cosmopolitanism has a 'proclivity to turn "the cosmopolitan" into a *fixed idea* or *abstract ideal* – to turn it into an "ism" and so divorce it from the social world of needs, passions and conflicts of which it is part. The new cosmopolitanism, as I read it, is not only a way of thinking that recognises the validity of cosmopolitan ideas in social theory; it also elevates the idea of the cosmopolitan to supreme status.' Fine, 2002a.

62 Kaldor, 1999, p 6.

We are concerned here with tracing a thread of law, politics and philosophy that challenges the idea that community must necessarily be defined in an exclusive way. It is a thread that opposes tyranny while remaining vigilant to the danger of creating new exclusions. It is a thread that has always challenged that side of the dialectic of modernity that threatens its own particularly menacing and characteristically modern form of barbarism. Cosmopolitan law is not a sequel to modernity but rather an element deeply embedded within it. It is also a characteristically modern form, based on the extension of the project of the universalisation of right. And neither is it a panacea, a cure for all ills, a new ideology for a new world order; it is simply a new form of law.

At Nuremberg, in The Hague and at Arusha, aspects of wars have been deconstructed by cosmopolitan legal processes into crimes. Following the attacks on the United States in September 2001, the Bush regime set about the construction of crime into war. Not only was it unwilling to consider prosecution for those thought to be responsible, it was even unwilling to respect the most basic principles of humanitarian law in its treatment of prisoners. Similarly the Israeli regime responds to the criminal bombing of its civilians by making war against a whole people.

The American and Israeli regimes distort reality in order to make it seem to fit into a model of orthodox international relations. This is necessary because they want it to appear legitimate for them to relate to the world as nothing but powers in pursuit of what they portray as national interest. These are both situations that cry out for a cosmopolitan response, but the response that is actually made is one of brutally denying and reshaping reality so that it first looks like, and then actually becomes, inter-state conflict. In our advocacy of cosmopolitan law, let us not pretend that history and progress are on our side. Let us not write off such defeats for our perspective as the final follies of the old order. Let us understand clearly that cosmopolitan law, while it has attained a genuine material existence, has not superseded state power but continues to develop alongside it and often in opposition to it.

Chapter Two
Individual responsibility and
cosmopolitan law

Chapters Two and Three examine two central advances made at the Nuremberg tribunals that followed the Second World War. The first is the establishment of the legal responsibility of individuals for their parts in violations of international humanitarian law committed by large state-like formations. The second is the codification of crimes against humanity and the establishment of universal jurisdiction for such crimes. These two innovations can be seen as the foundational acts of cosmopolitan criminal law. They constitute the subjects of cosmopolitan criminal law in individual perpetrators and individual victims, and they define the scope of such law with the concept of universal jurisdiction.

'We were only obeying orders' was not a valid defence at Nuremberg. Article 8 of the Charter of the International Military Tribunal at Nuremberg (1945) stated:

> The fact that the Defendant acted pursuant to order of his Government or of a superior shall not free him from responsibility ...[1]

Conversely, for those giving the illegal orders, the charter allowed no 'Acts of State' defence:

> The official position of defendants, whether as Heads of State or responsible officials in Government Departments, shall not be considered as freeing them from responsibility or mitigating punishment. (Article 7)

The tribunal added that a superior order would not serve even as a mitigating factor unless it was given under circumstances that left a defendant with no moral choice but to obey the order.[2]

The tribunal established a definite link between individuals and their actions, by treating so called 'cogs in a murder machine' as perpetrators, refusing the excuse of service to the state. It presupposes that choices are available to the perpetrators of such crimes. If no such choice is in fact available, that is, if the situation is one of 'kill or be killed', then this would constitute a legitimate defence or mitigation.

This insistence on the individual criminal responsibility of perpetrators was one of the most important and far-reaching precedents that were set at Nuremberg. It is a principle that since its establishment at Nuremberg is necessarily at the heart of cosmopolitan criminal law. The Nuremberg precedent has been followed and strengthened by the tribunals for Yugoslavia and Rwanda.

The question we[3] shall address in this chapter is how well this legal assumption of choice and responsibility fits with the sociological reality of the

---

1 Jackson, 1949, p 242.
2 Murphy, 1990, p 151.
3 This chapter was written jointly with Robert Fine and is based on a previously published article: Fine and Hirsh, 2000.

ways in which individuals make the decision to commit a crime against humanity. Is the decision to commit such a crime one for which it is reasonable to hold individuals to account?

The prevailing sociological explanation of such decisions in relation to the Nazi genocide is that provided in Zygmunt Bauman's *Modernity and the Holocaust* (Bauman, 1993). Bauman himself may not think of his work precisely in this way, but his basic proposition is that it is the dominance of 'rational choice' over moral response in the modern age that is the key to understanding how ordinary men and women commit such extraordinary crimes. Conversely, the key to overcoming this potentiality is seen to lie in the development of a postmodern ethics that subordinates the imperatives of 'rational choice' to a reconfigured 'moral point of view'. Bauman does not like a world structured around 'rational choice', but he accepts that this is the actuality of our present world; he looks to a way of thinking that overcomes the constraints of 'rational choice' and in its place revives our suppressed capacity to act in a moral rather than rational way. From this perspective, 'rational choice' appears as a form of human decision making that arises in the modern epoch and that has as its consequence the exclusion of ethical concerns. And 'rational choice theory' appears as a form of reified consciousness that hypostasises rational choice as a natural presupposition of social life and blinds us to its historical preconditions and demoralising consequences.

We are not going to defend rational choice theory against this very sharp line of criticism, but rather argue that this line of criticism is over-dependent on the rational choice model that it attacks. We want to argue first, that the reduction of 'modernity' to the imperatives of an amoral and instrumental rationality paints a one-sided picture of modernity that obscures the inner connections between modernity and the development of moral consciousness itself; secondly, that the reduction of reason to instrumental, technical or technological rationality distorts the meaning of reason and severs its connections with thinking, understanding, willing and judgment; thirdly, that the decisions of individuals to participate in crimes against humanity (including those synthesised under the name of the Holocaust) cannot be adequately explained within this framework; and fourthly, that the moral point of view itself is far from being a purely innocent or suppressed factor in decisions to commit crimes against humanity. Most of all, although we recognise that Bauman and those who think like him have undoubtedly revealed something extremely important about the nature of organised violence in the modern age, we must also be alert to the dangers of forcing the empirical phenomena into an over-determined theoretical straitjacket.

Modernity and the Holocaust: Bauman's critique of rational choice

In Zygmunt Bauman's conception, the modern world really does run the way rational choice theory says it runs: in terms of short term and instrumental preferences set within a given domain. Every aspect of social life encourages, coerces and impels individuals to act in accordance with their own short term, narrow, selfish interests. We live according to that 'principle' alone; we do that which we find rational in terms of immediate self-interest. This includes the search for means, obedience to orders, and conformity with social norms, regardless of their moral content. It also means the prioritising of self-advancement or self-preservation regardless of moral cost. We become a new type of bourgeois: not the Kantian who thinks and judges for himself, but the 'mass man' (to use a phrase borrowed from, among others, Hannah Arendt) who can kill without passion or enmity, simply as a job or in service to the state, because it is an efficient means to a given end or because he is commanded so to do or because that is what everyone else is doing. The making of merely 'rational choices', without regard for ethics, is the very mark of this social type. It is, Bauman argues, through the combination of many such 'rational choices' that the Jews of Europe were rounded up and murdered. As long as we remain within this 'rational' template, we are destined to play our part in the genocide.

The frighteningly domestic image through which Bauman portrays modernity is that of a 'garden culture' in which the extermination of weeds is the necessarily destructive aspect of the gardener's productive and aesthetic vision. A gardener has an image of how he wants his garden to be. He wants it to be well ordered and to conform to his own dreams of beauty and serenity. He likes certain plants and breeds them to fit in with his plan. He does not like other plants, which he designates as weeds and poisons or incinerates. In this scenario, the gardener sees the elements of nature instrumentally, in terms of how they affect him and may be affected by him, rather than as things endowed with an intrinsic value of which he is guardian.[4] In modernity human beings are themselves stripped of intrinsic value. Some are defined as weeds, others are selectively bred. Genocide is a kind of social weeding, and Hitler and Stalin were but 'the most consistent, uninhibited expressions of the spirit of modernity'.[5]

If the technologisation of conception is one aspect of the spirit of modernity, the other is the technologisation of execution. In this reading of the situation, it was the bureaucracy that executed the final solution, and even the 'political master', Hitler, found himself in the position of the 'dilettante' standing opposite the expert and facing the trained official.[6] There is no decision, as such, to commit crimes against humanity, simply the normal functioning of a bureaucratic state. In his discussion of Claude Lanzmann's *Shoah*,[7] Bauman tells us that 'by far the most shocking among Lanzmann's messages is the rationality of evil (or was it the evil of rationality?)'.[8] For the bureaucratic form of administration that prevails in modern society has a machine-like quality in which each bureaucrat follows detailed written rules unthinkingly and without responsibility for what the machine is doing as a whole. Bureaucracy is a machine for the exclusion of moral responsibility.

Bauman argues that the defining features of modern bureaucracy were not only well established in Germany during the Holocaust, but made the Holocaust possible. Government was conducted through a centralised,

---

4 Bauman, 1993, pp 91–92.
5 Bauman, 1993, p 93.
6 Bauman, 1993, p 15. Compare with Alan Bullock: '[Hitler] had a particular and inveterate distrust of experts. He refused to be impressed by the complexity of problems, insisting until it became monotonous that if only the will was there any problem could be solved.' Bullock, 1983, p 381.
7 Lanzmann, 1985.
8 Bauman, 1993, p 202.

hierarchical and bureaucratic state; respect was afforded to science, knowledge and expertise; rational behaviour was valued over irrational behaviour; the breaking down of tasks into small parts was prevalent; and the technology of factories and railways was well established. The Nazi regime appears in this reading as an extreme form of the modern state, and the administration that carried out the Holocaust as but an extreme form of modern bureaucracy. Even the choice of extermination 'was an effect of the earnest effort to find rational solutions to successive "problems"', and at no point did the Holocaust come into conflict with the principles of rationality:

> The 'Final Solution' did not clash at any stage with the rational pursuit of efficient, optimal goal-implementation. On the contrary, it arose out of a genuinely rational concern, and it was generated by bureaucracy true to its form and purpose.[9]

In Max Weber's exposition of modern bureaucracy, Bauman sees 'no mechanism ... capable of excluding the possibility of Nazi excesses ... nothing that would necessitate the description of the activities of the Nazi state as excesses'.[10] If it were the case that modern rational bureaucracy reduces the individual to nothing more than a cog in a machine, a blind applicant of rules, an actor only in the narrowest sense of making rational choices on exclusively instrumental grounds – if all this were true, then we could only conclude with Bauman that the condition of modernity robs people of any significant sense of moral responsibility, and that it is this negation of moral responsibility that is the condition of the possibility, as Bauman might put it, of the decision to commit crimes against humanity.

Bauman implies that neither the abstract conceptions of individual responsibility found in law nor the lack of any conception of responsibility in sociology offers a remotely adequate response to the enormity of the issue. Legal notions of individual responsibility are in this context only a legal fiction imposed on a recalcitrant technological reality, and in any event a court is itself a bureaucratic, rule-bound institution that judges questions of criminal guilt by abstraction from the complex reality of three-dimensional events. Putting the blame on a particular individual does little to confront the system of 'rational choice', for it is 'modernity' rather than individual killers that is primarily at fault. If perpetrators are guilty of not breaking free from this system, this is also the fate of the vast majority of people. Only the few have the courage and vision to risk everything by stepping out of society and confronting their unconditional responsibility for others.

As far as sociology is concerned, Bauman argues that it typically mimics the society that it purports to understand. The general absence of the concept of moral responsibility in sociology, Emile Durkheim's identification of morality with conformity to social norms, Weber's rationalisation of bureaucracy, the reification of rational choice by rational choice theory – all this in effect reflects the conditions of modern society. In opposition to the unheroic 'mass man' who succumbs to the pressures and constraints of rational choice, the only way to save ourselves from complicity is to hear the call to Being with Others, the call of alterity, the call to act morally, the call to go beyond the 'morality-silencing' bounds of reason and society and rediscover the pre-social sources of ethical life in the face of the other.

---

9   Bauman, 1993, pp 16–17.
10 Bauman, 1993, p 10.

Rationality and the Holocaust reconsidered

Two particularly problematic areas in Bauman's critique of 'rational choice' concern his focus on bureaucracy. First, in Weber's conception of bureaucracy individual officials *are* responsible for their actions and part of the immense power of bureaucracy is based on this responsibility for decision making and rule interpretation that is distributed throughout the hierarchy. If the Nazi organisation of terror and extermination constituted a typical modern bureaucracy, as Bauman argues, then individuals would have been expected to take responsibility for the tasks assigned to them and the leadership could not have relied on its employees to perpetrate murder simply as 'cogs in a machine'. As Weber recognised, the process of following a rule is always mediated through mind and consciousness, and the ethos of public service is the oil that allows the machine to run.[11] Secondly, the social organisations that conceived and executed the Holocaust were so different in both ideology and organisation from the 'Weberian' model of bureaucracy that they should not rightly be called 'bureaucracy' at all. They expressed a mode of rule that inherited elements of bureaucratic authority but reconfigured them in a way that cannot simply be understood in terms of Weber's analysis of rationality. The Holocaust was neither organised by typically 'modern formations' nor by anything approximating to an ideal Weberian bureaucracy.

Certainly, the analysis of totalitarianism in power offered, notably, by Hannah Arendt (in *The Origins of Totalitarianism*) and Franz Neumann (in *Behemoth*) paints a profoundly different picture of totalitarian rule. Totalitarianism was not the final culmination of the power of the modern state, but a revolution against the structures of the modern state. Movement rather than structure was its essence. Totalitarian rule was organised on the basis of the intermeshing of various state and party institutions and the proliferation of organisations within the party. Duplication was particularly apparent within the many police apparatuses, which all did similar work, spying on the population and on each other, without any clear knowledge of who would be rewarded and who would be purged.[12] In the complex duplication of organisations involved in the final solution, all were 'equal with respect to each other, and no one belonging to one group owed obedience to a superior officer of another'.[13] The only 'rule' according to the *Führerprinkip* was that formulated by Hans Frank: 'Act in such

---

11 Rules are nothing without interpretation. Bureaucracies are machines made up of people, each of whom takes decisions within given parameters. Weber writes: '... a system of rationally debatable "reasons" stands behind every act of bureaucratic administration, that is, either subsumption under norms or a weighing of ends and means.' Gerth and Mills, 1991, p 220.

12 See also Alan Bullock: 'There was always more than one office operating in any field. A dozen different agencies quarrelled over the direction of propaganda, of economic policy, and the intelligence services. Before 1938 Hitler continually went behind the back of the Foreign Office to make use of Ribbentrop's special bureau or to get information through Party channels. The dualism of Party and State organisations, each with one or more divisions for the same function, was deliberate. In the end this reduced efficiency, but it strengthened Hitler's position by allowing him to play off one department against another.' Bullock, 1983, p 381.

13 Arendt, 1994a, p 71. In September 1939, the Security Service of the SS, a party organisation, was fused with the regular Security Police of the State, which included the Gestapo, to form the Head Office for Reich Security (RSHA), commanded by Heydrich. The RSHA was one of 12 head offices in the SS, two others of which were the Head Office of the Order Police, which was responsible for rounding up Jews, and the Head Office for Administration and Economy (WVHA), which ran concentration camps and later the 'economic' side of extermination. [cont]

a way that the *Führer*, if he knew your action, would approve it.'[14] This 'categorical imperative' is the opposite of clear, rational, written rules. The 'leader principle' is not that of a bureaucracy organised on the basis of formal rules within a structured hierarchy, for the allegiance of the official is not owed to his or her immediate superior but to the leader himself.

The individual responsibility of the official is arguably even greater under the leader principle than in a regulated hierarchical bureaucracy in which responsibility and authority are distributed according to plan. On the one hand, to grasp the will of the *Führer* demands zeal and creativity far in excess of the old fashioned plodding bureaucrat, and wide latitude is given to sub-leaders for the execution of policies. On the other hand, each holder of position is held responsible for all the activities of his subordinates, even in cases of disobedience and failure. The perpetrators were not generally forced into the formations that implemented the Holocaust. Eichmann was keen to win promotion on his particular 'front line', and the members of the murderous police battalions (the *Einsatzgruppen*) were given the opportunity to withdraw from the killing actions.[15] When they accepted the authority of these outfits, they chose to do so even if the parameters of their choices were limited.

Authority in the modern sense of the term is not the same as power. People choose to defer to authority. To be sure, choices are never completely free; they are made within the limits of what is possible and of what alternatives are possible. There are always external constraints, yet rarely are those constraints so rigid that there is no choice; rarely is the structure so dominating that it removes all agency. Under the leader principle, authority works through the will of every member to know and act in accordance with the will of the leader, and to take responsibility for all the decisions taken in their field of operation. Bauman was right to tie his analysis of responsibility to the actual ways in which decision making was organised in the planning and execution of the Holocaust, that is, not to remain exclusively at the level of political philosophy or legal theory but to link such concerns with a sociology of decision making. However, the presumption of rationality in the substance of his analysis obliterates what Arendt called 'the horrible originality' of totalitarian rule.

It is commonly noticed about the Holocaust that one of its most striking features was its industrialisation of death. The Holocaust was of its time; it used the methods of its time and, particularly important to Bauman, are the methods of modern management through which the genocide was in part carried out. We say 'in part' lest the 'industrial' image of Auschwitz overtake our imagination of the Holocaust as a whole. We should remember that the Nazis devised two basic strategies for the annihilation of Jews: mass shooting and mass gassing. Special duty troops of the SS's (Schutzstaffel) Security Service and Security Police, called *Einsatzgruppen*, were assigned to each of the German armies invading the Soviet Union and were given the task of rounding up Jews and killing them through crude and primitive methods of shooting. These methods were the antithesis of Bauman's image of clean and

---

[cont] The RSHA contained Section IV, the Gestapo, divided into Section IV–A, dealing with 'opponents', and Section IV–B, dealing with 'sects'. The Higher SS and Police Leaders were in a different command structure to the 12 offices of the RSHA, while the *Einsatzgruppen* were under the command of the RSHA, but were not one of the 12 offices: Arendt, 1994a, p 70.

14 Arendt, 1994a, p 11.
15 Browning, 1993.

dispassionate white-coated technicians introducing gas into gas chambers. These were methods that confronted the killers with the blood, faces and screams of their victims. It is estimated that some two million Jews were murdered in this way. To murder the rest of European Jewry the Nazis built 'camps' with large scale gassing and sometimes crematorium facilities (Auschwitz, Belzec, Chelmno, Majdanek, Sobibor and Treblinka) and many other 'camps' that were designed to work their inmates to death. The technology used here was often barely more sophisticated than the brute violence of the *Einsatzgruppen* and it was only when death camps were combined with labour camps (such as at Auschwitz) that architectural relics of 'industrial killing' were left behind. All in all, about three and a half million Jews were murdered in this way. A further half a million Jews or so were killed through hunger, disease and exhaustion in the ghettos and as victims of random terror and reprisal. In short, we should be wary of the contemporary synecdoche that substitutes 'Auschwitz', or rather an industrialised representation of Auschwitz, for the whole.

Some elements of bureaucracy certainly existed in the Third Reich: people were sometimes numbered, processed using bureaucratic-style machines, placed under systems of surveillance; there were papers, form filling, official stamps and files of information kept on individuals. But there was no bureaucratic hierarchy of command or system of rules that would be recognisable to a student of Weber. Officials who were technically in positions of authority could be denounced and replaced by their juniors; one apparatus was liable to be liquidated in favour of another; the stability and hierarchy of genuine bureaucracy were absent. What was most significant about the execution of the Holocaust was not the presence of bureaucratic authority but rather the reconfiguration of these bureaucratic elements to construct a principle of rule such as the world had not experienced before.

When Bauman turns rational choice into a modern fatality, he also reduces it to its basest elements. He declares that 'most scientists would be prepared in exchange [for research grants] ... to make do with the sudden disappearance of some of their colleagues with the wrong shape of nose or biographical entry'.[16] He says that rational individuals would play their part in gassing millions, if it meant holding on to a good job. The rational individual would look the other way, stand by and refrain from intervening into affairs that were none of his business, that were not in his job description. This is not the individual who would devote her life to making sense of the world in all its boiling complexity. The shame we feel when we live in a world in which the Holocaust has happened is represented as the antithesis of reason. It is as if morality and reason were opposed armies, or the opposition of morality and reason that Bauman discerns under Nazism were true of modernity itself.

Bauman also totalises rational choice to explain the behaviour of those who conceived the genocide, those who organised it, those who perpetrated it and those who stood by without intervening. And the same mechanism also appears to have governed the behaviour of the victims:

> The Jews could ... play into the hands of their oppressors, facilitate their task, bring closer their own perdition, while guided in their action by the rationally interpreted purpose of survival.[17]

---

16 Bauman, 1993, p 109.
17 Bauman, 1993, p 122.

Bauman argues that the regime in power is always in control of the 'game' in such a way that the 'rational choice' from the point of view of the subordinates is also the preferred choice from the point of view of the regime. So it was that the Jewish administrators and police of the ghettos were enticed to co-operate with the Nazis in the deportation of Jews on the grounds that, however many Jews they produced, they were saving or at least delaying the transport of the rest. The Nazis were able to rely on the Jews to act 'rationally' and thus collaborate in their own extermination:

> In [the world of Auschwitz], obedience was rational; rationality was obedience … Rational people will go quietly, meekly, joyously into a gas chamber, if only they are allowed to believe it is a bathroom …[18]

Here the 'rationality' of the Jewish response that looked to make an accommodation with the Nazis is contrasted with the 'irrationality' of the Warsaw Ghetto uprising. But the choice was not between unreason and reason. We may prefer the heroism of the Warsaw Ghetto uprising to the conformity of the Jewish councils, but in both cases Jews were faced with an impossible choice. The accommodation strategy seemed reasonable to a conservative Jewish leadership who understood the Nazi threat as a continuation of an age-old antisemitism with which a *modus vivendi* could eventually be found. It was an attempt to give a little in order to save more. The 'rebellion' strategy adopted in Warsaw seemed reasonable when it became clear that the Nazis planned to kill everyone and that there was no exit. It does not increase our understanding of events to assign the epithet of 'rational' to one strategy and 'ethical' to the other.

There can be two interpretations of Bauman's overall thesis. The 'weak' one may be summed up by his observation that 'modern civilisation was not the Holocaust's *sufficient* condition; it was, however, most certainly its *necessary* condition'.[19] This interpretation brings to the fore the fact that the Holocaust was modern both in its conception and in its execution, and that the conventional view of Nazism as simply 'anti-modern' cannot hold. The 'strong' interpretation of this thesis is that the dynamics of modernity push towards genocide, that there is nothing in modernity that pulls away from genocide, and that even when genocide is not actual its potentiality is ever present. Bauman himself vacillates between these positions, but between them there is a lot of ground. The weak thesis reminds us that the Holocaust happened in a 'civilised' European country that was technologically and culturally advanced, and cannot be written off as an aberration or just another example of man's inhumanity to man. The strong thesis is that modernity brings us the uncoupling of human beings from moral choice and the tying of human beings to a narrow, short term instrumental rationality. People are made into unthinking cogs in the all-powerful structures of modernity. Bureaucracy brings us the human being who is incapable of seeing the bigger

---

18 Bauman, 1993, p 203. He adds: '[T]here are no scientific methods to decide whether the well-off residents of the Warsaw Ghetto could have done more to alleviate the lot of the poor dying in the streets of hunger and hypothermia, or whether the German Jews could have rebelled against the deportation of the Ostjuden, or the Jews with French citizenship could have done something to prevent incarceration of the "non-French" Jews.' Bauman, 1993, p 205.
19 Bauman, 1993, p 13.

picture. Science brings us 'a rule forbidding the use of teleological vocabulary'.[20] Rational choice becomes our fate.

Doubtless the technical-administrative success of the Holocaust was due in part to the skilful utilisation of 'moral sleeping pills' made available by modern science, technology and organisation; but it was also due to the skilful use of moral imperatives. The appeal by Nazi leaders to duty over private passion, economic utility and military need is now well established – whether in overcoming the resistance of 'ordinary men' to slaughtering other human beings or in overcoming the resistance of Generals to wasting much needed military resources on the killing of Jews. The 'moral point of view' was neither an innocent nor an excluded party in the decision to commit atrocities.

Police Battalion 101 and individual responsibility

In his book *Ordinary Men*,[21] Christopher Browning tells the story of Police Battalion 101, which was one of the formations that followed the German front as it invaded Russia in 1941 in order to kill the Jews who lived there. The personnel for the battalion was recruited from Hamburg during the war, after the youngest and fittest men, as well as the most politically committed, had already been drafted. Browning explores how these middle aged citizens of Hamburg were transformed into mass killers. In interrogations after the war, the men of the battalion identified a number of factors that led them to become killers: the wish to conform, to yield to peer pressure and to obey authority. They told of their desire not to be designated cowardly and not to evade their part in the dirty work that had to be done. Neither political indoctrination nor antisemitism seems to have been a major factor in these decisions.

The first assignment for the battalion was the rounding up of the Jews of Josefow. The men were to be sent to work camps and the women and children were to be shot. The Commander, Wilhelm Trapp, made it clear that no member of his battalion would be compelled to participate in the shootings: about a dozen of the men immediately decided not to take part, and others opted out later. However, about four-fifths of the men decided to participate. At first they found their task difficult to perform, but Browning argues that there was a 'toughening up' process that hardened the men to killing once they had already taken part. The 'decision' to commit crimes against humanity seems to have followed the first killings rather than to have preceded them. Once these men found themselves implicated in massacres, the group acquired an *esprit de corps* of mutual guilt. As we find among perpetrators of recent

---

20 Bauman, 1993, p 170. Take the case, which Bauman cites, of Dr Arthur Gütt, the Head of the National Hygiene Department in the Ministry of Interior who argued for selective breeding of human beings. Bauman comments that Gütt had no doubt that the policy he envisaged of 'selection-cum-elimination' was a logical extension, if not culmination, of the advancement of modern science. But Bauman does not discuss whether the theories of Dr Gütt actually constituted a logical extension of the work of the celebrated scientists, nor indeed whether there was any scientific basis whatsoever for his theorising. Gütt and his colleagues may have been recognised by the Nazis as genuine scientists, but that does not mean that we have to accept this recognition. The problem with eugenics was not that it was scientific but that it was not scientific. Bauman seems to accept that Nazi doctors are doctors: that their talk of hygiene, cleansing, blood and purification were genuinely within a medical tradition. But this is to take rhetoric at its face value.

21 Browning, 1993.

atrocities in Bosnia, the group regularly drank large amounts of alcohol in the evenings to 'blank out' their days and avoid having to think about their actions.

The members of Police Battalion 101 seem to fit Bauman's model better than that controversially advanced by Daniel Goldhagen,[22] that they were driven by an antecedent and virulent antisemitism. They decided to commit crimes against humanity under the influence of the command structure to which they were subordinated. In private life, they were no more predisposed to violence than any other randomly selected group. Yet this genocidal formation was able without much difficulty to incorporate most of them and use them as its agents. There was a role for deference to authority and for the unthinking following of orders. The individuals were explicitly given a choice and most of them made a positive choice to kill. Social factors, such as *esprit de corps*, peer pressure and the wish not to stand out, were all present in the making of these choices. However, the 'hands-on' massacres in which these men participated had nothing to do with social or technological distancing from unseen and faceless victims.[23]

There seems to have been some sense in which killing became an adventure for the members of the police battalion. They became caught up in an orgy of drink and violence and togetherness. It was, perhaps, similar to the explanation of Varnado Simpson for his behaviour at My Lai during the Vietnam War. Suffering from post-traumatic stress syndrome, he later described the events as follows:

> But like I say, after I killed the child, my whole mind just went. It just went. And once you start, it's very easy to keep on. Once you start. The hardest – the part that's hard is to kill, but once you kill, that becomes easier, to kill the next person and the next one and the next one. Because I had no feelings or no emotions or no nothing. No direction. I just killed. It can happen to anyone. Because, see, I wasn't the only one that did it. Hung 'em, you know – all types of ways. Any type of way you could kill someone, that's what they did. And it can happen.[24]

---

22 Goldhagen, 1996.
23 Bauman acknowledges this point. He writes: 'At the *Einsatzgruppen* stage, the rounded-up victims were brought in front of machine guns and killed at point blank range. Though efforts were made to keep the weapons at the longest possible distance from the ditches into which the murdered were to fall, it was exceedingly difficult for the shooters to overlook the connection between shooting and killing.' But Bauman immediately goes on to claim that this was why the administrators of the Holocaust found the methods inefficient and dangerous to morale: 'Other murder techniques were therefore sought – such as would optically separate the killers from their victims. The search was successful and led to the invention of ... gas chambers; the latter ... reduced the role of the killer to that of the "sanitation officer".' (Bauman, 1993, p 26.) It seems to me that this account misconstrues not only the order of succession between the face-to-face and the distanced (what about the 'death marches' at the end of the war?), but also the organisation of murder in the camps (as if the executioners did not have face-to-face contact with those they humiliated, tortured and killed). In the genocide in Rwanda in 1994, a rate of killing which exceeded that accomplished by the Nazis was achieved, using mainly clubs and machetes. In both Rwanda and Bosnia, it was common for perpetrators and victims to be well known to each other. The recent evidence does not show that either technological or social distancing are important factors in perpetrating crimes against humanity.
24 Bilton and Sim, 1992, p 7.

Adolf Eichmann and individual responsibility

Adolf Eichmann was a key bureaucrat and engineer of the genocide of the Jews. He was the man in charge of the whole programme of Jewish extermination. He was not forced into his job. In his case, there was no question of 'kill or be killed'. On the contrary, he was ambitious, keen to win promotion, and personified unquestioning recognition of the authority of the *Führer*.[25] At his trial he said that although he bore no ill feelings towards his victims, he simply could not have acted otherwise. He said that he had acted according to his conscience, and that his conscience would have troubled him only if he had questioned orders, a thought that seems never to have occurred to him.[26]

If we are to believe what Arendt wrote about him,[27] he was a rather pedestrian individual, with few motives beyond his diligence in looking out for his own career advancement. He had no ambition 'to prove a villain' nor was he even a convinced anti-Semite. He was simply a bureaucrat rooted in an everydayness that made him incapable of critical reflection or moral judgment. It was sheer thoughtlessness that predisposed him to become one of the greatest criminals of the modern age. The lesson Arendt took from Eichmann's Jerusalem trial is that we have to come to terms with the fact that the man responsible for the execution of the Holocaust was terrifyingly normal: '... the deeds were monstrous but the doer ... was quite ordinary, commonplace, and neither demonic nor monstrous.'[28]

Eichmann appears in this account as the very personification of Bauman's 'rational actor' driven by a narrow and petty self-interest to push aside any consideration of the moral substance of the job he did. When he offered the improbable defence that he had nothing to do with the killing of Jews, he seems not so much to have been lying as revealing that 'he merely never realised what he was doing'.[29] Since he conceived himself as a man who was 'only doing his job', acting not out of inclination but only in a professional capacity, he could not regard himself as a murderer. He saw himself merely as a 'cog in a machine' and so he was able to play his role without worrying about the purpose of the whole machine, or the ethical consequences of its work. He was an archetype of what Arendt called the 'mass man': the new type of bourgeois who presents himself simply as an 'employee'.[30] Eichmann stands at once as the exemplar of the claim that the perpetrators of the Holocaust were 'men like ourselves' who merely followed the norms of rational decision making, and as a rejoinder to conventional images of a world

---

25 Arendt, 1994a, p 45.
26 Arendt, 1994a.
27 It may be that Arendt was influenced too much by the persona that Eichmann wanted to present at his trial, which was not exactly the 'real' Eichmann. Yet it is precisely the persona which Eichmann presented at the trial which appears to fit so well with Bauman's rational bureaucrat picture. Arendt's picture of Eichmann could easily have been Bauman's inspiration for his account of the genocidal bureaucrat.
28 Arendt, 1994a, pp 3–4.
29 Arendt, 1994a, p 287.
30 Alain Finkielkraut argued in relation to the Barbie trial that the Holocaust was 'from Eichmann to the engineers on the trains ... a crime of employees' and that it was 'precisely to remove from crime the excuse of service and to restore the quality of killers to law-abiding citizens ... that the category of "crimes against humanity" was formulated'. Finkielkraut, 1992, pp 3–4.

dichotomised between our own absolute innocence and the unspeakable Nazi beast. He was living proof of what Karl Jaspers and Hannah Arendt termed the 'banality of evil', demonstrating that the perpetrators were endowed more with 'prosaic triviality' than with 'satanic greatness'.[31]

On the face of it, the case of Eichmann offers a strong case for Bauman's 'rational choice' argument. It also highlights, however, a major difficulty with his formulation of the problem. Arendt mentions one moment in the trial when Eichmann suddenly declared that he had lived his whole life according to Kant's moral precepts and especially according to a Kantian definition of duty. Arendt comments that this was outrageous, since Kant's philosophy was bound up with the human faculty of judgment, with thinking for oneself, and so rules out blind obedience. However, when pressed further, Eichmann revealed that he had read Kant's *Critique of Practical Reason*, and he came up with a roughly correct version of the categorical imperative:

> I meant by my remark about Kant that the principle of my will must always be such that it can become the principle of general laws.[32]

He added that, from the moment he was charged with carrying out the final solution, he knowingly ceased to live according to Kantian principles. Arendt comments that Eichmann did not merely cease to follow Kant's categorical imperative but rather that he distorted it in line with Hans Frank's formulation, which is mentioned above: 'Act in such a way that the *Führer*, if he knew your action, would approve it.' This meant that duty was duty, a law was a law; there could be no exceptions, not even for one's own friends. But when Eichmann said that he had given up on Kant, this also meant in effect that he had put his own self-advancement before any ethical concerns, and blind obedience to the leader before his own practical reason and reflective judgment. In saying this, he must have recognised at some level his own descent into thoughtlessness, lack of reflection, unreason.

This episode reveals the inversion of 'reason' and 'passion' in Bauman's reformulation of Kant. In place of Kant's identification of 'practical reason' with larger moral concerns and 'passion' with self-interest, self-advancement and self-preservation, Bauman reverses this order of association. Reason is now identified with self-interest, self-advancement and self-preservation, and ethics is now identified with one's emotional response to the face of the suffering other. In Kant's hierarchy of reason and passion, passion is subordinated to the demands of reason but is not denounced or damned. Bauman's hierarchy is more severe: it does denounce 'reason' (that which Kant calls 'passion') in favour of postmodern ethics (that which Kant calls 'reason'). The neo-Kantian turns out to be more Kantian than Kant. The effect of this inversion is not only to accept the disconnection of rational choice from ethics, but also to sever the relationship between thinking and understanding on the one hand, and moral judgment and decision making on the other.[33] There are many moments in the text when Bauman writes of the separation of reason and ethics under Nazism. This may well be true, though we would continue to

---

31 Arendt and Jaspers, 1992, p 62.
32 Arendt, 1994a, p 136.
33 The interconnections of thinking, willing and judging, and the dangers inherent in the separation of thinking from willing and judging, became the subject matter of Hannah Arendt's later investigations in *The Life of the Mind*: Arendt, 1978.

insist that the Holocaust had more to do with the 'eclipse of reason' (whether conceived in terms of economic, political or military utility) than with the triumph of reason, and more to do with the triumph of a horrible kind of racist morality than with the eclipse of morality. The main point, however, is not to turn this particular opposition of rational and moral choice into an unalterable fact of 'modernity', still less into a fact of life as such. This is the slippage that seems to dog Bauman's extraordinary analysis.

The case of Eichmann reveals a man who, when he became a Nazi, self-consciously gave up on 'practical reason' (thinking for himself, developing his reflective capacities, judging on the basis of universal criteria) and replaced it with mere obedience to orders, social conformity, rigid duty to order. This was his choice. It was a terrible one in the circumstances. But it had nothing to do with the effacement of a pre-social moral consciousness by the technical-rational norms of modernity. For the individual's capacity to think and judge for himself is as much a feature of 'modernity' as is the awesome power of 'society' over the individual.

Conclusion on individual responsibility

Bauman is not explicit about his attitude to trials for crimes against humanity,[34] though he does comment that he found the experience of the Demjanjuk and Barbie court cases 'embarrassing'.[35] His work could be read as a theoretical underpinning of an argument that it is impossible for a court of law to remove from crime the excuse of service as Alain Finkielkraut hopes. Indeed, Klaus Barbie's defence, and in fact also those of Eichmann and the Nuremberg defendants, were not incompatible with the substance of Bauman's work.

Barbie's lawyers, the Congolese M'Bemba, the Algerian Bouaïta, and the French-Vietnamese Vergès, constructed a 'left wing' and 'anti-imperialist' defence. Barbie's actions were not crimes against humanity; the Holocaust was simply a family quarrel amongst white Europeans; whites did to other whites what all Europeans routinely do to everyone else: so what? asks the rest of the world. By putting Barbie on trial you are simply trying to camouflage European history, to scapegoat the Nazis for that which you are all responsible.[36]

If the structures of modernity are as deterministic as in Bauman's account, then trials make little sense, since nearly everyone is guilty. Only those who took a moral decision to step outside the structures of modernity are, in this framework, not guilty. Bauman stresses the fact that this was possible; he gives examples of individuals who risked their lives to behave morally and 'irrationally'; but they are necessarily very rare and unusual individuals. Moreover, trials make little sense because courts are exactly the sort of modernistic, rule-bound, bureaucratic, rational institutions that Bauman argues are responsible for the Holocaust. Tribunals themselves, for Bauman, must surely fail to step outside the realm of totalitarianism.

---

34 At a lecture Bauman gave at Warwick University on 19 February 2001, I was twice able to ask him what his attitude was to crimes against humanity trials. I still do not know what his attitude is, since he seemed to go to some lengths to avoid giving a straight answer.

35 Bauman, 1993, p 206.

36 Finkielkraut, 1992.

So is the precedent set at Nuremberg, to hold individuals responsible for their actions, sustainable? What can we say about the ways in which decisions to commit such crimes are actually made?

First, we are not dealing with individuals who had prior, fixed preferences for antisemitism and were thus 'just on the look out' for propitious circumstances in which they could maximise these preferences at low cost to themselves. The making of a mass murderer is a social process in which there is an interplay between the act and the actor in which the commission of the deed may precede both its signification and its justification by the actors involved. Rather than the motive leading to the act, it was often the case that complicity in atrocity, torturing and murdering innocent human beings led to the search for good reasons – perhaps on the basis of the Pascalian principle that if you kneel first, then prayer will follow. There must be an emphasis on the malleability of preferences, on how experience changes them, on how 'ordinary men' turn into hardened monsters or at least become hardened in their monstrous acts.

Secondly, the making of a mass murderer is a social process in which there is also an interplay between structure and agency. Regarding structure, the *Führer* principle represented a new context (*contra* Bauman) in which 'ordinary people' are given new carrots to become 'extraordinary' by committing vile deeds. We see here a kind of ordinary – conformist and officially validated – extraordinariness. Once these incentives disappear, some become (like Eichmann) obedient servants to the authority of the court that tries them, and most become ordinary 'democratic' civil servants and businessmen. Regarding agency, it is clear that some people walked away from the 'incentives' to murder and exercised their own moral judgment. Such judgments were not entirely 'reflective' in the sense that there were no rules or standards to guide them, for individual subjects could still appeal beyond the particular normative order of the so called *Volk* to a humanist tradition – of thinking for yourself, of the right to subjective freedom, of universal equality – that is as much part of 'modernity' as instrumental rationality. We see here strong confirmation of the argument (*contra* Bauman) that not even this totalitarian epoch could reduce all action to instrumental rationality. On the contrary, totalitarian terror demonstrated ultimately the subordination of instrumental rationality to a certain 'moral' point of view in which (as Arendt has argued) questions of economic, political and military utility were self-consciously subsumed to the end of killing and degrading Jews.[37]

Put at its strongest, it is difficult to escape the conclusion that the moral point of view is *always* a crucial element of decision making in the modern world, and that no rational choice can be understood solely in terms of instrumental rationality. For without reference to moral concerns, we cannot explain how some people monitor their preferences, refuse all incentives to violate them and resist to the end lending themselves to the horrible processes we have described in the text. Value rationality works not just as an accidental or subordinate ingredient within preference formation and expression, but as a constitutive aspect of how 'we' – individuals thrown into a world without absolute foundations – make sense of, understand and judge the preferences we make.

---

37 Arendt, 1994b.

The reality is that not everyone was responsible for the Holocaust. Social structures were in place that put considerable pressure on many individuals to commit crimes against humanity. There was peer pressure; there was the pressure to pursue personal success and advancement; there was pressure to conform; there was pressure to submit to 'authority'; there was pressure to follow racist and genocidal ideology. There were risks, sometimes small, sometimes large, but very rarely life-threatening, in resisting these pressures. There were also more personal motives, such as killing as part of an adventure or as an outlet for psychological frustration and anger, and such as simple sadism or love of power. But whatever motives were to the fore in any particular case, it is clear that individuals made choices; sometimes choice was limited; sometimes other options were not attractive; sometimes they were difficult and dangerous. But perpetrators are never merely the puppets of the social structure within which they find themselves.

Chapter Three
Crimes against humanity:
the actualisation of a universal

Auschwitz has become the signature of an entire epoch – and it concerns all of us. Something happened there that no one could previously have thought even possible. It touched a deep layer of solidarity among all who have a human face.[1]

In this chapter I look at the Nuremberg process, the ways in which the charge of 'crimes against humanity' was used, and the codification of the term 'genocide' in the Genocide Convention (1948). I go on to look at the emerging academic discipline of 'genocide studies' and the ways in which it understands and defines these concepts.

The Nuremberg process, in spite of its inadequacies and flaws, was the beginning of the actualisation of the concept of cosmopolitan criminal law. It was the point at which power first coincided with supra-national authority in a successful legal response to mass killing. The acceptance of the new legal charge of crimes against humanity heralded the recognition of the principle that the most serious human rights abuses are the business of all human beings, and that the prosecution of such crime is therefore a supra-national matter. The development of cosmopolitan criminal law is a process that occurs within the sphere of existing global politics and diplomacy, and within the sphere of existing power relationships. It is a messy and uncertain development, always beset by the grossest hypocrisy. It is diluted and perverted by those states and heads of states who have reason to fear the consequences of universal jurisdiction. It is the opposite of utopian; it has a real existence and an organic development. It is not just the assertion of an abstract universal by critics but is the concrete development of a universal in the real world.

It was not a new problem that faced the four powers when they were confronted with the prospect of victory in 1945. Whenever the overthrow of an old regime is achieved, the problem is posed of how to deal with the old leadership in order to neutralise them as a threat, hold them to account for their actions, and build the foundations of the new regime in such a way as to make its difference clear to all. When Charles I and Louis XVI were executed, there was little doubt as to the legal irregularity of the institutions that decided their fates. It could not have been otherwise, since under all existing law regicide was the greatest crime. Otto Kirchheimer calls this 'trial by fiat of the successor regime' and the Nuremberg trial 'the most important "successor" trial in modern history'.[2] Part of its importance was in putting up a barrier

---

1 Habermas, 1991, pp 251–52.
2 Kirchheimer, 1969, p 323. Kirchheimer fits his discussion of the Nuremberg process within the context of the use by states of political trials, 'the most dubious segment of the administration of justice, that segment which uses the devices of justice to bolster or create new power positions': Kirchheimer, 1969, p vii. This places discussion of Nuremberg next to discussions of the Soviet show trials and the French military trials of their National Liberation Front (FLN) prisoners in Algeria.

between the past and the present. 'Experience shows that every successor regime feels intensely that in condemnation of the predecessors' practices lies the key to humanity's future.'[3] Post-war trials of Nazis, therefore, had clear benefits for the four powers in terms of legitimation, both of themselves and of the new regimes that they wanted to build.

However, as soon as they had allowed the genie of cosmopolitan law out of the bottle, they went to great lengths to control it, limit it and peg it back. The universality of the new form was perceived as threatening. No crimes were to be considered that had been committed by any of the Allies, such as the bombings of Dresden, Tokyo, Hiroshima or Nagasaki; the treatment of German civilians by the Red Army; the Russian complicity in the invasion of Poland; or French collaboration with the Nazis. The concept of crimes against humanity at Nuremberg was tied to crimes against peace and to war crimes, which were safer charges for the powers because they were more concerned with familiar questions of inter-state relationships and sovereignty.[4] The Allied powers tried to avoid allowing the universality of the crimes against humanity charge to set universal precedents. They did this by particularising the charge. The offence of crimes against humanity was linked to a particular nation, Germany, and a particular frame, that of the Second World War.[5] At Nuremberg, it was easy for the four powers to keep significant control over much of the process. In the end a conclusion as to the efficacy of international cosmopolitan law must focus on the question of its ability to find an autonomous space for itself. If cosmopolitan criminal law is able to attain a genuine life outside the control of the great powers, then this autonomy is achieved; if it remains nothing more than a façade erected for purposes of legitimation that remains forever under the control of the powerful, then it is not.

The International Military Tribunal at Nuremberg

In his report to the President of the United States, Justice Robert H Jackson, the chief prosecutor, said that the important achievements of the Nuremberg process had been to make explicit what was already implicit in international law with respect to war crimes, crimes against peace and crimes against humanity, and to incorporate these principles into a judicial precedent.[6] Perhaps he was downplaying the degree to which the process was innovative, since during the trials it had been important for the prosecution to undercut the *ex post facto* argument, which held that defendants were being tried for offences that did not exist in international law at the time of their commission.

3 Kirchheimer, 1969, p 325.
4 The Berlin Protocol of 6 October 1945 ingeniously limited the scope of crimes against humanity by means of replacing a semicolon with a comma in the London charter, which resulted in the fact that 'all the crimes against humanity enumerated therein were made punishable only in so far as they were ancillary or subsidiary to other criminal acts within the jurisdiction of the tribunal'. Also, the tribunal 'partly in disregard of the terms of the charter which gave it jurisdiction in respect of crimes against humanity "before or during the war", in so far as they were committed in connexion with or in execution of any crime within the jurisdiction of the tribunal, apparently declined to treat acts committed prior to the war as crimes against humanity'. Lauterpacht, 1950, pp 35–36.
5 For this point I am indebted to Alan Norrie: Norrie, 2002.
6 Jackson, 1949, p 437.

While the prosecution argued that the offence of crimes against humanity was in fact simply a distillation of existing law, the formulation and use of that charge set an important precedent.

The London conference of the USA, the USSR, Britain and France took place in summer 1945, and produced the charter of the tribunal. The trial of the major war criminals started on 20 November 1945 and finished on 1 October 1946 with three acquittals, seven prison sentences and 12 death sentences. There were eight members of the tribunal or judges, a senior and an alternate from each of the four powers. There were notable absences from the dock: Adolf Hitler, Josef Goebbels, Heinrich Himmler and Martin Bormann were dead. Gustav Krupp was intended to represent German industrial might in the dock, but was elderly and found by the court to be mentally incompetent. However, all of the leading Nazis who had been arrested were on trial.

The prosecution at Nuremberg charged the defendants with four counts. Count one, conspiracy, charged all 22 of the defendants with participation in a common plan to prepare and execute the substantive crimes enumerated in counts two, three and four:

> At the trial of any individual member of any group or organisation the Tribunal may declare (in connection with any act of which the individual may be convicted) that the group or organisation of which the individual was a member was a criminal organisation.[7]

Count one, charging defendants with conspiracy, is not outlined in the charter as the other three counts are: the language of conspiracy is included in Article 6(a) in relation to crimes against peace, but not (b) or (c) in relation to war crimes or crimes against humanity. The charter was the result of hurried negotiations in London and showed the effects of much patching and compromise.[8] Stanislaw Pomorski comments that 'one is at a loss to understand why conspiracy to prepare an aggressive war should be a crime per se while conspiracy to set up a death camp should not be'.[9] The ambiguity and confusion of the charter left considerable law making powers in the hands of the tribunal, and Jackson prepared the conspiracy count to include all the other substantive crimes, arguing that the tribunal should accept this even though it was not explicitly allowed by the charter itself. In the end the judgment of the tribunal rejected Jackson's expansion of the conspiracy charge.

The conspiracy/criminal organisation plan was conceived by a young lawyer from the American Department of War, Colonel Murray C Bernays, and was set out in a memorandum dated 15 September 1944.[10] Bernays opposed an administrative solution to the problem of 'de-Nazification', preferring a judicial one that was intended to grant due process. He proposed, first, that a court should judge that the Nazi government, party and agencies such as the SS (Schutzstaffel) and SA (Sturm Abteilung) were conspiracies to commit murder and other crimes. The same court should then try individuals considered to be representative of those organisations who would then be found guilty of the same offences on the grounds of their membership of these organisations alone. Once the conspiracy was established, 'each act of every

---

7   Smith, 1977, p 61; Article 9 of the London charter.
8   Smith, 1977, p 58.
9   Pomorski, 1990, p 222.
10 Pomorski, 1990, p 215.

member thereof during its continuance and in furtherance of its purposes would be imputable to all other members thereof'.[11] Thus any member of these criminal organisations could then be arrested and found guilty simply by virtue of their membership.

Jackson argued for the conspiracy/criminal organisation approach in order to 'reach a great many of the equally guilty persons against whom evidence of specific violent acts might be lacking although there is ample proof that they participated in the common plan or enterprise or conspiracy'.[12] Bernays' plan was adopted by the Americans with a little refinement and watering down.

Pomorski argues that the approach was important in that it allowed the tribunal to find that Hitlerism, as a social phenomenon, was criminal:

> If one perceives a deterrent and preventive function of criminal law in a broad sense, if one views it as a consciousness-building factor, the idea of organisational prosecution fulfilled its tasks very well.[13]

Renaud Donnedieu de Vabres, the French senior judge, set out his argument against conspiracy in two deliberative sessions (27 June and 14 August 1946) and with two memoranda.[14] First, conspiracy was, he argued, an Anglo-American legal concept, unknown to both continental and international law. Secondly, the prosecution had failed to prove the existence of a huge 25-year conspiracy beginning in the early 1920s; it had failed to establish that there was a common plan to prove that a group of people had, at a specific time and place, agreed on definite criminal objectives and the criminal methods they intended to use to attain them. Instead, the prosecution had merely gathered up various expressions of Nazi principles such as passages from the party programme and quotations from *Mein Kampf*, contending that these were the core of a fixed criminal plan. He argued that there had been no master plan, but a development of policy.[15] Thirdly, conspiracy was not a crime against international law at the time the acts were committed so that any charges would be ex post facto. Fourthly, the London charter had only listed three prosecutable crimes. At the end of Article 6, the mysterious short paragraph had been added stating that all those who participated in 'a common plan or conspiracy' to commit any crimes would be 'responsible for all the acts performed by any persons in execution of the plan'.[16] Donnedieu de Vabres argued that this paragraph was aimed at complicity and did 'not provide for a specific general crime' of conspiracy.[17] Fifthly, he argued that conspiracy required some degree of equality amongst the conspirators that did not exist in this case due to the overpowering weight of the Führer compared to the other actors. He wanted to convict for substantive crimes and, where necessary, also to punish accomplices and accessories, but to drop the conspiracy charges.

Some German observers welcomed Donnedieu de Vabres' opposition to conspiracy charges, since they implied collective German guilt, but he himself

---

11 Pomorski, 1990, p 215.
12 Pomorski, 1990, p 219.
13 Pomorski, 1990, p 224.
14 Smith, 1977, p 121.
15 If we understand Nazism through the work of Hannah Arendt, then the idea of a huge organised and coherent conspiracy is difficult to sustain. It is also clear that Nazi policy, for example in relation to the Jews, was not planned in advance but developed over time.
16 Smith, 1977, p 122.
17 Smith, 1977, p 123.

took the opposite position. He thought that to find the Nazi leadership guilty of the conspiracy would too easily absolve those Germans not directly involved. He was also worried that the Jewish conspiracy myth could be replaced by blaming a small secret Nazi conspiracy for Germany's problems.

The case of Karl Doenitz illustrates the complexities involved in the idea of conspiracy. He was Commander of the German submarine programme from 1935 until 1943, when he became Commander in Chief of the navy. He was convicted at Nuremberg on counts two and three – crimes against peace and war crimes – and sentenced to 10 years in prison. There was much discussion in his case about the attack on Norway, and whether this particular attack was aggressive or defensive, since there was evidence that the British were also planning to attack Norway. There was also much discussion about the waging of submarine warfare, and whether Doenitz had been responsible for a policy of failing to rescue or actively killing survivors of naval attacks. Biddle, the American judge, admitted that 'Germany waged a much cleaner [naval] war than we did'.[18] The case against Doenitz hung on things that were not centrally important, and that might have been carried out by either side in the war, such as the attack on Norway or the ruthlessness of submarine warfare. But was there not a case for charging Doenitz with being a part of the Nazi machine that planned to rule the world and commit crimes against humanity? There was a division of labour: some ran death camps; others took the territory that was to be cleansed of Jews; others patrolled the seas to keep them safe for Nazi shipping and dangerous for enemy shipping. Irrespective of particular crimes committed by the U-boat fleet, there was a good argument for finding that those who ran the U-boat fleet were doing so as part of a greater Nazi plan. Crimes against humanity or genocide are necessarily conspiracies. Though the court in general rejected the conspiracy prosecution, it may be argued that to find defendants guilty of the other substantive crimes contained the necessary element of conspiracy in a different form.

Count two of the prosecution was crimes against peace:

> All the defendants with divers other persons during the period of years preceding 8 May 1945 participated in the planning, preparation, initiation and waging of wars of aggression that were also wars in violation of international treaties, agreements and assurances.[19]

In 1927 the Assembly of the League of Nations had adopted the Declaration on Aggressive War, which declared aggressive war to be an international crime:

> All wars of aggression are, and shall always be, prohibited. Every pacific means must be employed to settle disputes of every description that may arise between states.[20]

In 1928 these propositions were incorporated into the Paris Pact for the Renunciation of War as an Instrument of National Policy, signed by 15 states and later adhered to by 48 others, converting it into a universal treaty. The Kellogg-Briand Pact (1933), the Convention for the Definition of Aggression, reaffirmed these principles. The tribunal at Nuremberg held that the Kellogg-Briand Pact in particular constituted international law against the waging of aggressive war. In its opinion, the renunciation of war:

---

18 Pomorski, 1990, p 261.
19 Smith, 1977, p 16.
20 Lukashuk, 1990, p 127.

... as an instrument of national policy necessarily involves the proposition that such a war is illegal in international law and that those who plan and wage such a war, with its inevitable and terrible consequences, are committing a crime in so doing.[21]

The tribunal also noted that Article 227 of the Treaty of Versailles (1919) provided for the establishment of a special international tribunal to try the former German Emperor 'for a supreme offence against international morality and the sanctity of treaties'. Article 228 provided for the indictment of others accused of having committed acts in violation of the laws and customs of war.[22]

Count three, war crimes, was the least controversial count since it relied on the most precedent. It added together the sections of the Hague Rules of Land Warfare and the Geneva Conventions that prohibited certain wartime actions, such as acts of mistreatment of prisoners, murder and devastation not justified by military necessity.[23] These conventions and treaties became part of customary international law that binds all states irrespective of whether or not they have ratified this or that particular convention. Common war crimes evolve into crimes against humanity if they are committed pursuant to orders drawn up in advance, thereby assuming a state-organised character, and also have as their objective the mass annihilation of people.[24] States have the responsibility to prosecute their own soldiers who commit war crimes. Clearly, when the state itself is criminal the prosecutions must come from outside the state.

Crimes against humanity

[N]amely, murder, extermination, enslavement, deportation and other inhumane acts committed against any civilian population,[25] whether before or during the war, or persecutions on political, racial or religious grounds in exception of or in connection with any crime within the jurisdiction of the tribunal, whether or not in violation of the domestic law of the country where perpetrated.[26]

The term 'crimes against humanity' first appeared in the declaration of 28 May 1915 by the governments of France, Britain and Russia concerning the massacres of Armenians in Turkey. This declared that all members of the government of Turkey would be held responsible, together with its agents implicated in the massacres.[27] However, in the end, it remained little more than a declaration.[28]

---

21 Murphy, 1990, p 149.
22 Murphy, 1990, p 150.
23 Smith, 1977, p 12. Conventions against war crimes include St Petersburg Declaration (1868); Hague Conventions (1907); Geneva Protocol (1929); Geneva Regulations on the Treatment of Prisoners of War, Wounded Sailors and the Civilian Population on Occupied Territory (1929); Geneva Conventions of 1949 and supplementary protocols thereto (1977).
24 Reshetov, 1990, p 169.
25 On 22 February 2001, three Bosnian Serbs were convicted at the International Criminal Tribunal for the former Yugoslavia for crimes against humanity. They had been involved in the perpetration and organisation of the mass rape of women during the war in Bosnia. The significance of this case is that the defendants were found guilty of crimes against humanity solely on the basis of the rape charges. This case added rape to the specific crimes which can constitute crimes against humanity: *Prosecutor v Kunarac, Kovac and Vukovic*.
26 Ginsburgs and Kudriavtsev, 1990, p 177.
27 Clark, 1990, p 177.
28 In April 1919, following heavy British pressure, an Ottoman court was set up in Constantinople to put the wartime Turkish leadership on trial for war crimes and for the genocide of the Armenians. Kemal Bey and Tevfik Bey were found guilty of acting 'against humanity and [cont]

To the extent that the crimes committed by the Nazi regime, particularly against the Jews, were unprecedented, the formulation of a law that was capable of addressing the particular unprecedented characteristics was required. Crimes against humanity are different from murder, not just quantitatively, but also qualitatively. The Nazis were not simply unwilling to share Germany with the Jews; they were unwilling to share the earth with them. State expulsions, murders and persecutions were not unprecedented; in the context of international law, expulsions had been considered as crimes against neighbouring states. Genocide is qualitatively different; it is a 'criminal enterprise against the human condition'.[29] As Hannah Arendt puts it, genocide is:

> ... an attack upon human diversity as such, that is, upon a characteristic of the 'human status' without which the very words 'mankind' or 'humanity' would be devoid of meaning.[30]

Genocide is a crime against every human being on earth because it is an attack on each person's status as a human being: it means that a person's recognition as a person is conditional; it means that they may be defined as insects or rats instead of human beings, and treated accordingly. To make an analogy with murder: a murder is not considered only to be the concern of the individual who is murdered or that person's family. In most contemporary legal systems, it is also considered to be the business of the state, and it is the state that has responsibility for prosecuting the murderer. Similarly, the Nazi genocide was not simply the concern of the Jews, but was a crime of direct relevance to the whole of humanity.

The formulation and prosecution of crimes against humanity by the four powers at Nuremberg was therefore a cosmopolitan act. It was a recognition that such a crime is not the property of any particular group or state, nor does it fall within the jurisdiction of any; it is the responsibility of human beings in general. Implicit within the logic of the term 'crime against humanity' is the need for an international court. Also implicit within the term itself is a particular, modern, universalist conception of 'humanity'. It is a conception that assumes a fundamental equality of right throughout the human community. It assumes that human beings are necessarily bearers of basic rights.

Robert Fine[31] looks at the ways in which the charge of crimes against humanity at Nuremberg was viewed by writers at the time of the trials. He identifies three distinct contemporary strands of opinion. First, there was a cosmopolitan point of view, such as that of Karl Jaspers. Jaspers defined four strata of responsibility for the genocide:[32] political responsibility, in that each human being had a responsibility for how they were ruled; moral

---

[cont] civilisation' for their parts in the deportation of Armenians. Kemal was hanged, but there was much nationalist opposition to the process and the Ottoman court freed many other prisoners without charge. In the end the British were also forced by the triumph of the nationalists in 1921 to free their prisoners. 'Constantinople is the Nuremberg that failed. What Constantinople shows, most of all, is that the enormous political difficulties of mounting prosecutions against foreign war criminals can be so great that a tribunal can crumble.' Bass, 2000, p 106.

29 Edgar Faure, in Finkielkraut, 1992, p 28.
30 Arendt, 1994a, p 269.
31 Fine, 2000.
32 Jaspers, 2000.

responsibility, in that each person would confront the 'countless acts of indifference' without which genocide would not be possible; metaphysical responsibility, in which every individual is held responsible for the fact that human beings are capable of such crimes; and legal responsibility. This last responsibility was to be addressed by criminal courts and would be assigned to those who had actually carried out crimes against humanity, whether with their own hands or from behind a desk. Jaspers argued that prosecution was centrally important in order to avoid the designation of collective German national guilt. The prosecution of mass murderers as mere criminals would remove their aura of satanic greatness and expose them in all their banality. The world would not allow such crimes to go unpunished.

Secondly, Fine identifies a 'realist critique' among contemporary writers, represented most strongly by the defendants themselves. This critique defined the Nuremberg process as nothing more than the application by the powerful of their own will, an application that was obfuscated behind a façade of due process. The charge is that the process was nothing more than victor's justice. Kirchheimer addresses this criticism in a way that acknowledges its strength: '... in all political trials conducted by the judges of the successor regime, the judges are in a certain sense the victor's judges.'[33] He focuses on the different attitudes that were taken to the trial by the USSR delegation and by the Americans at the London conference. The Russians wanted to set up the tribunal in such a way as to guarantee that all the defendants would be 'convicted' and executed. Jackson preferred an approach based on a separation of power between the tribunal and the prosecution, and on the independence of judges who would be in a position to evaluate the evidence presented and to come to a verdict based upon it.

Kirchheimer argues that in reality there was less of a difference between the cynical realism of the USSR and the American approach than there appeared to be. 'Occurring in the wake of a National Socialist defeat, the trial could not but take the defeat of National Socialist doctrine and practice as its starting point.'[34] There was not a contradiction between the existence of an independent judicial tribunal on the one hand and the manifestation of power on the other; rather, the manifestation of the power of the victors was expressed in the form of an independent judicial tribunal. The trial was not presided over by God, judging the Nazis from above and outside the world. It was organised by those forces that had defeated Nazism militarily and ideologically. It was organised by the victors over Nazism in the name of a set of values that it held to be superior to those of Nazism, namely, human rights.

This leads to the second of the realist critiques put forward by the defendants at Nuremberg: the *tu quoque* ('you likewise') argument. They attempted to normalise what they had done, arguing that there was nothing special about the inhumanities committed by the Nazis in relation to the whole history of man's inhumanity to man and in particular in relation to crimes carried out by the four powers. How could the two old imperialist powers, the regime that had perpetrated the Stalinist purges and the one that had just exploded two atomic bombs in densely populated cities, sit in judgment over the Nazis under the banner of human rights?

---

33 Kirchheimer, 1969, p 332.
34 Kirchheimer, 1969, p 334.

In a wider sense, the *tu quoque* argument could be levelled against any type of terrestrial justice. Only the archangel descending on judgment day would be exempt from the reproach that blame and praise have not been distributed according to everyone's due desert.[35]

Kirchheimer contends that this is an argument addressed to the public at large, and to future historians, rather than a serious defence in a court which, of course, in general refused to hear it. The *tu quoque* argument was a stronger argument against the Nuremberg process, whose charter disqualified in advance the examination of crimes committed by anyone other than the Nazis, than it is against more recent tribunals such as the International Criminal Tribunal for the former Yugoslavia (ICTY). While the ICTY's establishment by the Security Council still protects the great powers, who may use their vetoes, it has no such limitations in the body of law with which it operates. Serbs, Croatians and Bosnians may all be charged with crimes. The *tu quoque* argument becomes less relevant as cosmopolitan law gains strength and independence; the success of cosmopolitan law may be measured by the progress it makes in defeating the *tu quoque* argument, rather than, as at Nuremberg, simply ignoring it.

The realist critique also challenged the legality of the process: there were new 'laws' but no legislature, and the laws under which defendants were tried had not existed at the time of the crimes. The defendants also argued that they should not be made to take responsibility as individuals for offences that were carried out by the state and were legally authorised by it. Kirchheimer argues in response to this defence that such acts as making policies to select and kill individuals on the basis of their 'racial' characteristics:

> ... [do] not give such enactments the dignity of law. It is the negation of the purpose of law, which even in the form of the shoddiest enactment must still offer a password: the ordering of human relations ... The presumed validity of an enactment does not necessarily exculpate those who might consider invocation of the statute a foolproof defense mechanism. An enactment in itself is a mere cipher, whose real import and weight ... are determined by those who fashioned it or learned to mould it in constant practice.[36]

The third contemporary approach that Fine examines is Heidegger's argument 'against humanism'. Humanity itself was not innocent; many of the greatest atrocities had been carried out in the name of humanity against those designated to be inhuman or bearers of inhuman culture. Crimes against humanity were committed by Germans; crimes for humanity were committed by their accusers. Michel Foucault has persuasively charted the inhumanities committed in the name of humanism. For example, the development of the modern prison system was intended to replace ancient and inhuman corporal punishments with modern, reasonable and efficient methods designed to rehabilitate the souls of criminals: Foucault exposes the horrors and the anti-human nature of the modern humanistic approaches.[37] Similarly, the terrors of the French Revolution, and of Stalin's communism, were committed in the

---

35 Kirchheimer, 1969, p 337.
36 Kirchheimer, 1969, p 328. Franz Neumann also argues persuasively that there was nothing which could be rightfully characterised as law in Nazi Germany, and Lon Fuller argues that since Nazi enactments were retroactive and secret they could not be understood as laws: Neumann, 1963; Fuller, 1969.
37 Foucault, 1991.

name of humanity, against those sections of society that were held not to recognise the existence of any fundamental human community. Heidegger was against individuals being held criminally responsible at Nuremberg, arguing that the legal subject was a fiction that forgets the historicality and finite freedom of human existence and the homelessness of modern human beings. He argued, and Zygmunt Bauman was later much influenced by his argument, that the events of the Holocaust were the results of such a profound malady of modern society that any attempt to scapegoat a few individuals in a legal process would constitute nothing more than empty hypocrisy.

Fine argues, in summary, that the originality and strength of Arendt's understanding of the Nuremberg process was in the way she recognised the limited justification of each of these understandings of the Nuremberg process – humanist, realist and post-humanist – and wove them into a more critical and grounded cosmopolitan argument. What gives her discussions their force is the recognition of the equivocation of law and her readiness to embrace legal remedy in the knowledge of its risks.[38]

At the time of Nuremberg, Arendt wrote to Jaspers that the Nazi crimes were such that no law could prosecute them, that no mundane criminal process could achieve any sort of justice, or punish the perpetrators with anything but an inadequate sentence. '[T]his guilt, in contrast to all criminal guilt, oversteps and shatters any and all legal systems. That is the reason why the Nazis at Nuremberg are so smug.'[39] Yet 15 years later, in relation to the Eichmann trial, it was Arendt who defended the trial against Jaspers' scepticism. For her, that trial represented missed opportunities to push the bounds of cosmopolitan law, to institute an international court and to bolster the offence of crimes against humanity. Nevertheless, she defended the right of the Israelis to kidnap the indicted Nuremberg war criminal Eichmann from a state with a bad record for extradition, and to put him on trial. This action served the cause of justice, resulted in the punishment of Eichmann, gave many victims their day in court, and allowed the story of the Holocaust to be retold in an authoritative way to a new generation. Throughout her work, Arendt is aware both of the importance of the cosmopolitan project of international criminal law and of the many problems and shortcomings of its actuality. She wrestles with the perplexities and contradictions. She avoids what Fine[40] refers to as cosmopolitan utopianism as well as 'realist' cynicism while engaging positively with the question of crimes against humanity prosecutions.[41]

---

38 Fine, 2000.
39 Arendt and Jaspers, 1992.
40 Fine, 2000.
41 In a process which ran parallel to the Nuremberg tribunals, Allied military commissions condemned 920 Japanese to death and sentenced to prison terms 3,000 others who had been found guilty of crimes during the Second World War. The International Military Tribunal sat in Tokyo from 1946 to 1948, trying the 25 most senior Japanese defendants. The International Military Tribunal for the Far East (IMTFE) was set up by a 'special proclamation' of General MacArthur, Supreme Commander for the Allied Powers in the Pacific, with a charter similar to that for the Nuremberg tribunal. One important difference was that only persons charged with crimes against peace could stand before the tribunal; all others were to be tried by national or other courts. The Emperor of Japan, Hirohito, was not charged with any crimes. This seems to have been simply a political decision made by the Americans; they wanted Hirohito to remain as Emperor in their newly established regime. Political considerations, and the consolidation of a friendly and anti-Russian regime, took precedence over cosmopolitan law: Piccigallo, 1979.

During the preparations for the main trial at Nuremberg, the Russians had specifically wanted the inclusion of a charge relating to the massacre of Polish officers in the Katyn forest. However, the Americans found evidence showing that it was the Russians themselves who had committed the massacre. The scandal was hushed up by the court.[42] This incident, however, illustrates the fact that the Cold War was, during the trials, rapidly beginning to freeze. There had been a period of about a year when the interests of all the great powers had converged around the prosecution of the Nazis. This remarkable period, however, was short-lived. The struggle between the USSR and the USA for global hegemony began to take precedence over the establishment of a global legal order, and co-operation in the name of justice quickly crumbled. The Cold War saw the emphatic re-emergence of particular interest as against cosmopolitan order. The global bipolar struggle was everything. Both sides held that victory in the global ideological and military struggle was the prerequisite for any kind of justice.

During the American war in Vietnam, there was little question of any kind of jurisdiction over crimes committed by combatants, but there was one notable exception. A military court-martial tribunal found William L Calley guilty in April 1971 of the murder of 'at least 22' Vietnamese civilians at My Lai on 16 March 1968. Between 8 am and noon on that day, 504 non-combatant inhabitants of My Lai, everyone who was there, were killed by the American soldiers of 'Charlie Company'.[43] Calley was, even before My Lai, a sadistic killer. During a previous assault on a village, he had thrown a defenceless old man down a well and shot him.[44] At My Lai, he saw a baby crawling away from a ditch that was already filled with dead and dying villagers; he seized the child by the leg, threw it back into the pit, and shot it.[45] Nobody else was ever held legally responsible for the massacre: no other killers, no one higher up the chain of command. No one else was found guilty of any war crime during the entire Vietnam War. Calley was sentenced to life imprisonment with hard labour. He served his sentence under comfortable conditions, and was released on parole in 1974 by Judge Robert Elliott, who said: 'war is war, and it is not unusual for innocent civilians such as the My Lai victims to be killed.'[46]

While there was a lack of official tribunals and legal accountability, it is nevertheless true that during the Vietnam War one important weapon in the armoury of the anti-war movement was the appeal to international law. The war could legitimately be characterised as a crime against peace; there was much behaviour that could be characterised as war crimes and crimes against humanity. Bertrand Russell wrote a book entitled *War Crimes in Vietnam*,[47] for example, and Jean-Paul Sartre published a pamphlet[48] with the same name, arguing that the American war in Vietnam constituted genocide. In May 1967 in Stockholm, and November 1967 in Roskilde, Denmark, a tribunal was organised to investigate whether the USA was guilty of crimes under

---

42 Smith, 1977, p 104.
43 Anderson, 1998, p 1.
44 Bilton and Sim, 1992, p 1.
45 Bilton and Sim, 1992, p 1.
46 Bilton and Sim, 1992, p 2.
47 Russell, 1967.
48 Sartre, 1970.

international law in Vietnam. While this tribunal had no official legitimacy, it was supported by many well known individuals in the anti-war movement. Even at a time when the official international structures of cosmopolitan criminal law were non-existent, ideas of law and justice still constituted an element in the campaign against the Vietnam War. Cosmopolitan criminal law had an existence even outside official structures. The characterisation of acts in terms of their illegality or criminality can be a powerful moral and political weapon.

The Genocide Convention and the problems of defining genocide

The Genocide Convention (1948) was agreed in order to add further clarity to cosmopolitan law by defining genocide as a specific crime. Article II defines the following as genocide:

> Any of the following acts committed with intent to destroy, in whole or in part, a national, ethnical, racial, or religious group, as such:
>
> (a) Killing members of the group;
> (b) Causing serious bodily or mental harm to members of the group;
> (c) Deliberately inflicting on the group conditions of life calculated to bring about its physical destruction in whole or in part;
> (d) Imposing measures intended to prevent births within the group;
> (e) Forcibly transferring children of the group to another group.[49]

There is much dispute about the interpretation and the validity of this definition. Some writers, for example Elie Wiesel and Steven Katz,[50] have emphasised the uniqueness of the Nazi genocide of the Jews. They propose a narrow and specific definition of genocide, or a narrow and specific interpretation of the definition which includes only the Holocaust and excludes all other cases of mass killings. Alain Destexhe[51] puts forward a narrow definition of genocide such that there have only ever been three: the genocide of the Armenians in Turkey in 1915, of the Jews and Gypsies in 1942–45, and of the Tutsis by the Hutus in 1994. At the other end of the spectrum, there are social scientists who define genocide in a much broader and more inclusive way,[52] and who have established an academic discipline that they call 'genocide studies'.

Steven Katz says that, in this debate, writers must be careful not to claim 'for [their] own collective national catastrophe some pride of place',[53] though it appears that in this respect he is not himself excessively careful. He surveys a number of instances of mass killing and shows why each one, with the exception of the Holocaust, cannot be considered to be a real genocide. In the case of the destruction of the native people of North and South America, he argues that

---

49 Compare with the Nuremberg definition of crimes against humanity: 'Murder, extermination, enslavement, deportation and other inhumane acts committed against any civilian population, whether before or during the war, or persecutions on political, racial or religious grounds in exception of or in connection with any crime within the jurisdiction of the tribunal, whether or not in violation of the domestic law of the country where perpetrated.'
50 Katz, 1983. 'Auschwitz was a unique phenomenon, a unique event, like the revelation at Sanai.' Wiesel in Cargs, 1976, p 8.
51 Destexhe, 1995.
52 Eg Charny, 1994; Kuper, 1982; Fein, 1993.
53 Katz, 1983, p 296.

even though many millions were killed, and the death rate was about 40% of the population, there was no genocidal ideology or intent. In the case of the killing of the Armenians in Turkey in 1915, there was similarly no genocidal intent, but rather the killing was the result of an over-zealous nationalism. The purpose was ethnic cleansing, rather than killing. He makes a similar argument in the cases of the killing of the Ibo in Nigeria and of the native Brazilians. The Gypsies were killed by the Nazis but this did not constitute genocide:

> The overall Nazi policy toward the Gypsies was different in kind from that toward the Jews ... The Nazis did not ontologise the Gypsy into their metahistoric antithesis, nor did they make the elimination of all Gypsies from history a primal part of either their historic 'moral' mission or their metaphysical 'mythos'.[54]

Katz concludes: 'I believe enough evidence has been marshalled to suggest that in and through the category of "intention" we can begin to perceive at least one seminal individuating characteristic of the Holocaust.'[55]

Alain Destexhe also stresses that intent is an important defining characteristic. Raphaël Lemkin, argues Destexhe, invented the word 'genocide' in 1944, referring to the destruction of a nation or of an ethnic group, implying the existence of a co-ordinated plan, aimed at total extermination, to be put into effect against individuals chosen as victims purely, simply and exclusively because they are members of the target group. That means that they are not targeted simply because they are held to be in the way, like the Muslims in Bosnia or Kosovo, nor because they pose a threat, real or imagined, like the political opponents of Stalin or Mao; nor because they live in a state that is waging a war, like the inhabitants of Hiroshima. The point about the use of the word 'genocide' for Destexhe is that it describes a crime motivated purely by 'racial, national or religious considerations' and has nothing to do with the conduct of the war. Genocide contains no seed of utility: people are killed simply because they exist. It is 'a crime against the person as a person, against the very humanity of the individual victim'.[56]

Leo Kuper argues for a much wider definition because he is unhappy with the use of motive as a defining criterion. The Genocide Convention defined an act as genocide only when it is the killing of the ethnic group *as such*. This introduced motive as a central consideration. At the time when the convention was negotiated, the Russians insisted on the removal of the political motivation as being inconsistent with a 'scientific' definition of genocide.[57] The British insisted that intent was crucial, but motivation immaterial. The Venezuelans proposed the inclusion of the words 'as such'. This means that in order to count as genocide in the terms of the convention, the motivation must be proven to be purely non-utilitarian ethnic hatred. Kuper is critical of this inclusion of motivation on the grounds that it allows a defence to the charge of genocide. He gives two examples. The UN representative of Brazil, in reply to a charge of genocide against Indians in the Amazon region, argued that this could not be characterised as genocide since those carrying out the killing did so only for economic gain.[58] US army Chief of Staff, General Maxwell Taylor,

---

54 Katz, 1983, p 308.
55 Katz, 1983, p 310.
56 Destexhe, 1995, p 4.
57 Destexhe, 1995, p 4.
58 Kuper, 1982, p 33.

argued that the bombings of Hiroshima and Nagasaki did not constitute genocide, as people were killed because they lived in enemy strongholds and not because the Americans had the intention of killing them simply because of their ethnicity.

Destexhe wants to keep the definition of genocide narrow in order to focus attention on the most serious cases. He is worried about the dilution of the term 'genocide', believing that a process of verbal inflation is diminishing its power. When people campaign against a particular set of acts that they consider evil, they often use the word genocide in order to highlight the seriousness of their case. Racism against black people in the USA;[59] the selling of tobacco that causes millions to die of lung cancer; the abortion of millions of foetuses; the refusal by governments to fund AIDS research sufficiently – all have been characterised as genocides.

The genocide studies scholars, on the other hand, want to keep the definition broad in order to incorporate into their discipline all cases of mass killing:

> … [b]y 'genocide studies' we mean attempts to expose, comprehend, and prevent the phenomenon of genocidal killing as a subject in its own right and, ideally, in comparative perspective.[60]

Helen Fein carried out a study of introductory sociology texts from 1947–77, and showed that a minority of texts in all three decades defined and recognised genocide; those in the middle decade (1957–67) were least likely to mention genocide, while those published last (1968–77) were almost twice as likely to recognise genocide as those in the decade after the Second World War.[61] She goes on to say that 'the beginning of professional social scientific interest in genocide was in the 1970s', and that comparative research on genocide is almost wholly generated by scholars educated in the USA and writing in English.

These scholars reject the idea that the Holocaust was a profoundly unique or holy event that defies analysis and understanding. They situate themselves in a certain sociological and scientific methodological tradition that particularly values comparative studies.

Michael Freeman[62] formulates the rejection of the profound uniqueness argument by making a critique of Elie Wiesel's religious understanding of the Shoah and of his insistence on the primacy of survivor testimony over social scientific analysis. He quotes Wiesel's three reasons for holding that the Holocaust cannot be wholly explicable:

> (1) The events obeyed no law and no law can be derived from them; (2) complete understanding would require identification with all the victims and all the executioners, which is impossible; (3) no language is sufficient to communicate the Holocaust experience; the language of science, in particular, fails before the suffering of the victims.

His answers to Wiesel are, first, that contemporary social scientific forms of understanding are more sophisticated and flexible than simply the search for 'laws' of social behaviour; understanding can be derived from analysis, and

59 Weisbord, 1975.
60 Markusen and Kopf, 1995, p 5.
61 Fein, 1993, p 5.
62 Freeman, 1991, p 187.

that understanding does not need to aspire to a totalising quest for absolute knowledge. Secondly, while empathy is necessary for an analysis of genocide, it is also necessary to go beyond the subjective consciousness of victims and perpetrators, and to investigate the social structures in which they find themselves and which help to make them who they are, as well as simply focusing on their agency. Thirdly, the problem of language is a general problem about the representation of experience, which may be particularly acute in the case of the Holocaust; but it would be a greater error for social science to ignore this challenge than for it to attempt, sensitively and carefully, to confront it. Freeman also argues that, since Wiesel considers the study of the Holocaust to be important in order to prevent possible future genocides, then it is clear that past and future must have important elements in common. The Holocaust may be unique in certain ways, as is any event, but it also has features in common with other genocides, and other possible future genocides.

Markusen and Kopf similarly criticise those whom they call, following Alan Rosenberg and Evelyn Silverman,[63] Holocaust 'absolutists', who hold that the Holocaust was a profoundly unique event, outside history and outside the possibility of representation or comparison. They prefer to call themselves 'contextualists', which means that they see the Holocaust in its historical context and that they assert the validity of comparison.

It is the rejection of the idea of the uniqueness of the Holocaust, and the insistence that it is an event within, not outside, history, that allows genocide studies to broaden its focus from the single event and look also at similar social phenomena. Leo Kuper, one of the founders of the discipline, says that he has been driven to this terrain by the realisation that genocide is all too common in our own day, and that the organisation charged with its prevention and punishment, the United Nations (UN), responds with indifference, if not with condonation.[64] A central concern, then, of the emerging discipline is not the uniqueness, but the ordinariness of genocide. And, as Bauman argues, sociology's traditional neglect of the field as a pathological condition of society, rather than as an aspect of society's normal functioning, becomes untenable.

Israel W Charny argues as follows:

> What is needed, I would argue, is a generic definition of genocide that does not exclude or commit to indifference any case of mass murder of any human beings, of whatever racial, national, ethnic, biological, cultural, religious, and political definitions, or of totally mixed groupings of any and all of the above.
>
> I propose that whenever large numbers of unarmed human beings are put to death at the hands of their fellow human beings, we are talking about genocide.[65]

Frank Chalk argues that social scientists have a different set of objectives to those of international lawyers. Lawyers are concerned with successful prosecution, while sociologists are concerned with:

> ... outlining the boundaries of a set of cases which they want to study for the purpose of discovering their common elements and analysing the processes that brought them about. Perhaps these differences in objectives account for the differences in breadth and focus which one finds in the several definitions of

---

63 Rosenberg and Silverman, 1992.
64 Kuper, 1982, p 9.
65 Charny, 1994, p 74.

genocide that have appeared since the concept was first elaborated by Raphaël Lemkin in 1944.[66]

Assigning a high value to comparative studies is characteristic of genocide studies. Their methodology is fundamentally an empiricist one that flows from an empiricist tradition in American social science. It is concerned to distance itself methodologically from mystical or impressionistic approaches to the subject: from those approaches that assert the dominance of experience over analysis; from those that argue that the only possible response to genocide is silence; from those that cannot go beyond horror and moral indignation; and from those that seek to make genocides into the property of one or other group, to use them for political ends, and which seek to establish the place of one group or other at the top of the hierarchy of the oppressed. Focus on comparative study is an attempt to replace these approaches with dispassionate scientific investigation. It wishes to appear respectably scientific and scholarly.

The work by Eric Markusen and David Kopf,[67] who undertake a comparative study of the Holocaust and Allied strategic bombing in the Second World War, is typical of genocide studies. They compare two common types of contemporary governmental mass killing, and they find that they have many common features: enough, indeed, to allow them to call strategic bombing genocidal. This enables them to highlight the unacceptability of strategic bombing, a form of mass killing that is often regarded as a necessary evil and therefore defensible, by arguing that it is little different from genocide, which is universally condemned.

The comparison between the Holocaust and strategic bombing consists of discovering a number of traits that Markusen and Kopf argue are common to the two. They argue that important common characteristics are as follows:

(a) The dehumanisation of the 'other' – by the mass media, governments, the elite, the educational institutions, the killers.
(b) The role of the 'healing-killing paradox'. This means that people sometimes kill in the belief that they are protecting themselves, or their group.
(c) Scientific rationalisation; bureaucratic distancing.
(d) Technical distancing.
(e) Organisational loyalty. Air force decision makers are loyal to the air force, Nazi killers are loyal to their particular police outfits.

In investigating whether strategic bombing is genocidal, they use Helen Fein's criteria:[68]

(a) There is a sustained attack, or continuity of attacks, by the perpetrator to physically destroy group members.
(b) The perpetrator is a collective or organised actor or a commander of organised actors.
(c) Victims are selected because they are members of a collectivity.
(d) The victims are defenceless, or are killed regardless of whether they surrendered or resisted.

---

66 Chalk, 1994, p 46.
67 Markusen and Kopf, 1995.
68 Markusen and Kopf, 1995; Fein, 1993.

(e) The destruction of group members is undertaken with intent to kill, and murder is sanctioned by the perpetrators.

Markusen and Kopf find that, since all these criteria are present, strategic bombing is, indeed, genocidal. They do, however, quote Fein, who argues that '[t]o equate Hiroshima and Auschwitz belies the distinctive end and design of each plan and their distinctive effects'.[69] She argues, further, that they fail to consider whether the scientists and planners involved in nuclear strategising are actually 'value free', unthinking about the ends of their acts, or whether they take responsibility for involvement in the nuclear project – as some do – in order to prevent war. Thus, labelling their acts genocidal disregards the evidence that it is not their indifference to killing but their estimation of the risks of avoiding killing that is the issue separating anti-nuclear activists and nuclear engineers.

Both Markusen and Kopf's thesis and Fein's critique can be seen as illuminating examples of the methodology of genocide studies. The discovery and use of checklists of traits that are common to genocides can be seen to be problematic. The lists of traits or characteristics that are produced by genocide studies are in fact far from straightforward and require deeper analysis. Also, they rely heavily on definitions that are inevitably, at some level, arbitrary. This is, perhaps, why so much of the work produced by these theorists is concerned with analysis of, and argument for, certain ways of defining key terms, such as genocide itself, which even within the discipline is much disputed. There is also much creation of new terms, such as Leo Kuper's 'genocidal massacre',[70] Rudolph Rummel's 'democide',[71] 'sociocide', 'linguicide', and 'cultural genocide'.[72] Fein herself is critical of these last three inventions, arguing that 'genocide becomes not only unbounded but banal, an everyday occurrence'.[73] But the reason why definition comes to be such a focus for controversy is not only that the term 'genocide' contains great moral weight, and therefore great temptation to highlight this or that form of repression; it is also because the empiricist method of genocide studies relies on the definition and discovery of key characteristics, and seems unwilling to delve deeper inside the social phenomena themselves, an undertaking that would risk attracting a charge of unscholarly or unscientific investigation. The strictly scientific methodology always seems to be traceable back to an arbitrary definition.

Referring back to Markusen and Kopf's list of common characteristics between strategic bombing and the Holocaust, it is clear that the question of dehumanisation, for example, is complex, and requires deeper investigation. Dehumanisation is often posited as one of the key features of genocide.[74] And certainly human beings are often portrayed by genocidal formations as cockroaches, rats, or germs that need to be killed for the health of the greater society. Yet on the other hand, genocide, and specifically sadistic treatment and killing of victims, is not committed against non-humans but, emphatically, against human beings; human beings who are seen as threatening, potentially

---

69 Markusen and Kopf, 1995.
70 Kuper, 1982, p 10.
71 Fein, 1993, p 75.
72 Fein, 1993, p 17.
73 Fein, 1993, p 17.
74 Eg Freeman, 1991, p 190.

powerful, worthy of hatred and deserving of the most terrible punishment. Dehumanisation cannot be simply reduced to an unproblematic trait which can then be used as a measuring stick in some statistical analysis. Also, while they may have had certain aspects in common, the quality of Nazi racism against Jews was surely different from that of the Allied war machines against German and Japanese people; to package both of these distinct forms of anti-human ideology as 'dehumanisation' is surely to oversimplify and gloss over exactly the complexities that ought to be under investigation.

The 'healing-killing paradox' is another example of a term invented in order to show a common strand that runs throughout different genocides. It is grandly named, but the point is surely banal: often when people kill, they think, or they say, that they are killing in order to heal. It is just another way of saying that when people kill, they believe they have good justification to do so, that it is some form of self-defence.

Scientific rationalisation, bureaucratic distancing and technological distancing are also held to be traits characteristic of genocide. The genocide studies scholars appropriate these simple traits from Bauman's work, as if that work just added extra empirical knowledge to their own. The fact that Bauman's work is a thoroughgoing and vigorous critique of their whole methodology seems to be entirely unimportant. In any case, often genocide is carried out with very little bureaucratic or technical distancing; the *Einsatzgruppen*, for example, or the Rwandese machete *génocidaires*, acted without the need for any of Bauman's moral sleeping pills.

Fein's distinction between nuclear weapon designers and *génocidaires* is that the former believe they are acting to minimise killing, whereas the latter are indifferent to killing. But behind the façade of hard scientific methodology lurks the arbitrariness of hidden value judgment. Does not the healing-killing paradox tell us that all *génocidaires* also believe that they are acting to minimise harm?

All of these debates about the uniqueness of the Holocaust and the definition of genocide, as Norman Geras[75] has argued, leave one feeling uncomfortable. The heat of the debate feels disrespectful to the victims. There is a suspicion that there are hidden agendas, and that the participants in the debate are engaged in competition to define some mass killings as more profound or important than others. Norman Finkelstein[76] argues that some of the insistence on the uniqueness of the Holocaust is explicable for reasons connected with gathering political support for Israel. Yet on the other hand, some of the arguments against the uniqueness of the Holocaust downplay the enormity of this particular, world-changing event.

The arguments about intent are all, in the end, a little arbitrary. There is no 'pure' genocide, unsullied by the pursuit of money, land, political advantage; and there is also no purely utilitarian mass killing, untainted by a racist ideology that defines the worth of the lives of some as being less than others. The tribunals for the former Yugoslavia and for Rwanda have both made convictions for genocide. They seem less concerned about the niceties of definition, and seem to be happy to convict, for example, Radislav Kristic,[77]

75 Geras, 1998.
76 Finkelstein, 2000.
77 *Prosecutor v Kristic.*

without profound investigations as to the intent of the Bosnian Serbs, or as to the particular ratio of self-interest to exterminatory racism that motivated the killing and ethnic cleansing. The tribunals seem to be able to operate effectively enough with the existing definitions of genocide and crimes against humanity, even if they are theoretically unsatisfactory in some respects.

These genocide studies scholars are disabled by their self-imposed methodological restrictions. They fail to rid their analysis of value judgments, only succeeding in hiding such judgments behind a façade of respectable objectivity. They are trying to understand and analyse the social reality of genocide but they do not pay enough attention to the ways in which, as it were, the social reality understands itself. The existing social phenomena of genocide are being made sense of and given meaning by the existing social phenomena of the institutions, body of law, and ideas of cosmopolitan criminal legal processes. The abstract understanding that the genocide studies scholars impose on the world is too far removed from the structures that the world develops by itself to adequately address the phenomena in question. The existence of the crimes against humanity charge at Nuremberg and its general acceptance as law is more radical than any moment of utopian criticism.

Chapter Four
Peace, security and justice in the former Yugoslavia

In Chapters Four and Five, I look at three different approaches taken by the international community towards the conflict in the former Yugoslavia. In Srebrenica, security and justice were subordinated to a vain quest for peace and the avoidance of conflict. The wish to avoid at all costs any disruption of the peace ended in disaster for those who had understood that they were being promised life-saving help by the UN. In Kosovo, the international community in the form of the North Atlantic Treaty Organisation (NATO) focused on preventing and reversing the ethnic cleansing, yet with such a blunt use of force that peace, security and justice all suffered. The priority given by the intervening powers to avoiding putting their own soldiers at risk had not changed since Srebrenica, but the policy that flowed from it took a very different form. The establishment of the International Criminal Tribunal for the former Yugoslavia (ICTY) focused on justice, yet it was established under the Security Council's powers to work for peace and security. While the ICTY has been denounced from many different angles, I argue that its most important achievement is its existence; it is an empirical fact. Cosmopolitan criminal law exists, and in those three courtrooms in The Hague, as well as in Arusha, it conducts the daily business of putting people on trial for crimes against humanity and genocide. In Chapter Five, I look at two cases at the ICTY in detail.

Peace before justice: Srebrenica and Dayton

> [T]he so called safe area has become the most unsafe place in the world. (Alija Izetbegovic, referring to Gorazde.)[1]

In July 1995, a crime against humanity was committed by Bosnian Serb forces against the Muslims who lived in Srebrenica or who had fled there for safety. This crime was committed under the noses of UN forces, who did little to prevent it.

By the end of May 1992, Serb forces had occupied and ethnically cleansed a large part of eastern and western Bosnia, and the front line that was established then was essentially stable until the summer of 1995. There were, however, Bosnian Muslim enclaves that they had failed to defeat: Bihac in the west, and Gorazde, Zepa, and Srebrenica in the east. Refugees fled to these enclaves, swelling their original populations.

Between May 1992 and January 1993, Bosniak forces from Srebrenica attacked and destroyed Serb villages near the town. Serb forces responded with a counter-offensive, capturing some villages and severing the link between Srebrenica and Zepa.[2] The Bosnian Government put pressure on the

---

1   O'Shea, 1998, p 46.
2   *Prosecutor v Kristic*, para 14.

international community and UNPROFOR[3] to provide convoys of food and medical supplies to the civilians in Srebrenica. Two weeks after the first convoy had successfully arrived, the Bosnian army launched an offensive against the Serbs in Bratunac. The Serbs refused to allow further aid through, arguing that it would help the military capability of the Bosnian army. The Serbian offensive against the enclaves intensified, and by February 1993 the situation in Srebrenica was becoming desperate. A UNHCR report of 19 February described the situation in Srebrenica:

> There is no food such as we know it. They have not had real food for months. They are surviving on the chaff from wheat and roots from trees. Every day people are dying of hunger and exhaustion. The medical situation could not be more critical. People who are wounded are taken to the hospital where they die from simple injuries because of the lack of medical supplies. They have problems of epidemic proportion with scabies and lice.[4]

When General Morillon of UNPROFOR visited the besieged town, the inhabitants organised a protest by the women and children to prevent him from leaving. They demanded protection. Morillon jumped on top of his armoured car and addressed the crowd: 'We will not abandon you.'[5] The world saw this pledge on their evening news bulletins.

Following the 1991 Gulf War, a 'safe haven' had been declared by the victorious coalition in order to protect the Kurds in northern Iraq from the Saddam regime. The relative success of the policy had been dependent on three factors that did not apply in Bosnia. First, the safe haven was imposed by a coalition that had just dealt a crushing military defeat to the Iraqi army in Kuwait, so there was no need to negotiate with the Iraqi regime, nor to obtain its consent, nor to appear neutral between it and the Kurds. Secondly, the safe haven was large, and it bordered one of the allies enforcing it, so forces could easily be deployed and withdrawn. Thirdly, the terrain was relatively open, making air cover easier.[6]

By March 1993, Srebrenica was in danger of imminent defeat. On 16 April 1993, the Security Council passed a resolution that designated the town of Srebrenica and its surrounding area as a 'safe area', but the resolution was half-hearted and vague. Britain, France and Spain, the countries whose troops were most likely to be used in any action guaranteeing safety, were nervous:

> They made sure that Srebrenica was turned into a 'safe area', as opposed to a 'safe haven' ... The difference under international law was that safe havens need not depend on consent of the warring parties and could be enforced, while safe areas were based on consent.[7]

It seems, however, that the world did not really notice this nice distinction. It was understood that the UN was guaranteeing the safety of civilians who lived within these enclaves. But the Security Council had only placed a duty upon the Bosniaks and the Serbs to keep these areas safe; UNPROFOR's role would be to monitor the humanitarian situation.

---

3   United Nations Protection Force.
4   Honig, 1996, p 82.
5   'A Bosnian betrayal', *Dispatches*, Channel 4, 1996; *Prosecutor v Kristic*, para 15.
6   Honig, 1996, p 99.
7   Honig, 1996, p 104.

The UN was always in a contradictory position. No country was willing to commit soldiers capable of fighting against those who were doing the ethnic cleansing. In the absence of such a force, all international intervention had to gain the consent of all sides in the conflict, since everyone possessed a *de facto* veto on their activities. There was an arms embargo on all sides that helped the Serbs since they already had access to the arms of the JNA.[8]

Since Serb consent had to be won for any policy, a condition of the granting of 'safe areas' was to be the disarming of Muslim forces in the name of creating a 'demilitarised zone'. Serb forces were unwilling to allow the UN to transport supplies to the enclaves if they were being used as bases for the Bosnian army. On 17 April, 143 lightly armed Canadian soldiers entered Srebrenica. They were not mistaken by the desperate inhabitants for liberators. The Canadians were in a difficult position. They could not defend the town against a serious attack. They were supposed to disarm the Muslims; but if at some time in the future they were forced to withdraw, this would leave the Muslims even more defenceless. However, the Serbs withdrew one and a half kilometres and stopped shelling. Srebrenica appeared to have been saved, and the world's press looked elsewhere for its stories.

On 3 March 1994, 570 Dutch troops relieved the Canadians in Srebrenica. Most of their ammunition had been delayed when the ship carrying it to Croatia had broken down; by the time it arrived, the Serbs declared that the Dutch already had enough supplies, and declined to let it through. Convoys of fuel and food were also often delayed by the Serbs. Following a NATO air raid in November 1994, the Serbs took 70 Dutch soldiers hostage; General Mladic came to visit them, arriving in a Mercedes jeep that the Serbs had previously confiscated from a Dutch convoy. They were eventually released. During 1995, the Serbs continued systematically to undermine the operational capability of the Dutch force, particularly by restricting food and fuel supplies. Morale amongst the Dutch soldiers was poor.

In March 1995, Radovan Karadzic issued a directive to his forces in the Srebrenica area, ordering them to 'create an unbearable situation of total insecurity with no hope of further survival or life for the inhabitants of Srebrenica'.[9] The Serb forces were also ordered to:

> ... reduce and limit the logistics support of UNPROFOR to the enclaves and the supply of material resources to the Muslim population, making them dependent on our good will while at the same time avoiding condemnation by the international community and international public opinion.[10]

The final Serb attack on the safe area of Srebrenica began on Tuesday 6 July 1995. There was much small arms fire and shelling recorded by the Dutch from their observation posts that surrounded the town. One observation post in particular came under attack, and the soldiers inside it surrendered to the Serbs, who eventually allowed them to go back towards their comrades in the town in their armoured car. On their way back, they encountered a Muslim roadblock through which they drove without stopping. One soldier, Raviv van Renssen, was shot in the head and killed. A second observation post was attacked and overwhelmed by the Serb forces. The Serbs gave them a choice:

---

8   Yugoslav National Army.
9   *Prosecutor v Kristic*, para 28.
10 *Prosecutor v Kristic*, para 28.

they could either make their way back to their unit in Srebrenica or be taken prisoner. The soldiers opted to be taken prisoner. The Dutch Lieutenant Colonel Karremans did not yet understand that Srebrenica was in danger of falling to the Serb forces. By Saturday, the Bosnian army was decisively outgunned; they wanted NATO air strikes against Serb forces. Their strategy was to manoeuvre the Dutch into the line of fire, so that they would be forced to call for air support. They therefore made it difficult for the Dutch to withdraw from their observation posts into the town. But the Dutch soldiers preferred to surrender to the Serbs, who treated them well, than to remain in their positions.

At 10 pm on Sunday, the most senior UN Commander in the former Yugoslavia, French Lieutenant General Bernard Janvier, ordered the Dutch battalion to position their armoured cars around Srebrenica in order to stop the Serb advance. From Zagreb, Janvier and Yasushi Akashi, the UN Secretary General's special representative, sent an ultimatum to the Serbs: they were to withdraw from Srebrenica and release the captured Dutch soldiers, or else air support would be employed.

On Monday morning, there was increased shelling of the town, both of the Muslim civilians and refugees and of the Dutch soldiers, followed by a relative lull. By early evening, Serb soldiers were lining up above Srebrenica ready to advance into the town. Muslim civilians began to flee from the town towards the north. At 6.30 pm, the Serbs began to advance. Many Muslim civilians streamed towards the Dutch compound at Potocari, just outside the town, for protection, and broke into it. The Bosnian army was trying to stop civilians from withdrawing from the town to the base; they still wanted to force the Dutch to fight, and to call for air support. Most of the refugees remained in Srebrenica during the night of 10–11 July.

The Dutch requested air support at 7 pm during the Serb attack. Following much discussion and delay, Janvier promised that NATO would be ready to attack from the air by 6 am. The Dutch soldiers were informed that NATO had given an ultimatum to the Serbs that if they did not withdraw they would come under heavy air attack first thing in the morning. Janvier and Akashi, however, had only agreed to the air attack if the Dutch troops were attacked first.

Karremans announced to the Bosnian army and the civilian town council that the Serbs had been warned to withdraw on the threat of NATO air strikes. The Bosnians did not trust Karremans. Major Fahrudin Salihovic, of the Bosnian army, twice asked Karremans if he could guarantee that the attack would take place. Karremans twice answered 'don't shoot the piano player', which was translated by the interpreter as 'don't trouble the bringer of good tidings'.

NATO aircraft were in the air from 6 am, ready to attack. All in Srebrenica waited for the attack. UNPROFOR commanders were waiting to be contacted by the Dutch if they were being attacked by the Serbs.

The NATO aircraft, which had been airborne since 6 am, were forced to return to their base in Italy by 11.30 am. The Serb forces were made aware of this from radar bases in Serbia. Shortly after 11 am, the Serb attack resumed. The Dutch resumed the evacuation of refugees to their base. There were some limited NATO air attacks that afternoon. The Serbs issued an ultimatum of their own. If the air attacks were not stopped, the captured Dutch soldiers would be killed and the refugees and Dutch battalion would be shelled. The Dutch Government, Akashi and UNPROFOR quickly halted the air attacks. The Dutch withdrew to their base, and Karremans opened ceasefire negotiations with the Serb forces.

By the evening of 11 July, there were around 25,000 Muslim refugees, mostly women and children, crowded into the Dutch base. The highly organised and pre-planned Serb 'deportation' operation began. Ratko Mladic himself was in Srebrenica on 11 July, with a television camera crew, to organise the cleansing of the town in order to make, as he told the cameras, a present to the Serbian nation. His meeting with Karremans was filmed; Karremans raised a glass to toast the Serb victory. He was ordered by Mladic to return with 'representatives' of the Muslim refugees in order to organise the 'deportations'.

Conditions in and around the Dutch base were bad. At the trial at the ICTY of Radislav Kristic, the Chief of Staff of the Drina corps of the Bosnian Serb army, a resident of Srebrenica described the scene:

> The baby had its pram, and we left our belongings in the pram or simply lay down on the ground ... As we sat there, snipers would fire every now and then, and all this throng would then move to one side or the other, screaming.[11]

Above them was the village of Pecista where the Serb soldiers were setting houses on fire. At the sound of shelling, the whole crowd would 'simply dodge to one side or the other with frightened cries, and that is how we spent the night'.[12] The next day General Mladic appeared among the refugees with his television crew and handed out sweets to the children.[13] After the General had left, Serb soldiers mingled with the crowd, harassing people and carrying out some sporadic killings.[14] That night, a Dutch medical orderly witnessed two Serb soldiers raping a young woman. He testified that the rape was seen by many refugees but that nobody could intervene because of the presence of Serb soldiers.[15] Other witnesses testified that they had seen women being dragged away and that they could hear women screaming.[16]

The Serb forces organised buses to take the prisoners away. The Muslim men were separated from the women. Witness DD at the Kristic trial recalled seeing her young son for the last time as her family tried to board the buses:

> ... one of their soldiers jumped out, and he spoke to my child. He told us to move to the right side, and he told my son: 'young man, you should go to the left side.' ... I grabbed him by his hand ... And then I begged them, I pleaded with them. Why are you taking him? He was born in 1981. But he repeated his order. And I held him so hard, but he grabbed him ... And he took my son's hand, and he dragged him to the left side. And he turned around, and then he told me, 'Mommy, please, can you get that bag for me? Could you please get it for me?' ... That was the last time I heard his voice.[17]

The men were taken in buses towards Bratunac:

11 *Prosecutor v Kristic*, para 39.
12 *Prosecutor v Kristic*, para 39.
13 *Prosecutor v Kristic*, para 40.
14 *Prosecutor v Kristic*, paras 42–43.
15 *Prosecutor v Kristic*, para 45.
16 *Prosecutor v Kristic*, para 46.
17 *Prosecutor v Kristic*, para 55.

Over the next few days, Dutch soldiers held hostage in Bratunac reported seeing a number of buses filled with male prisoners. Most of the men sat with their heads between their knees, and when they did look up their expressions were of terror. The Dutch hostages also reported hearing frequent gunshots, particularly from the direction of the football pitch.[18]

The women and children were deported to Kladanj, in Bosnian Government territory. The *Kristic* judgment states that 'almost to a man, the thousands of Bosnian Muslim prisoners captured, following the takeover of Srebrenica, were executed'.[19] The judgment, drawing on evidence of missing persons lists, on forensic evidence from mass graves, and on the testimony of UN observers, states that:

> [T]he Trial Chamber is satisfied that, in July 1995, following the takeover of Srebrenica, Bosnian Serb forces executed several thousand Bosnian Muslim men. The total number is likely to be within the range of 7,000–8,000 men.[20]

Perhaps Srebrenica could have been saved if the Dutch battalion had been willing to risk lives in a heroic stand; perhaps it could have been saved if Janvier and Akashi had been more willing to offer air support; perhaps it could have been saved if other states had offered more troops as the Netherlands had done; but the UN's humiliation in Srebrenica was not an isolated disaster. The UN stood by and watched the ethnic cleansing in Srebrenica as it did in the rest of Bosnia; as it stood by and watched the genocide in Rwanda. In both cases it had intelligence reports telling it what was likely to happen, but it was unable or unwilling to protect people. In Rwanda, there were television pictures showing thousands of desperate, frightened people crowding around UN bases, and UN soldiers retreating, leaving those people to their fate. Failure at Srebrenica, while not inevitable, mirrored failure elsewhere. Most towns and villages in the 'Republica Srpska' did not even receive the token protection and the publicity that was afforded to Srebrenica, but were cleansed unnoticed by the world's news media.

Since the UN and the states who provide its forces were unwilling to risk the lives of their soldiers in an operation to prevent it, ethnic cleansing was carried out unhindered. There was much discussion at the time of the military and political impossibility of putting an international force in Bosnia that was capable of defending the victims of ethnic cleansing. There was also much political obfuscation: politicians argued that there were evils on all sides in the war. Douglas Hurd, the British Foreign Secretary, argued that it was impossible to go into other people's countries and run them: this was the lesson learned from the British Empire. The Balkans were portrayed as an exotic and inherently unstable place, and therefore, by implication, undeserving of help.

Given that a force to prevent ethnic cleansing was not forthcoming, the role that the UN gave itself in Bosnia was one of observation and of attempting to slow down and ameliorate the effects of ethnic cleansing. The UN forces found themselves in the position of constantly having to negotiate at a number of different levels. It was necessary to negotiate with leadership of the Bosnian Serbs; it was also necessary to negotiate with each group of Chetniks at each

---

18 Honig, 1996, p 36.
19 *Prosecutor v Kristic*, para 67.
20 *Prosecutor v Kristic*, para 84.

roadblock. While the UN did have, as its trump card, the possibility of calling in air support which was genuinely able to hurt the Serb forces, the Serbs developed trump cards of their own. They were able to take UN soldiers as hostages, and to threaten the increased shelling of civilians. The UN had no answer to these threats.

A flavour of the kind of negotiations that were constantly taking place can be obtained from a letter that Sir Michael Rose, the Commander of UNPROFOR, sent to Mladic, the General in charge of Serbian ethnic cleansing in Bosnia:[21]

Dear General,

Following your telephone conversation today with Brigadier General Brinkman [General Rose's Chief of Staff in Sarajevo], I would like to confirm that the UN always regrets the need to use force in its peacekeeping mission. As Commander B-H Command, I fully agree with you that we must in the future avoid all situations which necessitate the use of force, whether it be applied from the ground or the air. We can only do this through closer liaison and co-operation. As you know UNPROFOR ... is in B-H to help return this country to peace through peaceful means. It is not part of our mission to impose any solution by force of arms. We are neither mandated nor deployed for such a mission.

However, you will understand that everyone has the right of self-defence. If our troops are deliberately engaged by fire, then we have to respond, no matter who it was that opened fire. I am sure that as a soldier you will understand this point of view.

I believe that we must now return to the *status quo ante* in terms of the relationship between UNPROFOR and the Bosnian Serb army. These are difficult times for everyone, and we must not allow local tactical-level incidents to undermine the road to peace. I urge you now to give orders accordingly.

Yours Sincerely,

Michael Rose.

Rose, the brave SAS hero, defended his stance in a letter to *The Times* on the same day that they published his letter to Mladic. It isn't his fault, he argues; he is merely carrying out the orders of his political masters:

The mandate, and therefore the mission, is principally one of peacekeeping, not peace enforcement. The primary mission of the UN in Bosnia remains that of assisting UNHCR and other humanitarian agencies to sustain the lives of millions of suffering people in the midst of a war ...

It is not within the mandate of capability of UNPROFOR to impose a military solution on the country. Injudicious use of force would take the mission across the line which divides peace from war ...

If this happened, the enclaves of eastern Bosnia would fall, Sarajevo would return to the horrors of the last two winters, and the future of the Croat Muslim Federation would be put in doubt ...[22]

During late summer 1995, all sides in the conflict made significant gains. The Serbs took and cleansed the 'safe areas' of Bihac, Srebrenica, Zepa and Gorazde. The Croats took the Krajina from the Serbs, and there committed one of the biggest acts of ethnic cleansing of the whole war. The Bosnian army

---

21 (1994) *The Times*, 2 November, p 15.
22 (1994) *The Times*, 2 November, p 19.

retook some territory in central Bosnia. The Americans sensed that the new situation could be transformed into some sort of equilibrium, and, for the first time in the war, NATO launched a serious and sustained assault from the air against Serb forces.

In November 1995, the Americans organised the final negotiations at an air force base in Dayton, Ohio. They refused to deal with the indicted Mladic and Karadzic, preferring to negotiate with the real Serbian leader, Slobodan Milosevic. The Dayton deal was agreed on 12 November. On the one hand, Milosevic came under severe American military and diplomatic pressure to make the deal; on the other hand, the deal allowed the Serbs to keep the territory of Bosnia that they had cleansed, and allowed Croatia to keep the Krajina. Dayton ended the war, but on the basis of accepting the reality of the ethnic cleansing of a large proportion of Bosnia.

There were cosmopolitan institutions and forces positioned in Srebrenica and in the rest of Bosnia to which the victims of the ethnic cleansing and the outside world looked to stop the killing and the terror. There were armies and air forces; blue helmets and red crosses; diplomats, politicians and military leaders; there were promises and guarantees. Yet in this case, the cosmopolitan institutions were nothing more than a form that disguised an old fashioned 'realist' content. In this case, the radical critique of cosmopolitanism looks persuasive. Cosmopolitanism was the form of appearance of the great powers. The policies followed by them were based on little more than calculations of self-interest; there was no political will to defend human rights, nor to stop or reverse the huge injustices that were perpetrated against the Muslims of Bosnia. The policies of the great powers were hidden behind a façade of cosmopolitan forms and institutions. Even with the preponderance of the appearances and forms of cosmopolitanism, there were no sparks or flashes of genuinely cosmopolitan response. In Bosnia, what happened, contrary to appearances, was ordinary power politics.

Justice before peace: Kosovo

By 1999, the policy of the West in relation to ethnic cleansing had changed. Ten years earlier the limited autonomy that had been allowed to Kosovo by the Yugoslavian constitution was swept away by the Serbs. Albanians were dismissed from their jobs, denied education in their own language and forced to live under a brutally racist regime. 'Kosovo became a *de facto* Serbian colony where 90% of its population ... were ruled by less than 10%.'[23] Peaceful opposition to the new regime had little effect and gained little outside support. Following a massacre of more than 70 Albanians by Serb police in Drenica in March 1998, the Kosovo Liberation Army (KLA) markedly increased its membership and popular support.[24] During the autumn of 1998 and the winter of 1999, tension increased between the JNA, the ethnically Serb minority population, the Kosovar Albanian majority, and the KLA.

International monitors were sent into Kosovo in October 1998. In January 1999, in the village of Racak, armed Serb police units killed 45 civilians.[25]

23 Demjaha, 2000, p 33.
24 Demjaha, 2000, p 34.
25 Demjaha, 2000, p 35.

Twenty-two unarmed men were shot in a gully; 23 others, including women, were killed in the streets. It became clear to the monitors that the Serb strategy was to intimidate civilians into fleeing strategically important areas. As well as police units, the regular army was now involved.[26] Reports of particular incidents of ethnic cleansing coming out of Kosovo accelerated.

On 19 March 2000, the talks began at Rambouillet. Madeleine Albright, the American Secretary of State, proposed that the province of Kosovo be given autonomy, but short of independence, and that NATO troops be allowed into Kosovo to guarantee that autonomy and freedom from ethnic cleansing for the population. Although many Kosovars wanted independence, their representatives signed the agreement that kept them within the Yugoslav state. The Serbs, however, were unwilling to sign. The talks went on for three weeks, while the process of ethnic cleansing on the ground in Kosovo gathered pace. Milosevic wanted to pursue the same strategy that had allowed the Serbs to cleanse half of Bosnia. He wanted to negotiate, to make agreements and ceasefires, while at the same time his troops and paramilitaries were doing their irreversible work.[27] It was American insistence on NATO troops being allowed into Kosovo to guarantee the agreement which Milosevic could not accept. The Serbs were given an ultimatum: agree to the deal or face air strikes. Milosevic preferred air strikes to erosion of his sovereignty in Kosovo.

NATO began air attacks on 24 March. The Serbs saw this as a signal to begin an uninhibited campaign of ethnic cleansing against the entire Kosovar population. While the bombing campaign slowly accelerated, hundreds of thousands of Kosovars were terrorised out of their homes and out of the country. They were sent across the borders, stripped of their money, their homes, their identity papers and their citizenship. Hundreds of thousands arrived in refugee centres in Macedonia and Albania.

NATO was unwilling to send any forces into Kosovo to defend the population, since this might have resulted in the deaths of some of their soldiers. Instead, they clung to the strategy of bombing strategic targets in Serbia until Milosevic agreed to the terms of the Rambouillet agreement.

In the case of Kosovo there was the political will to respond with force to the threat of ethnic cleansing. NATO had changed its stance since the campaign in Bosnia. It now demonised Milosevic, a policy that contrasted with its previous attempts to build him up into a position where he could control and 'civilise' the Bosnian Serbs. NATO did not allow its troops to be put in a position where they could be taken hostage. The policy that it pursued in Kosovo was simply the blunt use of enormous force. The result in the end was that the campaign of ethnic cleansing in Kosovo, unlike that in Bosnia, was unsuccessful; the

---

26 'The killing of Kosovo', *Panorama*, BBC1, 1999.
27 'Disunity within the international community means that its statements and actions are weak, watered down to the lowest common denominator. As Slobodan Milosevic knows and exploits, it also means that international condemnations, sanctions, and threats are often empty. Deadlines can be broken, conditions only partially, cynically fulfilled, and there will be only limited repercussions.'
At the 25 March 2000 meeting of the Contact Group, US Secretary of State Madeleine Albright warned her colleagues: 'During the Bosnian war, how many times did one party or another appear to accept our proposals, only to walk away? We say that in the former Yugoslavia, promises mean little until they are implemented with safeguards. Incentives tend to be pocketed; warnings tend not to be believed. Leaders respond not to the distant threat of sanctions but to the reality of sanctions.' Quoted in Human Rights Watch, 1999, p 113.

Kosovars were allowed to go back to their homes with some guarantees of safety. But the cost was enormous; to the Kosovars, who had to endure the most appalling campaign of ethnic cleansing before the Serb forces finally conceded defeat, and to the 500 Serb and Kosovar civilians who died during the 78 days of bombing, as well as the presumably higher number who were wounded.[28]

While there was some component of cosmopolitan motivation in the Western response to the ethnic cleansing of Kosovo, there was also a large component of self-interest, particularly the wish to avoid 'domino' destabilisation and mass movements of refugees towards the West. The overriding concern to avoid any risk to Western soldiers undermined the effectiveness of what was possible in terms of protecting populations from the ethnic cleansers. In Kosovo the great powers used less cosmopolitan forms than they had used in Bosnia – NATO rather than the UN, aerial bombing rather than peacekeeping forces – but the content of the policy was more effective in aiding the victims of ethnic cleansing.

Omarska: an intimate concentration camp

Before looking in detail at the setting up of the international tribunal, another of the strategies employed by the international community to address events in the former Yugoslavia, I will give a brief sketch of the kinds of crimes that were being committed in Bosnia in 1992.

In 1997, Rezak Hukanovic published his memoir[29] describing his experiences at Omarska. Omarska had been an iron mining and ore processing complex and was near Prijedor, a small north western Bosnian city. It was officially called an 'information centre' for men suspected of being members of the government army. In reality its inmates were Bosnian Muslim or Croatian civilians plucked out of their homes during ethnic cleansing. They were chosen purely on the basis of their designated nationality or ethnicity; Omarska was a concentration camp.

Hukanovic's memoir of Omarska is written in the third person, centred on a character, clearly himself, called Djemo. Djemo was at home in Prijedor, worrying about his wife's unhappiness with his tendency to flirt with women and remembering Serb against Muslim football matches, where the losers paid for the beer and food at the following barbecue. He was taken from his home at gunpoint by a Serb militia to a building where people were interrogated and beaten. From there he was taken to Omarska. He estimates that over the next two days more than 3,000 inhabitants of Prijedor arrived there, including his son and some of his cousins.[30]

All through his memoir he comes across people he knows, both prisoners and guards. There was no bureaucratic distancing or pseudo-scientific dehumanisation. Omarska was a very intimate concentration camp.

The prisoners were crowded together and systematically starved. There were routine and constant beatings; in the dormitories, on the way to and from

---

28 Human Rights Watch, 2000, p 2.
29 Hukanovic, 1997.
30 Hukanovic, 1997, p 26.

the canteen or the latrines, all the time. The guards used clubs, thick electrical cable, rifle butts, fists, boots, brass knuckle-dusters, iron rods.

Prisoners were tortured into false confessions: a doctor who had no cellar was forced to admit that he stole drugs from his clinic and hid them in his cellar; a man who was widely known to suffer from progressive blindness admitted that he had been a sniper.[31] The sounds of these torture sessions were heard daily from the dormitories. In the hot summer, the prisoners were kept thirsty; the guards would throw small bottles of water into the dormitories because the frantic struggle between the prisoners amused them. The prisoners were routinely forced to sing Chetnik songs.

> When somebody took a leak, the others gathered around to cup their hands and catch the urine, wetting their chapped lips with it and even drinking it.[32]

A group of 10 prisoners was taken out by drunken guards and ordered to strip naked. One man who had been a prisoner for quite some time, refused to strip. The guards knocked him to the ground and cut off his penis and half of his behind with a knife; they then directed a strong jet of water from a fire hydrant at his wounds and later doused him with petrol and set him alight in a garbage container.[33]

The prisoners were completely and constantly infested with lice.

Every night, after midnight, the guards called out the names of one or more prisoners. These prisoners were taken out and beaten bloody, their bones often broken and their skin punctured. A 60-year-old man was ordered to rape a young woman; he refused, and after being tortured, was killed.

Hukanovic tells of a soldier by the name of Zoka, who would ask a prisoner which eye he would like to keep, or which ball, and would remove the other one.

A white building at Omarska, known as the White House, was used for routine torture and killing. Djemo was taken there on 10 June 1992. He was beaten by four men who were drunk. He was ordered onto all fours 'just like a dog'[34] and hit incessantly by a man named Ziga on the back of the head with a club 'that unfurled itself every time he swung it to reveal a metal ball on the end'.[35] A man called Saponja, who knew Djemo quite well, appeared and began kicking him in the face with his boot. All through the torture the guards were screaming abuse and making jokes. Djemo, unlike many, survived the White House and was sent back to the dormitory.

One of the prisoners was a mathematics teacher called Abdullah Puskar. A guard, who had been Puskar's student, often came to collect him at night. He harangued him as he beat him. 'I listened to you long enough, now you'll listen to me for a while ... I'm gonna beat that math out of you or die trying!'[36] It was Puskar and not his student who died.

Hukanovic tells the story of a few guards who were good, honest men. 'But after a couple of days at Omarska, most such men were sent to the front lines ... That was the last anyone would hear of them.'[37]

---

31 Hukanovic, 1997, pp 28–29.
32 Hukanovic, 1997, p 32.
33 Hukanovic, 1997, pp 33–35.
34 Hukanovic, 1997, p 62.
35 Hukanovic, 1997, p 62.
36 Hukanovic, 1997, p 74.
37 Hukanovic, 1997, p 77.

He tells of many more brutal tortures and deaths, always humiliating and unimaginably painful. It is clear that at Omarska murder and torture were routine. Bodies were regularly taken away in yellow trucks.

Djemo was taken from Omarska on a crowded, thirsty bus journey to a camp called Manjaca. Here there were also terrible, crowded conditions, hunger, thirst, and lice; but brutality, while it still existed, was less tolerated by the Commander in Chief of the camp, who interrupted a beating with the words: 'Enough. That's the kind of thing you were supposed to do in Omarska, but you can't do it here.'[38] There were visits from the Red Cross, who provided diesel for the collection of water, but the prisoners still got little and dirty water.

In the end, Djemo was released in an exchange of prisoners organised by the Red Cross and UNPROFOR. He and his fellow prisoners alighted from the buses into a scrum of the world's press and TV reporters, and then went into exile.

Ed Vulliamy was a journalist who was in the first group of any outsiders – press, Red Cross or United Nations (UN) – to see Omarska, on 5 August 1992. He quotes a witness, Nedzad Jacupovic, who survived the White House, as follows:

> They would bring people from the big red hut at eight in the evening, 40 of them each night, to the White House. There, they would beat them until they were dead; it could take a day, three days or five days, ripping clothes off with knives, cutting people and then just kicking and beating them to death over a period of days. Then they would arrive with lists of others in the White House who were not yet dead, for execution. They would record the men's details, take them out, one every 15 minutes, towards the Red House, where they were butchered. I was counting the numbers; sometimes 18, 20 or 30; the record was 42. They were killed just in front of my windows.[39]

Vulliamy quotes another survivor of the White House, Sakib R, who calculated that 612 men disappeared from the hut during 12 days in July 1992:

> I saw people loading the dead onto lorries and they were dropping bodies down the mine shaft. On one occasion, 12 Croats were taken out to the toilet. I went in there, and saw bits of their bodies on the floor.[40]

Vulliamy says that '[t]he testimonies are willing and endless, but the evidence these two men submit is typical, cogent and can be corroborated'.[41] 'One survivor … estimates that he was personally forced to help deposit 600 bodies down the mine shaft at Omarska.'[42] Vulliamy estimates that something like 6,000 men were at Omarska at any one time, and several thousand of them were brutally murdered. He adds that there were other similarly brutal camps, for example one at Kereterm, established at a disused tile factory on the edge of Prijedor and known as 'Room Three', and the Luka camp outside Brcko. Here, a university lecturer called Mirsad was held and he told the following story:

---

38 Hukanovic, 1997, p 111.
39 Vulliamy, 1994, p 109.
40 Vulliamy, 1994, p 111.
41 Vulliamy, 1994, p 111.
42 Vulliamy, 1994, p 108.

... the guards allowed a pretty young woman called Monika to torture prisoners. She took pleasure in the task and laughed as she performed it: 'Monika was the daughter of a local whore, whom we all knew. She was 18 years old, and was the most cruel torturer of young men. She would break a glass bottle and cut open their stomachs while the guards watched and laughed. She had a soft, gentle face. We never expected someone like that to do such things. But she enjoyed doing it ...'[43]

Hukanovic describes how one day all the prisoners, including the beaten and the sick, were taken out onto the tarmac and stood against a building. There were, he estimates, about 3,000 of them:

The soldiers positioned themselves around the prisoners, ready to fire. One guard, known for never parting from his machine gun for even a second, climbed to the roof of the building across the way and began loading the magazine of his gun with cartridges ... he aimed the barrel at the runway and lay down next to it, taking aim at the men ... the guards kept their guns trained on the prisoners for over an hour. Then they were all taken back to the dormitories.[44]

Omarska was utterly different from Zygmunt Bauman's picture of the genocide of the Jews, the picture of the principles of scientific rationality coldly and dispassionately designating the goal of extermination, and a bureaucratically and technologically efficient execution of the plan. At Omarska, killing was passionate and inefficient. Many of the guards knew personally many of the victims. It often took hours or days to kill a single prisoner.

Hukanovic tells us that:

On weekends regular troops from Banja Luka came to the camp. The guards called them specialists, and they were indeed specialists at breaking arms and legs, tearing out organs, and smashing skulls against walls. The weekends at Omarska were orgies of blood. One day ... one of the regulars said, loudly, so everyone could hear: 'Today is my 25th birthday, and I've only killed 23 Muslims.'[45]

Regular soldiers came to Omarska at the weekends to torture and kill Muslims. Was this a way to wind down after a hard week at the front?

The main objective of the concentration camps, especially Omarska, but also Kereterm, according to a UN commission of experts:

... seems to have been to eliminate the non-Serbian leadership. Political leaders, officials from the courts and administration, academics and other intellectuals, religious leaders, key business people and artists – the backbone of the Muslim and Croatian communities – were removed, apparently with the intention that the removal be permanent. Similarly, law enforcement and military personnel were targeted for destruction.[46]

When Djemo was being taken to freedom, one exchange of prisoners failed to take place. The prisoners were taken to a cell block in the prison of a military barracks. Their guards went off to sleep, leaving the prisoners in the hands of the locals, the 'Knin Boys'. They were left in the hands of this gang for a day and a night, who tortured them, humiliated them and forced them to sing

43 Vulliamy, 1994, p 113.
44 Hukanovic, 1997, pp 50–51.
45 Hukanovic, 1997, p 52.
46 Final report of the United Nations Commission of Experts established pursuant to Security Council Resolution 780, 1992, para 175: cited in Honig, 1996, pp 76–77.

Chetnik songs. The gang was allowed to amuse themselves with a bunch of Muslims while they were in town, while the guards rested.

Vulliamy's story about the young woman torturer reinforces this picture of killing and beating for recreation. In very many of the testimonies of brutality the perpetrators are drunk and laughing, enjoying themselves. They amuse themselves by forcing prisoners to sing for them, and by haranguing them with witty and ironic comments while they are murdering them.

There is an abundance of sexual torture, one prisoner sometimes being forced to torture another. One prisoner was forced to bite another prisoner's testicles off.

On 7 May 1997, Dusko Tadic was found guilty of crimes against humanity. 'He was found to have played a part in almost all of the assaults on prisoners described by [Omarska] survivors during the one-year trial.'[47] The detailed judgment upholds the view of Omarska that I have summarised from Vulliamy and Hukanovic. The judges said that 'women who were held at Omarska were routinely called out of their rooms at night and raped'. One woman was 'taken out five times and after each rape she was beaten'.[48]

The UN response: the ICTY

In the summer of 1996, a NATO spokesman was widely quoted as saying that 'arresting Karadzic is not worth the blood of one NATO soldier'. Geoffrey Robertson comments that:

> [T]his was not so much a case of dereliction of duty as of correctly divining the real purpose of the Hague Tribunal in the minds of the Security Council representatives who set it up, which was never to put major criminals like Karadzic and Mladic behind bars, but to pretend to an anxious and appalled world that something was being done.[49]

David Forsythe agrees, arguing that the tribunal was set up fundamentally to placate public opinion, and lacked the support from those states that set it up that it required in order to be successful. Britain and other states failed to give this support since it might have interfered with diplomatic efforts to end the conflict.[50] But he does concede that it may not be entirely useless: 'The equivalents of Goering and Eichmann, much less Hitler, will not be tried, but neither will they be free to visit Disneyland on vacation.'[51]

However, social structures have emergent properties, and they are shaped by social agents; they have possibilities that are different from those intended; they have the possibility of growing and developing. Institutions do not always become what those who conceived of them had hoped. The ad hoc ICTY was set up with a certain degree of autonomy from the UN Security Council. This was inevitable, since it was set up as a court of law in the Western tradition, and such courts necessarily have a degree of independence from the powers in whose name they operate. The separation of powers

---

47 Traynor, 1997; *Prosecutor v Tadic*.
48 Vulliamy, 1994, p 117.
49 Robertson, 1999, p 265.
50 Forsythe, 1994.
51 Forsythe, 1994, p 419.

between the executive, the legislators and the judiciary are deeply ingrained principles, even if there are many mechanisms by which the separation can, in practice, be eroded or diminished. Even if the ICTY was set up by the great powers in order to feign a concern for justice, that does not necessarily restrict the existing institution to remaining a token gesture. The Nuremberg process was given life by the young idealistic lawyers who made it work, and who, as far as was possible, strove to use it to leave a set of precedents of cosmopolitan criminal law in place.[52]

Both the prosecutors at the ICTY and the judges have a belief in the importance of the work they are doing, and they do it with commitment and energy. Many of the central actors, for example Antonio Cassese and Cherif Bassiouni, are well renowned legal scholars, people who have been writing, almost since Nuremberg, about the possibility and necessity of international criminal law. They were brought in from an academic wilderness and given an institution to build. What the judges lack in actual trial experience they make up for in enthusiasm and vision.

At the Tadic appeal, there was an instructive little exchange. Defending Tadic was a British barrister, William Clegg, the same man who had defended Sawoniuk.[53] He was presenting an argument about what constitutes an international conflict. He made an analogy with lend-lease during the Second World War and said, rather clumsily, 'the Americans lent *us* armaments and money but this didn't necessarily mean that they were themselves participants in the conflict'. Judge Shahabuddeen pulled him up immediately, saying that he should speak more clearly: he should not say 'us', but Britain; he should remember that people will be reading these transcripts in 50 years' time, and he should express himself in such a way as to make himself intelligible to those future students of international law. Shahabuddeen was aware that the discussion in the *Tadic* case regarding the definition of an international conflict was ground-breaking; the court was making law for the future. Even if the ICTY was set up by the Security Council as an empty gesture, those involved were determined to make it work. Even if it was to end in failure, they were thinking about future generations of lawyers and students who might be reading those transcripts. The same can be said for the prosecutors: 'What Richard Goldstone and his successor ... have demonstrated is the optimistic fact that enterprises of this sort have a tendency to develop a momentum of their own.'[54] Cosmopolitan law is not simply an expression of the will of the great powers. It can be influenced, limited or corrupted by them; but it is a sphere of social life that necessarily has some degree of autonomy from the particular interests of the powerful.

Yugoslavia broke up in the summer of 1991. Croatia and Slovenia declared independence and fighting broke out between Croats and Serbs in Croatia. Serbia sent arms, supplies, and the JNA to Croatia. In October 1991, Bosnia held a referendum on independence but the Bosnian Serbs took control of

---

52 Franz Neumann, Otto Kirchheimer and Herbert Marcuse, for example, were all members of the prosecution team at Nuremberg: Salter, 2000.
53 See Chapter Six.
54 Robertson, 1999, p 267.

'their' territory in Bosnia. During the spring and summer of 1992, the Serbs began the process of ethnic cleansing against the Muslims in Bosnia.

In February 1992, the UN Security Council adopted Resolution 721, authorising a special peacekeeping force, UNPROFOR, for Bosnia. The Commission on Human Rights convened the first exceptional session ever on 13 August 1992 to discuss the ethnic cleansing. A special *Rapporteur* was appointed in August 1992, who subsequently issued four reports to the General Assembly and the Security Council.[55]

The first report, on 28 August 1992, confirmed that ethnic cleansing had been pursued throughout Bosnia by Serbs, that there had been torture and systematic execution and that 3,000 Muslims had disappeared after the fall of Vukovar. The second report, in October 1992, following a visit by the *Rapporteur* to Bosnia, stated that Muslims had clearly become victims of aggression and ethnic cleansing. Displaced persons were in a desperate situation, especially in the Travnik area; before their arrival in Travnik, many had been taken to the front lines, subjected to beatings, robbery, rape and sometimes shooting. There had also been ethnic cleansing in Pijavija, Prikepolje, and Proboj. On 6 October, the Security Council voted to establish a 'commission of experts' to gather evidence of war crimes in the former Yugoslavia.[56] The third report of the *Rapporteur*, on 17 November 1992, highlighted violations of the various parties' legal obligations under international law. Ethnic cleansing, it argued, followed the political objective of the Serbian nationalists of the creation of a Greater Serbia. It concluded that one and a half million out of four million Bosnians had become refugees, 75% of these refugees being children and elderly. The fourth report, the most comprehensive, concluded that the serious and large scale violations of human rights and international humanitarian law were not by-products of war but were deliberate policies of the Serbs. It also reported that there was discrimination against Serbian civilians in Croatia, and against Albanians in Kosovo.

Dame Ann Warburton was sent by the European Community to Yugoslavia in December 1992 and January 1993, and she reported on 3 February 1993 to the UN Secretary General. She found that the rape of Muslim women had been perpetrated on a wide scale and in such a systematic way as to be considered part of an intentional war strategy. She estimated that there had been 20,000 rapes, but said that it could be between 10,000 and 60,000, with about 1,000 pregnancies. She reported testimony that 'a repeated feature of Serbian attacks on Muslim towns and villages was the use of rape, often in public, or the threat of rape, as a weapon of war to force the population to leave their homes'.[57]

The Security Council's 'commission of experts' was slow, academic and stuffed with 'old fogeys'.[58] It was chaired by Frits Kalshoven, a retired

---

55 The four reports are cited in Bland, 1994.
56 Bass, 2000, p 211.
57 Joyner, 1994. On 22 February 2001, three men, Dragoljub Kunarac, Radomir Kovac and Zoran Vukovic, were found guilty of crimes against humanity at the ICTY for organising and perpetrating mass rape and sexual slavery. The judgment of the 11-month trial confirmed that, in the summer of 1992, rape houses had been set up in sports halls and other places. Rape was seen by the judges as a method of ethnic cleansing, aimed at spreading terror, and also at impregnating Muslim women with 'Serb' babies. *Prosecutor v Kunarac, Kovac and Vukovic*.
58 Bass, 2000, p 211.

professor of law at Leiden who admitted to having serious qualms about convening war crimes trials. Roy Gutman reported that Kalshoven 'tells visitors he does not know why he got the job'.[59] Kalshoven was the only full time employee of the commission who did not have the resources to carry out investigations. Gutman also reports that Kalshoven says that he was told by 'authoritative persons' at the UN not to investigate Milosevic or Karadzic.[60] Cherif Bassiouni, an Egyptian-American law professor at DePaul University who was on the commission, described Kalshoven as an 'indoor scholar', and he started pushing hard to make something of the commission.[61] Bassiouni raised money for the committee and began collecting documentation and a database of evidence of crimes committed in Bosnia. Kalshoven, complaining about British and French foot-dragging, resigned in August 1993 leaving the committee in the hands of Bassiouni, but it was closed down in April 1994.[62]

On 22 February 1993, however, the Security Council had adopted Resolution 808, which formally decided that an international tribunal should be established for the former Yugoslavia. On 25 May 1993, the Security Council adopted Resolution 827, formally establishing the tribunal. The tribunal was set up under the UN Charter (1945) in relation to keeping the peace, not directly in relation to justice or to prosecuting crimes against humanity. It was established under authority of Chapter VII of the UN Charter, which provides that the Security Council shall 'decide what measures shall be taken ... to maintain or restore international peace and security'. Under Article 48(1) of the charter, '[t]he action required to carry out decisions of the Security Council for the maintenance of international peace and security shall be taken by all the Members of the United Nations'. All member states were thus obligated to adhere to the requirements imposed on states in the Security Council resolutions governing the activities of the tribunals.[63]

The Security Council argued that atrocities in Bosnia constituted a threat to international peace, and that the tribunals would contribute to the restoration of peace. It was on this basis, pursuant to Chapter VII of the UN Charter, that the Security Council decided in its Resolutions 808 and 827 to establish such a tribunal. The singling out of violations of humanitarian law as a major factor in the determination of a threat to the peace creates an important precedent. The establishment of the tribunal as an enforcement measure under the binding authority of Chapter VII, argued Theodor Meron, may foreshadow more effective international responses for violations of international law.[64]

The Security Council's resolution binds all member states to co-operate with the tribunals. The general obligation of states to co-operate can be found in operative paragraph 4 of Security Council Resolution 827 and operative paragraph 2 of Resolution 955, the resolutions establishing the Yugoslav and Rwanda tribunals respectively, and setting forth their structure, jurisdiction and procedures. These provisions both read as follows:

> [The Security Council] Decides that all states shall co-operate fully with the International Tribunal and its organs in accordance with the present resolution and

---

59 Gutman, 1993, p 151.
60 Gutman, 1993, p 150.
61 Bass, 2000, p 211.
62 Bass, 2000, p 212.
63 Kushen and Harris, 1997.
64 Meron, 1994.

the Statute of the International Tribunal and that consequently all States shall take any measures necessary under their domestic law to implement the provisions of the present resolution and the Statute, including the obligation of states to comply with requests for assistance or orders issued by a Trial Chamber under Article 29 [Article 28 for Rwanda] of the Statute.[65]

The specific obligation to surrender fugitives is found in Articles 28 and 29, which read as follows:

1   States shall co-operate with the International Tribunal in the investigation and prosecution of persons accused of committing serious violations of international humanitarian law.
2   States shall comply without undue delay with any request for assistance or any order issued by a Trial Chamber, including, but not limited to:
     ...
     (d)   the arrest or detention of persons
     (e)   the surrender or the transfer of the accused to the International Tribunal.[66]

The agreements to surrender suspects to the court are analogous to bilateral extradition treaties.[67] Because the Security Council has powers to act and to obligate states to act under the section of the charter relating to the maintenance of peace and security, this was a convenient and effective method of founding the court. The political will existed in the Security Council, and the legal powers were discovered with which to enact that will.

It is not obvious that the Security Council in fact had the legal right to set up the tribunal under Chapter VII of the charter. Neither is it clear that the Security Council could bestow upon the tribunal the authority to command states to co-operate, since it was claiming to be independent even though its authority originated from the fact that it was a subsidiary body of the Security Council. The establishment of the tribunal has also been seen as the assertion of political supremacy of great powers over small states, since this mechanism for setting up an ad hoc tribunal could only be used against less powerful states.[68] A subsidiary body could not have competence falling outside the competence of its principal, and it is questionable whether the General Assembly is competent to administer justice. The Security Council, it could be argued, is similarly incompetent to administer justice, but it is competent to handle matters relating to peace and security. Perhaps more importantly, the General Assembly is unable to make binding decisions – to make it mandatory for states to co-operate with the tribunal, for example – whereas Article 24(1) of the UN Charter obliges all member states to accept and carry out the decisions of the Security Council.[69]

These kinds of legal objections to the institution of the court have a similarity with some of the formalist objections to the Nuremberg process. It seems clear enough, however, that it is not the cogency or correctness of any particular legal argument that carries the day. If there is a coincidence of political will between the great powers and others to set up an international tribunal, then they are able to discover legal mechanisms with which to do it. The ICTY was set up under a section of the UN Charter that was clearly never

---

65 Meron, 1994, p 511.
66 Meron, 1994, p 511.
67 Kushen and Harris, 1997.
68 Cotic, 1994, p 223.
69 Kolodkin, 1994, p 388.

intended to empower the Security Council to institute a court. Yet the Security Council discovered a mechanism for doing what it wanted to do. Perhaps the Nuremberg tribunal suffered from significant flaws; perhaps it was vulnerable to the *tu quoque* argument, and perhaps also to the 'retrospective justice' argument. However, after Nuremberg, the Nuremberg process itself constitutes a clear unambiguous precedent. Innovation is necessarily unprecedented. Similarly, the ICTY was perhaps created on the basis of a piece of legal trickery. Once created, however, it constitutes a precedent.

The structure of the tribunal consists of three principal organs: the chambers, the prosecutor, and the registry. The chambers comprises three-member trial chambers and a five-member appeals chamber charged with adjudicating cases. The prosecutor investigates allegations and prepares indictments for cases to be prosecuted. The registry assists both the prosecutor and the chambers, in addition to performing other administrative duties, such as requesting governments to provide information on the identity of the accused, to serve documents and to extradite the accused.

The tribunal retains concurrent jurisdiction with the national courts of states that have emerged from Yugoslavia since its collapse. States have the right to put a suspect on trial, but the tribunal has the power to retry such a suspect. Article 210 of the statute prohibits trials *in absentia*.

Today, as we watch the trial of Milosevic himself unfold, the tribunal can appear to be a successful manifestation of Western, or American, power and resolve. It is not true, however, that there was a policy decision at an early stage by the Western leadership to create such a tribunal. When the tribunal was first constituted by the Security Council it was done so ambivalently. It is impossible to know exactly what the intent of Western leadership was when the court was set up, to know exactly how components of different motivations were balanced. There was a wish to pursue justice; there was a wish for the appearance of justice to cover an unjust policy; there was a wish for an instrument of apparently legitimate power that could punish the enemies of the West. And then there is no such thing as an 'intent of the Western leadership', but rather a coalition of individual approaches by states with different amounts of influence, and by individuals within regimes also with differing amounts of influence. Western policy swung wildly from the humiliation in the Sudan, to the timidity in Bosnia and Rwanda, to the thunderous response in Kosovo; the uses the West wished to make of the ICTY must also have swung wildly during this period, a period also of transition from Bush to Clinton to Bush, and from Major to Blair. Policy towards the court also became more favourable when Yugoslavia became more stable and when the possible threat to the fragile equilibrium held in place by NATO troops decreased; in other words, when the risk to stability and to the lives of NATO soldiers decreased.

One thing is clear: that the ICTY was first established without the resources or the power necessary to succeed in bringing to justice those primarily responsible for ethnic cleansing in the former Yugoslavia. Its growth into such a body was the result of a combination of factors. There was the work and vision of the prosecutors and judges who built the institution because they believed in it. There were the developments in the former Yugoslavia, such as fall of the Milosevic regime and the liberalisation of the Tudjman regime after his death. There was the increasing reliance by NATO on human rights rhetoric during the Kosovo conflict. There was the good luck of the ICTY in obtaining defendants, from the chance arrest of Tadic in Germany to the extradition of Milosevic, following his overthrow, encouraged by the promise of dollars to the new Serbian regime.

In November 1993, the 11 judges took office in The Hague. Antonio Cassese later said that the Security Council had thought that the tribunal would never become operational. 'We had no budget, we had nothing. Zero.'[70] The selection of a prosecutor was a protracted and politicised process, since the prosecutor would have control over the indictments of the court. In July 1994, the Security Council appointed Richard Goldstone. In 1993–94, the UN proposed a budget of $562,300 for investigations, including witness travel, interviews with refugees, forensic experts, translators and protection,[71] although in the end the General Assembly gave the tribunal $5.6 million for the first half of 1994 and $5.4 million for the second half. By 1999, in comparison, the budget had risen to $94 million.[72] In those early days morale and confidence at the ICTY were low, and there was a danger that the whole process might fold. A member of Goldstone's staff is quoted by Gary Bass: 'A, you can indict Milosevic and be shut down, or B, you can do low level [indictments] and do a few trials.'[73] Even the indictments of Mladic and Karadzic, issued on 25 July 1995, were bold moves by Goldstone, who said: '... it was really done as, if you like, an academic exercise. Because our duty was clear. We weren't going to be dissuaded from doing it by any prognostications – good or bad – as to what effect it would have.'[74] The autonomy of the prosecutor and of the court was, perhaps, not seen as a problem by the West since its power was very small.

The morale and sense of purpose at the ICTY strengthened greatly. It developed from a body whose central actors felt that it existed only to fail in 1993, to a body capable of indicting the (almost) top perpetrators of ethnic cleansing as an academic exercise in 1995, to a body capable of convicting Tadic in 1997. After the Tadic conviction there was a different feeling around the court. There were three courtrooms trying cases and a queue of defendants waiting in the cells. By 1999 the court was ready to indict Milosevic himself, and by June 2001 it held him prisoner. This trajectory of development would have astounded everyone in 1992 when the Security Council constituted the court. The relentless increase in leadership, competence and self-confidence within the institution has been mirrored by a gradual change in policy by the Western leadership in its favour.

The ICTY is an empirical fact; it exists. The court building is opposite the main conference centre on the edge of Den Haag, a couple of miles away from the seafront at Scheveningen. The brown stone 1950s-style building is surrounded by a metal fence, behind which UN security staff can be seen patrolling from time to time. Their uniforms are reminiscent of American police uniforms, but UN pale blue. They carry guns on their belts. They are recruited from police forces and armies around the world, but are not working for those forces; they work for and owe their allegiance directly to the UN and to the court. I spoke to guards from Nigeria, Scotland, Italy and Venezuela.

70 Bass, 2000, p 217.
71 Bass, 2000, p 221.
72 Bass, 2000, p 221.
73 Bass, 2000, p 229.
74 Bass, 2000, p 230.

There is airport-style security on entering the building. There are armed guards in the foyer and in the public galleries. They sit on either side of the defendants at all times behind the bulletproof glass separating the court from the public.

The building feels like an international court. It flies blue UN flags outside; it has blue UN flags and insignia behind and above the judges. Daily, it proceeds with the business of conducting trials. It conducts slow and long trials, but trials nevertheless. Cosmopolitan criminal law is not some utopian concept; it exists in this building in The Hague, even if only in an embryonic form.

On a routine day in the court, when there is no verdict to be announced, no new indictment, nothing dramatic happening, there are not many visitors. Even for the Milosevic trial, the public gallery is typically less than half full. There is a small press room, a handful of journalists. There is a young man in the press room whose job it is to feed the television pictures of the trials onto the internet. Proceedings in each of the three courts can be watched, with a half hour delay, from anywhere in the world.

I arrived at the court shortly after the end of the Sawoniuk trial in London. There, I had become accustomed to gossiping about the progress of the case with the others in the public gallery between sessions; there were the few who followed the case throughout, and the ones who came to look, occasionally, or just for a day or two. On my first morning at The Hague, I was watching the Blaskic trial. During the break, I approached one of the few other observers. I asked how the trial was going, what were her impressions. She looked at me with disdain, and said, shortly, that she was not about to explain the whole complex case to me, and walked off. A while later, I approached three men who were there, and attempted, a little more subtly, to talk to them. They looked at me with suspicion. They asked me who I was, what I was doing there, and why they had seen me talking to a Croatian journalist. I suddenly became aware that the whole atmosphere at The Hague was different from that of the Old Bailey. The woman had been a Croatian, covering the trial of Blaskic for a Zagreb paper; the three men, I noticed later, left the courthouse every day in a large black BMW with Bosnian diplomatic number plates. The events dealt with here were much more current and fresh than at the London trial. There was an atmosphere of suspicion. There were 'supporters' of all sides present; those who had direct experience of being 'cleansed' and those whose profession it was to deny and lie about ethnic cleansing. A small part of the war was still being fought, here, in the court building. The buildup to the NATO bombing in Kosovo was happening at that time.

The three Bosniak men told me that they were spies 'like James Bond'. They watched the trials, taking long and detailed notes. I spent some time trying to gain their confidence, hoping that perhaps I would be able to interview them. They became more friendly, and a little less suspicious, but they had their work to do; they answered questions either in riddles, or with the official Bosnian Government 'line'.

The staff who work in the building speak mainly English as they sit in the foyer near the coffee machine. I spoke to Americans, Canadians, British, Dutch, French, Germans, South Africans, and others. They are lawyers, ex-cops, translators, clerical workers, students doing internships. Being a sociologist, I attempted to strike up conversations with people, to find out what they had to say, to build up an impression of them and how they were thinking; to form an idea of the general morale of the staff and the institution; to do a little amateur ethno-methodology. I found them, in general, rather tight-lipped. It was only a few days later, when I was approached and questioned by the head of security at the court, that I realised that each member of staff who I had tried to talk to had subsequently gone to him to report the conversation. He knew my name, who I had been talking to, how long I had been around, and which trials I had been observing. All of this bolstered my impression of the seriousness of the court. They take themselves seriously and they take security seriously.

The UN existed in Srebrenica as it exists at The Hague, with the same blue flags and helmets; it had similar institutional forms and appearances. The content, however, of the supra-national interventions was significantly different. At The Hague, the UN institution is based on due process, justice, respect for human dignity and for human rights. It has a real, if limited, independence from the powers that set it up. It is self-consciously building on the fragments of cosmopolitan criminal law and practice that were bequeathed to it by previous processes. The ICTY quietly conducts its ground-breaking business. It contrasts starkly with UN negligence and indifference during the war in Bosnia. Even if the ICTY was set up by the Security Council in order to fail, the reality, in a limited way, is defying expectations. This UN institution has attained some real humanitarian content. What exists in the ICTY is a spark of genuine cosmopolitanism; in Srebrenica, behind the cosmopolitan façade, there was only darkness.

Chapter Five

The trials of Blaskic and Tadic at the ICTY

In this chapter, I present outlines of two trials from the International Criminal Tribunal for the former Yugoslavia (ICTY) based on my own observations at The Hague, on internet broadcasts of the trials, and on the trial transcripts and judgments. Tihomir Blaskic, a Croatian General, presented himself as a professional soldier, and at the time of his conviction was the highest ranking person to have been convicted at the ICTY. Dusko Tadic, an ideologue and torturer in a small town, was the first person who pleaded not guilty to be found guilty at the ICTY. Cosmopolitan criminal law is not an abstract ideal but a developing reality. It is important to anchor discussion of theoretical debates in the actuality of events: first, events that constitute the subject matter of cosmopolitan criminal law, in these two cases ethnic cleansing itself; secondly, events that constitute the substance of cosmopolitan criminal law, the extraction of individuals from machines of terror, the designation of their acts as crimes and the routine business of their prosecution. It is important to look at trials not only as legal cases but in a more rounded way as social processes. These discussions of trials are intended to give an insight into the mechanics of the processes of cosmopolitan criminal law. The concepts of cosmopolitan right, supra-national authority and due process attain their worldly actuality in the quotidian professional business of lawyers, judges, investigators, translators, security officers and journalists. As was shown in the last chapter, cosmopolitan forms do not necessarily coincide with genuine cosmopolitan content. The relationship between the lofty concepts and their worldly actuality is therefore a fundamental point of investigation.

The trial of General Tihomir Blaskic

The trial of Tihomir Blaskic opened on 24 June 1997 and ran until 30 July 1999; judgment was passed down on 3 March 2000. He was, at the time of his conviction, the highest ranking person to be found guilty at The Hague, and was sentenced to 45 years' imprisonment. He was the first to be found guilty who had not committed violent acts with his own hands, but was held responsible for such acts due to his position in the military structure of the Croatian army in Bosnia. He was in his late 30s at the time of the trial. He was charged with having committed, ordered, planned or otherwise aided and abetted in between 1 May 1992 and 31 January 1994:

(a) a crime against humanity, persecution (attacks upon cities, towns and villages; killing and causing serious injury; destruction and plunder of property; inhumane treatment of civilians; forcible transfer of civilians);
(b) crimes against humanity, wilful killing and causing serious injury;
(c) grave breaches of the Geneva Conventions;
(d) and violations of the laws or customs of war, for killing, serious bodily harm, destruction and plunder of property, destruction of institutions

dedicated to education or religion, inhuman or cruel treatment of detainees, including the taking of hostages for use as human shields, all this against the Muslim population of central Bosnia and in particular the Lasva Valley, that is more specifically in the municipalities of Vitez, Busovaca, Kiseljak and, to some degree, Zenica.

He was, in any case, charged with not having taken reasonable measures to prevent crimes or to punish the perpetrators thereof although knowing or having reasons to know that the crimes were about to be committed or had been committed. He was found guilty on every count, except that he was not held responsible for the shelling of civilian homes in Zenica, though the trial chamber concluded that this crime was probably committed by his forces in the HVO.[1]

The Blaskic trial was held in a small courtroom which appeared to have been constructed on the mezzo floor of the building, on the landing of the large grand staircase. The glass that separates the court from the public does not seem to cut the courtroom in half but rather to give the impression of a zoo, as though the court is in a glass cage and people can come along and look whenever they like. The public gallery feels as though it is outside the court. There are three sections of seats, for the public, for journalists, and for VIPs. The VIP section is in the middle, and at the front of this section the chairs are particularly comfortable. The small electronic boxes into which you plug your headphones work well; there are settings for French, English and BCS (Bosnian-Croatian-Serbian). The glass barrier is soundproof, and one can only hear what is being said through the loudspeakers or through one's headphones. There are also television screens either side of the glass partition that constantly show proceedings. Every now and then, the court decides to go into private session; suddenly, the microphones and television screens are switched off, the blue blinds are lowered over the glass partition, and the public gallery is entirely excluded from proceedings.

Inside the courtroom, there is a feeling that one is in the presence of a genuinely international court. The judges are from France, Portugal, and Guyana. The team of prosecutors is led in cross-examination by Kehoe, a man with a New York accent who is reminiscent of a tough, streetwise, rather intimidating cop. The defence team is smaller, consisting of a Croatian and a young American who, in contrast, seems to be rather 'Ivy League'. When the two Americans clash fiercely across the courtroom the French judge in the middle looks exasperated at this American adversarial combat, and yet again, but vainly, appeals for a little 'synthesis' from all sides: 'We don't want still to be here at Christmas.'

The area in which Blaskic was responsible for ethnic cleansing was the Lasva Valley, 30 kilometres north west of Sarajevo, surrounded by hills, through which the main road towards Travnik and Vitez passes. According to the 1991 census, the municipalities of Vitez, Busovaca and Kiseljak, which are in the Lasva valley, had been roughly evenly divided between Croat and Muslim populations, with a small Croat majority.

In early 1992 Blaskic was in Vienna, having left the Yugoslav army (the JNA). In February 1992, the municipal council of Kiseljak, the town in which

---

1 The HVO was the army of Croatians in Bosnia; the HV was the army of the Republic of Croatia.

Blaskic had been born, invited him to organise the defence of the municipality against the Serbs. This was initially organised with both Croat and Muslim participation. On 6 April 1992, the Republic of Bosnia-Herzegovina declared its independence, and it was formally recognised by Croatia the next day. The UN Security Council called for external forces to leave the territory of Bosnia. It demanded that the JNA and Croatian army units withdraw, place themselves under the authority of the Bosnian Government, or be disbanded. But the now Serbian JNA was nearby, at Jajce, and was also advancing towards the Lasva Valley from the south east. The Croatian nationalists, with the backing of Zagreb, gained the leadership of the HVO, the Croatian Defence Council in Bosnia, against the wishes of those Croatians who supported multi-ethnicity, or cohabitation, with the Muslims. The Bosnian Territorial Defence (the TO) was formed on 9 April 1992 and was 'outlawed' the next day by the 'President' of the Croatian community in Bosnia, Mate Boban. The Croatian General Anto Roso confirmed this in an order on 8 May, and on 11 May Tihomir Blaskic implemented that order by pronouncing the TO unlawful in the territory of Kiseljak. The joint Muslim and Croatian defence of the Lasva Valley, therefore, was only ever notional, and was quickly replaced by a Croatian nationalist leadership that planned a campaign of ethnic cleansing against the Muslims in the area. They were not prepared to allow Muslims to participate in the defence against the Serbs since it would have been necessary to allow them access to weapons.

Blaskic's defence contained a number of strands but centrally he argued that he was in charge of a poorly trained, hurriedly mustered force; he was under siege from the Serbs, communications between himself and his forces were difficult, and there were many Croatian paramilitary and police outfits operating in the area over which he had no authority. There were atrocities committed of which he did not approve and over which he had no control. He further argued that some of the atrocities committed against Muslims were in fact either committed by Serbs or by Muslims themselves. He argued that Muslims were committing atrocities against Croats, and that it was not surprising if Croat forces beyond his control retaliated in a similar manner. His defence argued that he had repeatedly issued written orders that his forces should respect humanitarian law. And the defence maintained that the use of work teams made up of prisoners to dig trenches was legal at the time of the conflict.

Blaskic presented himself in court as an experienced and meticulous army officer. He was always courteous. He played the part of an isolated professional soldier trying valiantly but unsuccessfully to discipline his untrained civilians into a modern and professional army. During his cross-examination, Kehoe would always greet him with a gruff 'good morning, General'. Blaskic would answer with 'good morning, Mr Prosecutor'. And they would get down to business. Kehoe would introduce a document, maybe a copy of an order that Blaskic had received or issued. Blaskic would require 10 minutes to read the order. Kehoe would ask him what the order meant. Blaskic would take five minutes to explain in great detail the meaning of the order, explaining everything in it except for the part that was relevant. It became increasingly clear under cross-examination that his professional attention to detail and rules was a screen behind which Blaskic was hiding the reality of his job in the Lasva Valley. He had a legalistic, unrealistic and pedantic way of reading documents, and attempted to use this as a shield against the accusations. He tried to drown the court in detail. This cross-examination went on for six weeks.

In May 1992, tensions between Muslim and Croatian populations had intensified in the Lasva Valley. The Croatian flag was being flown on public buildings that the HVO controlled; mosques and Muslim houses were beginning to be attacked, and there were some ethnically motivated murders. Some officers of Croatian origin were kidnapped by Muslims. Muslims were beginning to be pushed out of their homes by Croats, and there were many Muslim and some Croatian refugees moving into the area from places where Serbs had pushed them out. Blaskic was appointed Commander of the Central Bosnian Operative Zone of the HVO on 27 June 1992.

The Vance-Owen plan was put forward on 2 January 1993. It proposed the creation of 10 provinces in Bosnia that would each have substantial autonomy. The Lasva Valley was located mainly in Province 10, with the rest in Province 7. Though the Vance-Owen plan was never implemented on the ground, the tribunal judged that the Bosnian Croats understood that Province 10 was to be given to them, and that they also understood that they would have an interest in incorporating the Croatian areas of Province 7, which were predominately Muslim. '[T]he Bosnian Croats,' argued the judgment, 'bore a heavy responsibility in conducting the war in anticipation of its implementation [the Vance-Owen plan] and in willing its unilateral execution.'[2]

Mate Boban ordered Muslims to hand over their arms by 15 January 1993, and the HVO proceeded with a campaign to 'Croatise' the territories by force. Hundreds of Muslims were arrested and many were imprisoned in Kaonik, where they were badly treated. These Muslim prisoners were used to dig trenches, often under inhuman conditions and exposed to enemy fire; they were also used as human shields.

In April 1993, at a televised public meeting, Blaskic said that HVO soldiers had been attacked in Nadioci, and in a written order he commanded the HVO brigades and the Bitezovi special unit to fire back if attacked; he ordered the HVO brigades and the Military Police 4th Battalion to defend themselves against 'Muslim terrorist attacks'. On 16 April 1993 at 1.30 am, he issued a 'combat order' to the Vitez Brigade and the Tvrtko independent units to 'prevent the attacks of extremist Muslim forces'. They had to be ready to commence shooting at 5.30 am on 16 April. These statements and orders were thinly encoded announcements of the plan to begin the campaign of ethnic cleansing in earnest. At that time, and over the following days, the campaign was carried out in the Lasva Valley. Civilians were killed and wounded, houses burnt down, minarets brought down, mosques destroyed, women and children separated from the men and left to flee; women were raped and men imprisoned, beaten and led off to the front to dig trenches.

Ahmici was a largely Muslim village and was well known for its practice and teaching of the Muslim religion; its largest mosque had just been rebuilt. The Croatian inhabitants left the village on the evening of 15 April. At 5.30 am on 16 April, artillery began to bombard the village. Many Muslim men, women and children were forced out of their homes and shot, many others were burnt alive in their houses. This was the village where the British UN peacekeepers led by

---

2 *Prosecutor v Blaskic.*

Colonel Bob Stewart, who gave evidence at the trial, found the bodies of many people. Stewart was interviewed at the time on television news. His anger, disgust and frustration at the scene his men had found in Ahmici penetrated his English and military reserve. The interview was moving and memorable. No soldier in the HVO, the military or paramilitary police units was ever punished for the events at Ahmici by the Croatian authorities. This reaction can be contrasted with the fact that on 16 April, the very day of the attack on Ahmici, Blaskic sent a protest to UNPROFOR because a United Nations (UN) armoured vehicle had knocked down a church fence. Many other villages in the Lasva Valley met the same fate on 16 April and the following few days. Inhabitants were taken prisoner, forced to flee or murdered. There were attacks on Muslims all through the spring and summer of 1993 that constituted the campaign to 'Croatise' the territory.

The prosecution contested Blaskic's two central lines of defence, which were that he had difficulty in communicating with his troops[3] and that the crimes were committed by paramilitary units that were not under his control. The judges found that Blaskic had been successful in setting up a solid chain of command throughout the territories for which he was responsible. That chain of command incorporated paramilitary and police outfits that were not part of the HVO but that were shown during the trial to have operated under the authority and direction of Blaskic.

The HVO was not simply an army, but also had a civilian structure. The distinction between the military leadership and the civilian or political leadership was not sharp. Blaskic often appeared in public meetings, alongside Mate Boban, Dario Kordic,[4] Anto Valenta and other political leaders, who sometimes wore military uniforms; he was part of the leadership of the HVO, and was clearly aware of the fact that the programme of the HVO was one of 'Croatisation' and the ethnic cleansing of Muslim people, places of worship and businesses.

Much time was spent during the trial by the prosecution to show that the conflict was an international one, and not simply a conflict between Croats and Muslims within Bosnia. This was relevant for two reasons. First, some of the laws and customs of war, particularly the Geneva Conventions, only apply to international conflict, so that it was necessary to prove the existence of an international conflict in order to convict Blaskic of breaking those laws. Secondly, it was shown during the trial that the HVO and Blaskic were carrying out the policy of the Republic of Croatia in working towards the 'dream' of a Greater Croatia. Franjo Tudjman had met with Slobodan Milosevic in March 1991 to discuss the sharing of Bosnia between themselves. The chain of command was shown, in the trial, not only to be strong from Blaskic downwards to the troops on the ground carrying out the ethnic cleansing, but also upwards, all the way to Tudjman. A fiction of HVO

---

3   In fact, it was shown that cellular phones were working in the area at the time.
4   At the time of the cross-examination of Blaskic, the trial of Kordic was beginning in the courtroom upstairs. Kordic, the political leader of the Croats in the Lasva Valley at the time, was found guilty on 26 February 2001 for his part in the ethnic cleansing of the territory, and particularly for ordering the attack on Ahmici and other villages in April 1993. He was not found to be a prime mover or an architect of the overall campaign, but was found to be an important politician in the area. At the time of his conviction, Kordic was the most senior political leader to have been found guilty at the ICTY. *Prosecutor v Kordic and Cerkez.*

independence from Croatia was maintained, but it did not constitute a reality. Many HV personnel operated within the HVO, and documents produced during the trial show that they were ordered to change their insignia to those of the HVO. Later, Blaskic himself was transferred from the HVO to the HV on the orders of President Tudjman. It is true that Croatia, initially at least, gave some aid to Bosnia, but its links with the HVO were much closer, involving the interchange of personnel and the donation of a million Deutschemarks a day. Fundamentally, the Republic of Croatia was involved in a cross-border military campaign with the eventual aim of annexing parts of Bosnia.

The trial of Blaskic took over two years, heard 158 witnesses and received nearly 1,500 exhibits. It is perhaps a measure of the novelty and immaturity of the system of international criminal law that this trial, which was not fundamentally very complex, took so much time, money and resources. It is possible that with increasing self-confidence and experience the ICTY will be able to try cases more quickly and efficiently. William Clegg, the barrister who defended Tadic at his appeal, and who also defended Andrei Sawoniuk, expressed the opinion in an interview[5] that it should be possible to try a case such as this in six weeks. He argued that it would be better for the prosecution to pick its five or six clearest incidents with which to prove its charges, instead of attempting to prove every single allegation. It is also true that these first few trials have been concerned to prove larger issues than the guilt or innocence of the accused. For example, in the Blaskic and Tadic trials, much time was spent proving the complicity of Croatia and Serbia in the conflict in Bosnia and proving that genocide and crimes against humanity were being committed. Such issues, it is to be hoped, need only to be proven comprehensively once.

The trial of Dusko Tadic

Dusko Tadic was the first person who had not pleaded guilty to be convicted at the ICTY. He was found guilty in May 1997 and sentenced to 20 years' imprisonment. Tadic was arrested in February 1994 in Germany, where he was then living, on suspicion of having committed offences at Omarska, including torture and aiding and abetting the commission of genocide, which constitute crimes under German law. Proceedings at the ICTY against Tadic started on 12 October 1994 when Richard Goldstone, then the court's prosecutor, filed an application that the Federal Republic of Germany should hand over Tadic to The Hague and that the German courts should defer competence to the international tribunal. A public hearing was held on 8 November 1994, after which the indictment of Tadic and an arrest warrant were produced in February 1995.

Tadic was charged with individual counts of persecution, inhuman treatment, cruel treatment, rape, wilful killing, murder, torture, wilfully causing great suffering or serious injury to body and health, and inhumane acts alleged to have been committed at the Omarska, Kereterm and Trnopolje camps and at other locations in Opstina Prijedor in the Republic of Bosnia-Herzegovina. Germany enacted the necessary legislation for his surrender, and he was transferred to The Hague on 24 April 1995. He pleaded not guilty to all

---

5 Interview conducted by the author in The Hague, 21 April 1999.

charges. Following many pre-trial hearings about rules, procedure and other technical matters, the trial of Dusko Tadic began on 7 May 1996.

Mira Tadic gave evidence to the tribunal. She had married Dusko in 1979, after living with him for a year. At the time that she gave evidence she was 35. She was a nurse; Dusko only had secondary school level qualifications. Between 1980 and 1986 Tadic worked in a factory, assembling electrical equipment. In 1986 Mira got a job as a nurse in Libya and Dusko went with her. They were divorced in 1987 because, she explained, she wanted to get work in Switzerland as a nurse, and it was easier for single people to get such work than for married people. While they continued to live together, however, she never got the job in Switzerland. In 1987 Tadic formed a construction company which got some work in Croatia, but the business ended in the summer of 1989. Next, Tadic spent time working on his own house, with some periods in Germany working for his brother's construction company in Munich. Tadic opened a café in early 1991. Mira told of a letter that they had received from Muslims that 'was threatening, saying that we should leave Kozarac and if we did not leave Kozarac within three months that we would be killed, and it was signed by the "Young Muslims from Kozarac", that is the party of SDA …'. On two occasions the shop window was broken, and at one time the café was broken into and burgled. Mira Tadic gave evidence as follows:

> **Kay**: As we enter 1992 and some five months before the conflict in Kozarac, what was the state of relations like in the town amongst the different ethnic groups?
> **Mira Tadic**: The relations were tense. Apparently, we would say 'hello' and talk, but there were no close contacts or visits. Everybody was just minding their own business.
> **K**: What was causing this tension?
> **MT**: Because people were simply afraid of one another.
> **K**: Were you or your husband adding to this tension? Were you or your husband adding to this climate?
> **MT**: We could not add to it because we were a minority. We were more or less the only ones there …
> **K**: Why did you leave on 1 April 1992?
> **MT**: Because at that time in Kozarac it was not safe any more. We were in a minority. The Muslim people became organised. They had their barracks, they wore uniforms, held arms. I was afraid for my life and for the life of my children, and that is why I left Kozarac.[6]

The presentation of the prosecution case lasted for 47 sitting days and ended on 15 August 1996. During this period 76 witnesses gave evidence and 346 prosecution exhibits were admitted, including video tapes of the region and a model of the Omarska camp, together with a further 40 exhibits from the defence. The defence case began on 10 September 1996, ending on 30 October. Forty witnesses were presented and 75 exhibits admitted. Tadic testified for three days from 25 October 1996.

The judgment produced by the tribunal in the *Tadic* case was about 120,000 words long. It is a comprehensive account of the trial and of the events for

---

6 *Prosecutor v Tadic*, 9 October 1996, transcript, pp 6746–47.

which he was on trial. It spends many pages giving an outline of the history of Yugoslavia and its political breakup, focusing on the growth of the idea of the Greater Serbia and the development of ethnic cleansing as an instrument of national policy. It is a self-conscious attempt to provide an objective, authoritative and impartial narrative concerning the breakup of Yugoslavia, ethnic cleansing in Bosnia and of the small part played by Dusko Tadic.

Tadic was born on 1 October 1955. His mother had been deported during the Second World War to Jasenovac, the notorious concentration camp run by Croat Ustasa forces in alliance with the Nazi regime. This son of a concentration camp survivor was to become a *génocidaire* and torturer himself. He came from a prominent Serb family in the small town of Kozarac. His father was a decorated Second World War hero. Tadic taught karate and was the father of two daughters. Ninety per cent of the inhabitants of Kozarac were Muslims prior to the conflict. Tadic testified that most of his friends had been Muslim.

He joined the SDS, the Bosnian Serb political party, in 1990. A witness testified that Tadic's café became a centre for Serb nationalists, who were becoming increasingly racist against Muslims and who used to gather there, singing Chetnik songs. Tadic's brother's ex-wife testified that Tadic admired Milosevic, and had said that if his next child was a boy he would call him Slobodan. After the ethnic cleansing of Kozarac had been accomplished, Tadic became the political leader of Kozarac, was elected president of the local board of the SDS, and was appointed as acting secretary of the local commune in September 1992, also becoming its representative to the Prijedor Municipal Assembly.

Tadic began service as a reserve traffic police officer at the Orlovci checkpoint on 16 June 1992, and was thereafter assigned duties as a reserve policeman in Prijedor. He went to some lengths to resist being drafted for military service; when, after more than one attempt, he was successfully drafted to the war zone, he escaped the following day and went into hiding. He was arrested several times during the ensuing months for desertion but always managed to escape. In August 1993 Tadic travelled to Nuremberg, then to Munich, where he stayed with his brother, who operated a club there, and was reunited with his wife. He was arrested by German police on 12 February 1994.

One of the central charges against Tadic was that he was involved in killing, sexual torture and rape at Omarska. The incidents of sexual torture, as described in the previous chapter from the account of Rezak Hukanovic, were widely reported. In the trading of atrocity stories that surrounded the conflict in Bosnia, the story of one prisoner being forced to bite off another's testicle attained a certain centrality. The tribunal found that the beatings of the five named prisoners and of Senad Muslimovic did take place at Omarska and that witnesses G and H at the trial, whose identities were protected, had been compelled to and did take part in the sexual assault on Fikret Harambasic, and that G was compelled to sexually mutilate him by biting off one of his testicles. These events took place on 18 June 1992. The judgment describes the assaults and the beatings in detail, relying on a large body of witness testimony.

Tadic was identified by the witnesses as being involved in the beatings. One witness knew Tadic before they met in Omarska and also identified him in court. Another witness had previously identified him from a 'photospread' procedure, an identification accepted by the tribunal. Witness Senad Muslimovic said that Tadic was among those kicking him severely when he was tied to a large tyre, and that Tadic threatened his eyes with a knife, threatened to cut his throat and to cut off his ear, and he testified that Tadic in fact stabbed him twice in the shoulder. Tadic was seen by nine witnesses on the day of 18 June, calling prisoners out, beating prisoners, and torturing prisoners. The judgment gives details of this testimony, with names of witnesses and victims. Tadic's defence in relation to these allegations was that he was not present at Omarska. He said that he had never visited Omarska, and that on that day he was working as a traffic policeman. The judges were satisfied that Tadic did take part in the beatings and that he was present at, but not necessarily a participant in, the sexual mutilation.

Hase Icic testified in great detail to events at Omarska on 7–8 July 1992. He had known Tadic at school and had also played football with Tadic's brother. He testified that Tadic was present when he was taken into a room, a noose was tightened around his neck, and he was beaten unconscious with iron bars, whips made out of heavy electric cable and other weapons. The trial chamber accepted Icic's evidence. Sefik Sivac testified that he had once been good friends with Tadic until there was an incident when he had thrown Tadic out of his café. He threw him out because he had been saying that there 'would be a Greater Serbia, it would be theirs and that we, Muslims, will not be there, that there will be no place for them'.

Sometimes the judgment describes conflicts of evidence, places where the evidence of different witnesses was incompatible. The judgment details the conflicts and states clearly on which version the judges rely, if any, giving reasons for the preference, and giving the logical process by which the tribunal reached its conclusions. The judgment details each incident described by the witnesses, the alleged role of the defendant, the defence argument, and then its conclusions as to fact. Elvir Grozdanic testified that he had known Tadic for 10 years before the war, and that he had taken weekly karate lessons from him. He told of many abuses in Omarska, including Muslims being forced to chew grass and 'grunt as pigs do' and also to drink water from the ground 'as dogs do'. He told how he had seen a prisoner pushing an apparently lifeless body in a wheelbarrow, and how he had seen Tadic insert the hose from a fire extinguisher into the mouth of the body.

The defence evidence once again consisted of Tadic's alibi that he was on duty as a traffic policeman, and his claim that he had never visited Omarska. The defence produced witnesses to say that he had often been seen at the checkpoint, and that his superior officer had often checked to make sure he was on duty; they testified that Tadic did not have the right to use the police car for his own purposes, and so could not have travelled to Omarska. They also argued that, since it is not known whether the body in the wheelbarrow was alive or dead, then it was not necessarily an offence to insert a fire extinguisher hose into its mouth. A number of witnesses testified that they had seen Tadic at the Trnopolje camp. Tadic admitted having visited Trnopolje on five occasions for innocent reasons, usually accompanying Red Cross visitors.

The judgment discusses in some detail the charge that the motivation for the behaviour of the accused was discrimination on the grounds of race and of politics, and was part of a plan to build a Greater Serbia without a significant Muslim population. Tadic had been one of the early members of the SDS, whose policy it was to cleanse the Republica Srpska. He was a supporter of the policy of ethnic cleansing and understood it fully. Acceptance of this policy and the discriminatory means to achieve it was considered to be a requirement for advancement in the SDS. There was much evidence given about Tadic's personal commitment to the project of the Republica Srpska and also about his own increasing nationalist sentiment and his anti-Muslim racism.

The next charge related to the selection of five named Muslims from a forced march on 27 May 1992. The first witness described the selection of two of his brothers, his son and two others, who were held near a kiosk. The second witness testified that some minutes later he saw the five men being held at gunpoint near the kiosk. The third witness passed the kiosk a couple of hours later. He recognised four of the five men and said that another was taken from his column. When he was about five metres away from the men he heard two bursts of loud firing and he saw the men falling, one remaining standing for a few moments before he fell. All three witnesses testified that Tadic was the one making the decisions about who to select from the column, and the last witness testified that it was Tadic who gave the order to kill them.

Witness U for the defence testified that he was marching with the column but that he did not see Tadic at all during that day. It came out under cross-examination, however, that U now lives in a house that belonged to a Muslim and that was assigned to him by a Serbian committee on which Tadic used to sit. Witness W also testified that he had not seen Tadic at all during that day; however, two prosecution witnesses testified that they had seen witness W at the Kereterm camp, calling people out for torture. Witnesses V and A, also friends of Tadic, testified that they had not seen him in the town during that day. V and W, however, did confirm that Muslims were taken out of the marching column and killed that day. Due to some crucial inconsistencies in the prosecution evidence relating to this incident, the trial chamber did not find Tadic guilty of selecting and killing these men, though they are sure that Tadic was on the scene and that men were selected and killed.

The next charge related to events in the villages of Jaskici and Sivci on 14 June 1992. Armed Serbs, including Tadic, were accused of going from house to house in these villages and calling out residents, separating men from women and children and killing a number of named men. The population of these two villages had already been swollen by the arrival of a number of Muslim refugees from Kozarac, which had previously been attacked by Serb forces. In Sivci, 350 men were taken out of their houses after the village had been shelled by Serb tanks. They were made to run to a collecting point and at intervals were ordered to lie down in the road, where they were kicked and beaten by armed Serbs. Their money and identity papers were stolen as they were tortured. At the collecting point some were beaten again, and they were put onto buses and taken away to the Kereterm camp.

The experience of the smaller village of Jaskici was similar. All the men were marched away; after they had left the women of the village found that the bodies of five of the men had been left behind. Many of the women then left, but some remained, and witnessed the repeated return of the Serbs, who stole everything from the houses, from tractors to liquor. Two of the older men who had been left behind attempted to bury the bodies of the five men but were obstructed by the Serbs and were eventually obliged to bury them in one single grave. Subsequently all the houses of Jaskici were burnt, leaving only ruins.

There were five witnesses, four of whom already knew Tadic, who saw him in Sivci or Jaskici on 14 June in spite of the fact that he claims not to have left Banja Luka. The tribunal was satisfied that Tadic was amongst the armed men who entered these two villages. One witness, who had known Tadic, described him beating men from the village with a stick, and pouring water over those who had fainted in order to revive them. She also described Tadic beating her father. She has never seen the men of her family since that day, although she has made efforts to trace them. This witness's sister described Tadic beating men with a rifle butt. Both witnesses independently described Tadic as having a beard and wearing a camouflage uniform. The other witnesses identified Tadic, and described him taking part in classical ethnic cleansing behaviour, beating, threatening and terrorising people out of their houses.

Though there were some inconsistencies in the detail of the evidence – for example in their descriptions of Tadic's uniform and the uniforms of the other armed men with him – the tribunal was satisfied that Tadic had been an active participant in the ethnic cleansing of the two villages, but the tribunal was not satisfied that the five men had been murdered by Tadic or the armed men with him.

The next incident that Tadic was alleged to have been involved in was the attack on Kozarac and the surrounding hamlets on 24–27 May 1992. Witness Q worked at the hospital in Kozarac. On the way home from the hospital on 24 May he saw Tadic with another man jumping over a fence into some gardens. Moments later he saw a flare being launched from the vicinity of the gardens, illuminating the hospital so that the Serbian artillery and tanks could shell it and seriously damage it. The defence showed that witness Q had previously given a different sequence of events in his witness statement, that he had said that he was on his way to the hospital, not on the way home. He explained the discrepancy by saying that he had not thought the details were important when he gave his statement and that the account he now gave to the tribunal was full and authoritative. The tribunal accepted Q as a reliable witness. Other witnesses testified that they had seen Tadic in Kozarac during the time of the attack and participating in the attack. One witness testified that Tadic had said to him that Kozarac was going to be part of a Greater Serbia, saying that he had 'liberated Kozarac and nobody is going to take anything out of Kozarac, only over my dead body'.

The judgment discusses a number of issues regarding the nature of the evidence at the tribunal, and possible problems with it. This was the first contested case before the ICTY. The rules of evidence and of procedure were being developed by the tribunal and the appeals chamber during this and following cases, aiming to draw on 'best practice' from the world's legal systems.

The first problem discussed concerned difficulties regarding access to evidence. Both parties encountered problems due mainly to the fact that the authorities in the Republica Srpska were unwilling to co-operate with the tribunal. Most prosecution witnesses were living in western Europe, whereas most defence witnesses were resident in the Republica Srpska. At the trial, use was made of video conferencing to link the courtroom with the Republica

Srpska. Some witnesses were guaranteed anonymity, and others were guaranteed immunity from arrest while travelling to and from the court.

The second problem concerned the lack of specificity of the charges, particularly in terms of time. Some counts allege that crimes have been committed 'on or about' a particular date. This makes it difficult for the defence to establish alibis but is, in many jurisdictions, usual practice in criminal trials.

Thirdly, the tribunal discussed the need for corroboration. The defence argued that the court should not be able to convict when the only evidence is from one uncorroborated witness (*unus testis, nullus testis*: one witness is no witness). The tribunal rejected this principle, arguing that it is established practice in many jurisdictions that a court may convict on the evidence of one witness alone.

Fourthly, most of the witnesses for the prosecution were also victims of the conflict, and the defence argued that witnesses were likely to be less reliable if they were also from the ethnic group that had been victimised. Similarly, most defence witnesses were Serbs, which might also be thought to affect their credibility. The tribunal's answer to this point is that the credibility of each witness should be judged independently, after having seen their testimony and their cross-examination.

The fifth problem was pre-trial media coverage and the infection of testimony. The tribunal admitted that this could be a problem, and said that they took this issue into account when deciding on the credibility of witnesses when the issue of media coverage had been raised in cross-examination.

The sixth was the issue of identification evidence. Identification was crucial in this case because Tadic's alibi was that he was never present at the camps and the scenes of crimes. The tribunal was able to rely upon identification evidence of those who had known Tadic since childhood, and who were therefore able to identify him more certainly. They also relied upon four witnesses who identified Tadic from a series of photographs of men.

The seventh problem relating to the types of evidence available to the international court was exemplified by the testimony of Dragan Opacic. This incident was dramatic. Opacic was an important witness, and he made many allegations against Tadic. One allegation was that he swore that he had been present when Tadic murdered his father. 'But isn't your father still alive?' the defence asked on day three. Opacic insisted that he had watched him die. 'But this man is your father,' said the cross-examiner, calling to court an old man who rushed to embrace the witness.[7]

The prosecution withdrew all reliance on Opacic. His identity had been protected, and he had been known only as witness L. The defence had managed to identify him, in spite of his anonymity, and, because of this identification, had been able to show him to be a liar. The defence argued that many witnesses were not investigated in the way that Opacic was, and that others might be equally unreliable. The tribunal argued that Opacic was the only witness who was discovered by the Bosnian authorities while he was in custody. No other witnesses shared the same provenance and so Opacic could be treated as an individual case. But the general possibility of problems with

---

7 Robertson, 1999, p 292.

allowing anonymity to witnesses, and with receiving witnesses from the custody of states hostile to defendants, was well illustrated.

The eighth problem discussed was the issue of hearsay. It was decided not to make hearsay evidence inadmissible, but to allow the tribunal to hear the evidence and give it the weight that they judged it deserved.

All of these problems are considerable, although they are often present in ordinary criminal trials. The judges have great power both because of the flexibility of the rules and because of the absence of juries. Rules on admissibility are much less strict than they are in most jury trials, because the judges can give appropriate weight to evidence according to its provenance and admissibility, and can trust themselves to do so in a much more professional way than a jury. Judges, however, unlike juries, have to account for their decisions, and for the weight that they assign to each piece of evidence, in a detailed written judgment. Their decisions are also subject to the appeals chamber. It is clear, however, that thoughtful, impartial and aware judges are even more centrally important at the ICTY than in ordinary criminal trials where there is the added safeguard of a jury.

Much time in the *Tadic* case, as in the *Blaskic* case, was spent by the prosecution in trying to show the existence of an international armed conflict. However, the court held, by majority, that it had not been shown in this case that there was an international armed conflict taking place in Bosnia after 19 May 1992. There were 11 counts that relied on the fact that they constituted 'grave breaches of the Geneva Conventions'. Since the tribunal held that there was no international armed conflict existing after that date and that the Geneva Conventions only applied to international armed conflict, Tadic was found innocent on these 11 counts.

It was also necessary for the prosecution to establish a link between the actions of the accused and the wider armed conflict, since international humanitarian law has no jurisdiction over crimes that are not thus linked. Tadic's actions in Kozarac, Sivci and Jaskici were clearly linked to the overall campaign of ethnic cleansing being carried out by the Serb forces in Bosnia. His acts in the camps established by the Republica Srpska were also clearly carried out with the connivance or permission of the authorities, so here, also, his crimes are directly connected to the armed conflict.

Article 5 of the Statute of the International Tribunal concerns crimes against humanity, also proscribed by customary international humanitarian law. The tribunal held that, since the Nuremberg charter, the customary status of the prohibition against crimes against humanity and the attribution of individual criminal responsibility for their commission have not been seriously questioned. The tribunal argued that this finding is implicit in the appeals chamber decision, which found that '[i]t is by now a settled rule of customary international law that crimes against humanity do not require a connection to international armed conflict'.[8]

There are many sceptical arguments put forward regarding the ICTY. The small, unpublicised court in The Hague contrasts starkly with the oceans of terror and misery caused by the events in the former Yugoslavia. Mladic, the man who personally organised the cleansing of Srebrenica and the rest of Bosnia, and Karadzic, the mad psychiatrist who was the political leader of the

---

8 *Prosecutor v Tadic*, Appeal 1995, para 141.

racist campaign against Muslims, still enjoy their freedom. Tudjman, the architect of the campaign of 'Croatisation' in Bosnia and the Krajina, died peacefully in his bed. The court in The Hague, say the sceptics, was set up by the 'ethical imperialists'[9] who fought for hegemony in the Balkans under the cover of the language of human rights; it was set up spuriously by the great powers in the Security Council under the law authorising them to take measures to protect world peace and security. The court is bureaucratic and slow. The system gives great power to a politically motivated set of judges who are allowed to base their decision on many kinds of evidence that would usually be deemed by national criminal courts to be inadmissible, including hearsay, contaminated identifications and anonymous witnesses. This sceptical argument has been dealt a blow by the arrest of the big boss himself, Slobodan Milosevic. Many sceptics had felt that it was impossible for the ICTY to try the real leaders, that they would always be given *de facto* immunity by the great powers. The argument, however, has simply slipped a little, and now portrays the man who gave a million Kosovars hours to leave their country as an unfortunate scapegoat.

Alternatively, it is possible to see the ICTY as a step in an inevitable process towards international order and human rights. The story of humanitarian law and human rights is one of constant progress, banishing the darkness of inhumanity from the bright new modern cosmopolitan civilisation. The law has been written; it is in place. Finally, the world is in a position to deal with those who seek to deny others the status of human beings.

The evidence from The Hague does not really show either of these views to be true; or, perhaps, it shows them both to be true. The most important thing about the court is that it exists as an empirical fact. Cosmopolitan law cannot any longer be regarded as some sort of dream, but demands to be recognised as a reality. It has demonstrated that it is possible for an international court to hold trials under the universal jurisdiction of international criminal law. There is something enduring in this demonstration. We know that people can walk on the moon; we know that an international criminal court is a possibility. Once these things are demonstrated to be possible, they are possible forever.

Tudjman's successors in Croatia have grudgingly accepted the jurisdiction of the court and its legitimacy. Mladic and Karadzic had no place at the negotiations at Dayton, and were subsequently removed from power in the Republica Srpska. Karadzic's successor, Biljana Plavsic, now lives in a cell in The Hague as she awaits her trial, and Milosevic is being tried. The fact that Milosevic was indicted as a criminal must have been a significant boost to those fighting to depose him. Even if the Serbian opposition was more interested in his crimes against Serbs than his crimes against humanity, it must have helped that he was officially accused by the international community of being a criminal. It is not insignificant that these people could not travel abroad: they could not make a living on the lecture circuit, nor could they come to Harley Street for medical attention in their old age. It is not trivial to be indicted as a war criminal. And the ICTY is having more success than had seemed likely at one point in making significant arrests.

What of the charges against the court related to its flawed predecessor, the Nuremberg tribunal? What is to be said about the tribunal's foundation in a

---

9   Coates, 1999.

legal trick by the Security Council? What can we say about its own efficiency or fairness as a court? These problems bring us back to the central point: that of its existence. The court has a clear set of rules that it enforces. The provenance of its existence and its rules may be questionable; there are answers to those questions, however, and its existence is no longer in doubt. Neither are the central precedents of Nuremberg any longer in doubt. Individuals are responsible in law for their crimes, even if obeying orders, even if committed as head of state. Crimes against humanity and genocide are criminal offences that may be tried under universal jurisdiction. No principles in law are clearer now than these, even if they were open to dispute in 1945.

There are some questions that may be asked about the fairness of the court. For example, Geoffrey Robertson is worried about the lack of a clear demonstrable physical and political separation between the prosecution and the judges.[10] We may also cite the incident of Dragan Opacic when he gave anonymous evidence which was only discovered to be false at the last minute. As Caroline Buisman argues, the inequality of resources available to the defence and the prosecution, and the liberal rules of evidence, which are self-policed by the judges, are also possible sources of problems.[11] It is an empirical finding of this book, however, that the trials that I have observed and studied have been relatively fair trials; that is to say, they have been unfair only to the extent that ordinary criminal trials may be judged unfair. There is a clear body of law and rules upon which the ICTY operates; there is the opportunity for defendants to conduct a defence; there are opportunities to appeal against decisions made by the judges to a separate appeals chamber; there is due process; there are opportunities to cross-examine witnesses; there are honest and competent judges. Of course, the fact that trials are fair and that cosmopolitan law is clear does not tell us that there is a settled and just system of cosmopolitan criminal law in place. But it does tell us that cosmopolitan criminal law is possible and that it is not simply utopian.

---

10 Robertson, 1999.
11 Buisman, 2001.

Chapter Six
The Sawoniuk trial:
a cosmopolitan trial under national law

In Chapters Six and Seven, I look at two court cases that took place at the very end of the 20th century. Both cases were concerned with one of its defining events!, the Holocaust. One was the trial of Andrei Sawoniuk, a man who had been involved in carrying out the genocide in a small town in Belorus. The other was a defamation trial, in which David Irving, a British 'revisionist' historian, sued Deborah Lipstadt, an American academic, for calling him a Holocaust denier. Both cases were looking back at the event from the distance of more than half a century. Both courts, therefore, found themselves writing the history of the Holocaust as well as judging more specific issues. Both were judging men who had chosen to allow the genocide to define who they were, who had been seduced by the glory and power of the Nazis, yet who were not exactly Nazis themselves. Both trials were in Britain, perhaps the country in Europe least touched by the events themselves.

A central task of both trials was to tell a story, or a history, of what had happened, and to assign responsibility: to reproduce a narrative of much-narrated events. But the courts were charged with producing narrative with a unique form of authority. When courts make judgments they have the power to enforce those judgments; they have at their disposal the power to award damages as well as a monopoly on legitimate violence. Their judgments, therefore, claim a particular authenticity; legal processes claim to be, and hope to be recognised as, producers of impartial judgments. These cases were both concerned with events that happened outside the territory of the UK; events, in fact, that happened outside any particular national territory. But the Holocaust was not only cosmopolitan in the sense that it happened throughout Europe: it was also cosmopolitan in a whole range of other senses, which I have discussed in this book. It was the business of the whole of humanity. So when it is the task of courts to make judgments concerning the Holocaust, they find themselves having to judge cosmopolitan events from a cosmopolitan point of view: that is, from an impartial, and therefore not from a national, point of view. These two cases had many of the characteristics of cosmopolitan trials but were held in British courts under English law.

The main trial at Nuremberg was only the spearhead of the international process of judging those responsible for the Nazi crimes. As well as the 12 other trials organised by the international tribunal, there were many national post-Nuremberg trials organised by the successor regimes in countries that had been occupied, such as Poland, Hungary, Yugoslavia, Greece, Russia and France. These trials prosecuted those whose crimes could be localised in particular jurisdictions.

The trial of Adolf Eichmann in 1962 was fundamentally one of these national post-Nuremberg trials, although it had a number of peculiarities. Eichmann's crimes could not be localised in a particular jurisdiction, since his job was in the organisation of the genocide of the Jews across Europe. Yet he had not been considered an important enough criminal to be included, even *in absentia*, at the time of the main trial at Nuremberg. Thus, the trial of Eichmann in Israel follows the pattern of the other national trials. His crimes were against Jews, and so he was tried by the national courts of the Jewish state: not because he had committed his crimes there, but because, retrospectively, he had committed his crimes against its citizens. The Jews, in the absence of an international criminal court, argues Hannah Arendt, 'had as much right to sit in judgment on the crimes committed against their people as the Poles had to judge crimes committed in Poland'.[1]

The trial of Klaus Barbie in 1987 for crimes against Jews in France, and also crimes against the French resistance during the war, was more straightforwardly a national trial, even though the charge was actually crimes against humanity. Barbie had been the head of the Gestapo in Lyon, and so it was France that assumed the right to extradite him from Bolivia and put him on trial.

These post-Nuremberg trials have contained a strange mixture of national and cosmopolitan law. They followed the legal precedents set by the Nuremberg process, and they convicted for the cosmopolitan offence of crimes against humanity. But the courts were national criminal courts and relied on the normal processes and institutions of criminal justice. There was always a tendency for the trials to drift back from a cosmopolitan to a national perspective. Arendt was critical of the Eichmann trial when it drifted away from its central concerns with Eichmann and the Holocaust towards issues more concerned with Israeli nationalism and the legitimacy of the state of Israel, and when it glossed over issues concerned with Jewish collaboration with the Nazis.[2] Alain Finkielkraut, similarly, was critical of the Barbie trial when it drifted away from its cosmopolitan focus towards the needs of French nationalism and the continuation of the French national myth of resistance to Nazism.[3]

The trial of Andrei Sawoniuk in 1999 may also be seen as a Nuremberg successor trial. It was, however, carried out in Britain, not because the crimes were committed in Britain or against British citizens, but because Sawoniuk himself had settled in Britain and had British citizenship.

Since the Nuremberg trials, it has been an accepted norm of international law that jurisdiction over war crimes and crimes against humanity is universal. Such crimes, like those involving slavery and piracy, are understood in international law as an attack not only on the particular state in which they were committed but also on the international order. Any state, therefore, has the right to try a suspect for such crimes under the universality principle. However, when the British Home Secretary, Douglas Hurd, was faced with calls for the prosecution of suspected war criminals living in Britain in February 1998, he summarised his position as follows:

> We would normally deal with alleged crimes in foreign countries by way of extradition. However, all the cases in question relate to crimes committed in territories now controlled by the Soviet Union, with whom we have no extradition treaty. Nor do the courts in the United Kingdom at present have jurisdiction to try

---

1   Arendt, 1994a, p 258.
2   Arendt, 1994a.
3   Finkielkraut, 1992.

offences of murder and manslaughter committed abroad when the accused was not a British citizen at the time of the offence. If we were to prosecute in these cases we should need to legislate to extend the jurisdiction of our courts.[4]

He set up an inquiry that proposed new legislation to empower British courts to utilise a jurisdiction already available to them under international law.[5] Under international law, Sawoniuk could have been put on trial at any time since he entered Britain in 1946. Authority for such a trial was only granted under UK law by the War Crimes Act 1991. This Act limited the charges that a suspect could face to murder or manslaughter in contravention of the laws and customs of war, and so did not allow suspects to be charged, more appropriately, with crimes against humanity or genocide.[6]

Sometimes the USA,[7] Canada and Britain have simply deported suspected war criminals without a full trial, thus exposing them to whatever consequences they might have to face in the country to which they are deported. The British, by passing the 1991 Act, took responsibility to try such suspects themselves, even though they subsequently deported Konrad Kalejs in January 2000, claiming that there was insufficient evidence for a trial, although it seems that they had not searched very hard for such evidence.[8] It must be right only to contemplate deportation to jurisdictions able and willing to conduct a fair trial. Where this is not possible, a trial rather than a deportation must be preferable. There had been one prosecution in Britain under the 1991 Act before the Sawoniuk trial, that of Szymon Serafinowicz, but the trial was abandoned when the defendant became ill. This decision was vindicated when he died shortly afterwards.

The trial of Sawoniuk was a hybrid of national and cosmopolitan law. It was tried under English law and in a British court; but the crimes had not been committed in Britain, so the legitimacy of the trial relied on the fact that such crimes, according to the principle of universal jurisdiction, may be tried anywhere and by any state.

The ordinary and extraordinary Andrei Sawoniuk

Andrei, Andreivich or Anthony Sawoniuk was, in many senses, an ordinary man. Physically, he was not tall. Aged 78 at the time of his trial, he had white hair which was carefully barbered, and a round baby face with blue-grey eyes peering through his up-to-date glasses. He was always dressed smartly, in a

---

4   Hansard, 1988.
5   '[T]o enact legislation in this country to give the British courts jurisdiction over murder and manslaughter committed as violations of the laws and customs of war would not be to create an offence retrospectively. It would be making an offence triable in British courts to an extent which international law had recognised and permitted at a time before the alleged offences in question had been committed.' *Report of the War Crimes Inquiry*, 1989, p 97, para 9.27.
6   The report argues that any 'attempt to legislate to provide for prosecutions with respect to acts of genocide allegedly committed during the Second World War would be retrospective', since genocide was not defined as an offence in international law until 1948. *Report of the War Crimes Inquiry*, 1989, p 96, para 9.23.
7   '[T]o this day, crimes against humanity have not been incorporated into the federal law of the United States. Instead, the INS sought to deport resident aliens or naturalised citizens ... not as war criminals, but as persons who lied on their emigration forms and thus never should have been permitted to enter the country in the first place.' Douglas, 2001, p 197.
8   Dodd, 2000.

blazer, creased trousers, and shiny shoes, like the old Polish soldier and British Rail ticket collector that he was. He limped, and used a stick, but did not seem particularly fragile. He seemed to be a man who knew how to look after himself. He sat in court next to his solicitors, not in the dock, since he was on bail. He followed the transcript of the proceedings as it appeared on the laptop computer in front of him. He occasionally whispered, rather loudly, perhaps because of his partial deafness, to his solicitors. They seemed friendly and called him Tony. Not once in the whole trial did Sawoniuk look to his right towards the press gallery, or to the public gallery above it.

He was born in Domachevo, a small, ordinary town that is currently in Belorus, near Brest-Litovsk, and that was just inside the Polish border of the old Soviet Union. When he was born there on 7 March 1921, it was in Poland. Domachevo's main business was tourism. It had a spa and some hotels and guest houses. Domachevo conformed to the strange ethnic division of labour that was common in eastern Europe. The town itself was almost entirely Jewish, while the surrounding villages where the peasants cultivated the land were almost entirely non-Jewish. The Jews supplied goods and services to the farmers, as well as to visitors. The farmers sold their produce to the Jews in the market. Everyone who testified at the trial, the non-Jewish witnesses and Ben-Zion Blustein, one of the very few surviving Jews from Domachevo, said that the two populations lived together in harmony. As well as the Russian Orthodox church in Domachevo there was a Catholic church, where those who considered themselves Polish worshipped. Domachevo was a town like many hundreds of others that was soon to be engulfed by the Shoah in an entirely typical way.

Sawoniuk himself was born, and lived his childhood, outside the established division of labour, or perhaps underneath it. His family did not have land to tend, and so they lived in the town itself. His mother made a meagre living by doing laundry and other casual work for Jews, and when he was old enough he also worked for Jews, doing odd jobs where he could find them. He never knew his father, and his mother died when he was a child. He was regularly called a 'bastard' and was subjected to a certain amount of bullying on that account. After his mother died he lived with his grandmother and his brother Nikolai, or Kola. For these reasons he must have experienced a certain amount of alienation from the society in which he lived and in which he did not really have an established place. He left school at the age of 14. He was known by everyone in Domachevo simply as Andrusha, a diminutive of Andrei; Little Andy. He was still known by this diminutive when he was the commandant of the local Nazi-organised police force.

The German invasion of Russia started on midsummer night 1941, and within hours had swept well past Domachevo, which was one of the first small towns it encountered. Within a very few days, the Germans had organised a local police force that Sawoniuk and a handful of other local men joined enthusiastically. He was 20 years old and had experienced two very difficult years under Russian occupation. For the first time in his life he had a job, and a place in the world.

Sawoniuk has lived in Britain since 1946. He moved around a little, mainly on the south coast, before settling in London, just off the Old Kent Road. He worked for British Rail, and retired in 1986. He married twice after the war, both short marriages, and had a son with his second wife, but they parted shortly after his birth. In Britain he has been, as the police testified, 'of good character'.

On 9 March 1999, he appeared in court 12 at the Old Bailey. In many ways it was a routine trial. The defendants in the courts next door were accused, one of rape, and the other of murder. There was no bulletproof glass screen to protect him from assassination. There was no simultaneous translation apparatus in the courtroom. It was the usual English courtroom. The barristers wore wigs. The judge sat underneath the large royal crest on the front wall in his rather grander wig. Sawoniuk was not accused of anything exotic or un-British like genocide or crimes against humanity. He was accused of four counts of murder 'contrary to the common law' under the conditions specified in the War Crimes Act 1991. The ad hoc tribunals for the former Yugoslavia and for Rwanda have recently convicted for both genocide and crimes against humanity;[9] and Belgium has shown that it is possible for national courts to make convictions for genocide.[10] The fact that Sawoniuk was simply charged with murder, albeit with conditions attached, added to the impression that this was an ordinary Old Bailey trial.

For the individuals involved in the rape and murder trials in the neighbouring courts, however, those cases were in no way routine or mundane. They concerned events that must have made profound changes to the lives of those affected. Criminal trials give extraordinary events a routine form: they abstract them, shape them and civilise them. The rapist and the murderer, as well as Sawoniuk, both wore shiny shoes and well pressed suits. Their counsel spoke for them eloquently and persuasively. The judges politely offered them drinks of water. If the Sawoniuk trial was made to look routine, that is partly because that is a general function of a criminal trial. But the contrast between the businesslike quality of the trial and the horror of the events that it concerned was greater, because the events were extraordinary in a more profound sense than an ordinary rape or murder.

There are many senses in which this trial was entirely extraordinary. It was the first and only trial to be completed in Britain of someone accused of taking part in the Nazi genocide of the Jews. It was the only prosecution under the War Crimes Act 1991. It was the only time that a British court has sat in judgment of crimes committed outside Britain, and the only time a British court has travelled outside Britain. The trial happened 57 years after the crimes in question. The crimes were part of the Holocaust, which is perhaps the biggest and most extraordinary crime yet committed.

This juxtaposition between the ordinary and the extraordinary is a theme that runs throughout this particular trial, and it echoes a similar dialectic that many have detected within the Shoah itself. Claude Lanzmann[11] is fascinated by the ordinariness of the trains that transported so many to their deaths. Zygmunt Bauman[12] focuses on the bureaucratic individuals and procedures that organised the mass killing. Karl Jaspers[13] and Hannah Arendt[14] wrote about the banality of evil.

---

9 Eg *Prosecutor v Kristic*.
10 *Le Monde*, 8 June 2001.
11 Lanzmann, 1985.
12 Bauman, 1993.
13 Arendt and Jaspers, 1992.
14 Arendt, 1994a.

Sawoniuk was an ordinary kid, a nobody who joined the police force in order to become a somebody. When the real function of the police force became clear, some, including his brother, left; he chose to stay. When the *Einsatzgruppe* came to town to kill the Jews on Yom Kippur 1942, Sawoniuk helped. The Nazis left to kill the Jews in the next town, and the local police were left the job of hunting and killing those who had escaped the main massacre. Sawoniuk took a central part in this hunt and kill operation for a few months until it was complete. He killed maybe 50 or 100 or 200 Jews at this time, and he did so with more enthusiasm than most. There must have been many tens of thousands like him. They were a necessary part of the machine that committed the genocide. It was the locally recruited police forces who knew the Jews, and who knew where they might be hiding, much better than the invaders did. When it was all over, he found a life for himself in Britain, and lived it. On 21 March 1996, he was arrested by Metropolitan Police detectives, interviewed, and put on trial.

It was William Clegg, Sawoniuk's barrister, who raised the question of Sawoniuk's ordinariness. One of Clegg's central strategies was to try to make the prosecution look ridiculous and far-fetched. He often employed an ironic and satirical tone, and with some success; he is a warm, witty man with a sense of comic timing. The prosecution presented the enormous tragedy of the Holocaust. The barrister for the Crown, Sir John Nutting, a stereotype of an English establishment figure, tall, with an antiquated upper class accent, slow and methodical, had begun his case. He had used Christopher Browning as an expert witness to paint an outline of the Nazi plan to kill the Jews, of its development and execution. He had followed Browning with a succession of elderly witnesses. All these witnesses told the same background story, about Sawoniuk, about the German invasion, the setting up of the local police force and the ghetto, and most had added a particular testament to particular atrocities committed by Sawoniuk. Clegg constantly had to try to change the mood of proceedings for the jury. He had to pull their attention away from the greatest crime in human history and towards the specific charges made against his particular client. He pleaded with the jury, as follows:

> Let's be realistic and sensible. It was a ramshackle defence unit. He was just an ordinary policeman. He was no decision maker. There was nobody of lower rank than him. He was 20 or 21 years old. You may have felt that there's been an attempt to elevate his position. What has Browning's evidence about Hitler and Himmler to do with him? Hitler didn't have a hot-line from Berlin to his hut in Domachevo. It's like comparing Churchill to Pike in *Dad's Army*![15]

Later, in his closing statement, Nutting, the prosecutor, returned to Clegg's *Dad's Army* theme and to Browning's evidence:

> He told us of the *Einsatzgruppen* and their murders in the Brest region: 1,280 Jews in July; 3,123 Jews in August. You have heard eye witnesses' views of the ghetto. Mr Blustein's evidence of the fear, deprivation, restrictions, confiscations, collapsing morale, the preparedness for collective death. The ghetto was policed from the new police station at its gate. The defendant and Kazic Millart beat up Rachel Schneider for smuggling potatoes. The police patrols to prevent escapes. [*with rhetorical force*] This defendant was no Pike! This police unit was no *Dad's Army*![16]

---

15 19 March 1999. This date and those that follow in the footnotes to this chapter refer to the author's notes, taken while attending trial. The dates refer to the relevant days of the trial.
16 24 March 1999.

Inevitably, the trial raised the question of responsibility for the genocide. Who was responsible? Who can be responsible for a crime so huge that it can only be perpetrated by the mobilisation of the resources of a whole state? Daniel Goldhagen[17] argues that the responsibility for the Holocaust rests firmly with Germany, the German people, and their political institutions. They are the ones who are responsible. They were 'Hitler's willing executioners'. Indeed, Nutting made use of Goldhagen's phrase in his summing up:

> ... the defendant played an effective part in the search and kill operation after 20 September 1942. Hitler needed willing executioners. The Crown's case is that the defendant in one town and with the killing of a limited number of Jews played a part, however small, in carrying out this policy.[18]

Goldhagen wrote his book in order to prove German collective guilt, and thereby everyone else's collective innocence, yet Sawoniuk was not German. In Domachevo, the main massacre of the Jews was carried out by a unit of *Einsatzgruppe* men, who were German. They were assisted by a number of Ukrainians, and also by the local police. It is inconceivable that Sawoniuk was not present, since he was an important member of the local police, and this was the biggest event requiring 'policing'. He claimed that, by chance, he went away for the weekend to visit friends. ('I can't remember the name of their village, I can't remember the names of the friends.') Yet the central perpetrators of the main massacre were indeed German. This was a theme that Clegg touched on more than once: the Germans killed the Jews; the local police carried out normal police duties and the war against the partisans. This, however, was not true. Germans led the killing of the Jews of Domachevo, perpetrated the massacre, but relied on Ukrainian and local support both for the main massacre itself and also for the subsequent search and kill operation.

It is the function of the court of law to extract Sawoniuk from the enormous machine of the Third Reich. The Nazi movement committed the crime, but in a court the individuals who were part of that movement are transformed from footsoldiers and bureaucrats back into responsible human beings. The extraordinary history of Europe in the middle of the 20th century had transformed Sawoniuk as a young man from an ordinary human being into a sadistic killer. He had succeeded in transforming himself back into an unremarkable railway worker after the war. But the court demanded more of him. It demanded that he take responsibility for those crimes he had committed during the time when he was part of the genocide machine.

At one point during his cross-examination Sawoniuk lost his temper. He shouted at the jury:

> Andrusha Andrusha Andrusha. They say only Andrusha Andrusha. No one else killed no one. Only Andrusha. Everyone else just watches and claps. Only they pick on me.[19]

Nutting might have replied: 'No, Mr Sawoniuk, it isn't fair, is it? So many were guilty and it is only Andrusha who stands trial.' There must be many thousands of old men in Europe who committed crimes worse than those committed by Sawoniuk. Some of the members of the *Einsatzgruppe* who

---

17 Goldhagen, 1996.
18 24 March 1999.
19 22 March 1999.

actually committed the main massacre in Domachevo must still be alive, reading about the case in the newspapers. So Sawoniuk is certainly unlucky to be held accountable in this way.

The Sawoniuk trial was emphatically a post-Cold War trial. The KGB (Committee for State Security) had been interested in Sawoniuk since their forerunners had first carried out investigations during the Russian reoccupation of Belorus in 1944. But it was not until 1959, when they intercepted a letter that Sawoniuk wrote to his brother Kola, that they knew he had settled in Britain. It was only in 1988, at the very thaw of the Cold War, that they passed Sawoniuk's details to the British Government. It took the British another two years to trace him, because they had more important wartime criminals to chase, and also due to a mistranslation of his name.[20] The trial required the co-operation of Belorussian, Russian and Polish authorities. It is difficult to imagine the old Soviet Union allowing British police officers to interview suspects, or a British court to sit in Domachevo.

Sawoniuk was charged with four counts of murder 'contrary to the common law'. In order to convict under the War Crimes Act 1991, the prosecution had to show:

(a)   The crime was committed during wartime (1939–45).
(b)   It was committed in the territory occupied by Germany.
(c)   It was in violation of the laws and customs of war.
(d)   The defendant lived in the UK before 1991.

Each count related to an incident of murder, and each was alleged by a different witness.

Following the testimony of the expert witness, the whole court travelled to Domachevo: the judge, the lawyers, the jury, the stenographers, court officials and the press. The court list at the Old Bailey in London read 'Court sitting in Domachevo'. During his opening statement, Nutting had given the jury many photographs of Domachevo and had taken much time going through them, explaining each one. There were aerial photographs, including one taken by Allied bombers during the war, photographs of the town as it is today, and photographs of the paths travelled by the witnesses who alleged counts of murder. During the trip to Domachevo, the court followed the paths travelled by the witnesses and gained an overview of the town. Fedor Zan, a central witness, had been sworn in before the trip, and showed the jury where he had seen Sawoniuk shooting people.

Domachevo was under snow at the time of the visit. Much effort seems to have been made to keep the jury away from contact with the press and the locals. A newspaper report tells that the jury were 'held virtual prisoners in the Intourist Hotel, a hostelry exuding all the charm of a tax office' while the prosecution and defence teams enjoyed the hospitality of the only Indian restaurant between Warsaw and Moscow. The same report tells us that during the tour of Domachevo, Nutting 'strode about in the manner of a grand Shakespearean actor-manager', puffing on his pipe; the judge wore a 'pointed red hat with ear-flaps as though it were an Arctic-grade judicial wig', and Clegg made do with a brightly patterned Austrian ski jacket.[21]

20 Cesarini, 1999.
21 Hamilton, 1999.

The problems involved in the Sawoniuk prosecution may be divided into two types. First there are the problems that relate to the legitimacy of the whole legal process, and secondly there are the practical problems. I have discussed many of the first type already in this book, such as problems of individual responsibility, charges of victor's justice and *tu quoque*, and the impossibility of rendering justice in a court for crimes on such a scale.

Some of the many practical problems that arose in this case will arise routinely in cosmopolitan trials, while some of them are specific to this trial. In an ordinary murder investigation, the police may have control of the crime scene, often very soon after the crime is committed. This is unlikely to be the case where the crime is being carried out by a social formation that has state power. Thus the immediate identification and interviewing of witnesses and suspects will often be more difficult, as will the gathering of fresh forensic evidence. Another difference is that in an ordinary murder investigation, it is unlikely that there will be widespread support for the murder among potential witnesses, as there may be in these cases. In the *Sawoniuk* case, nearly all the possible Jewish witnesses were dead, as a result of the crime. In this case, the crime was being investigated by the British police, but within the jurisdiction of Belorus and of Poland. Potential witnesses were always interviewed in the presence of officials of the local state. Clegg[22] said that he felt that potential defence witnesses were intimidated by local officials, who were keen to secure conviction. This intermeshing of different jurisdictions is likely to be a common source of problems in these cases. The jurisdiction that is carrying out the investigation does not hold state power.

Difficulties of communication will also be a frequent problem faced by these trials. Often, evidence and interviews have to be mediated through interpreters. At the least this is a source of great expense, and may present more fundamental barriers to the process.[23]

There was a further practical problem in the *Sawoniuk* case which, it is to be hoped, will not arise commonly: that is the problem of the trial taking place so long after the crime. All the witnesses were elderly, struggling to recall details of traumatic crimes that they committed, witnessed, or suffered from as young people. Their memories must be mediated by 57 years of remembering and retelling the story and of hearing accounts, gossip, and accusations. The accuracy of the memory of witnesses is often an important issue in criminal trials; the problem was exacerbated in this trial by the unusually long time gap between the crimes and the trial.

---

22 Interview conducted by the author in The Hague, 21 April 1999.
23 In a study of court proceedings in the USA which used translators, Susan Berk-Seligson found that the process of translation could pose a number of problems. Interpreters, she found, can skew the meaning or the presentation of evidence or of questions. 'For the most part these changes are made unconsciously. On the whole, when interpreters make such fine alterations in the conversion of one language to another they seem completely unaware of the important impact that these alterations can have on judges and jurors. On the other hand, an interpreter who has either unconscious or conscious biases can take full advantage of such linguistic mechanism to suit her own purposes, and where there is a conflict of interest but it is not perceived as such by court personnel, the interpreter's interpretations can and do serve to slant what a speaker is trying to say.' Berk-Seligson, 1990, pp 2–3.

Ben-Zion Blustein: Holocaust memoir and legal testimony

On its return from Domachevo to the antique wood panelling of the Old Bailey, the evidence presented by the prosecution started with the only Jewish witness, Ben-Zion Blustein. Blustein seemed to me to be a typical Jewish Holocaust survivor. He appeared tough, but now old and a little stiff. He had a definite confidence in his story, combined with a nervous vulnerability; the vulnerability of one who knows that nothing in life is safe and that no safety is absolute. Many Holocaust survivors have a typical way, a genre perhaps, of telling their story. What made Blustein so uncomfortable in the Old Bailey was the fact that he was not allowed to tell his 'usual story'. Blustein has told his story often. He has told it at Yad Vashem. He has told it to a ghostwriter who created a book from it. He has told it to students and to schoolchildren. He has told it to family and to friends.

Primo Levi[24] writes of the way in which his inner drive to tell of what happened at Auschwitz was part of his motivation for keeping alive. He also writes of the importance of testimony, and the importance of being believed. His recurring nightmare at Auschwitz was to tell his story to friends and family and for people simply to ignore his voice, or not to hear his voice; the fear that people on the 'outside', in the 'real world', would be incapable of even hearing; the fear that Auschwitz was, literally, another universe.

Blustein must have been telling his story, attempting to 'represent' the dead Jews of Domachevo and of Europe, for his entire adult life. It is certain that when he does so in Israel, he is met with silence, with sympathy, and with sorrow. He is a survivor-hero in Israel, amongst Jews, and to anyone with any kind of human feeling who hears his story.

However, a court of law is not guided by human feeling; it is guided by its own rules and function. The court was not centrally interested in Blustein, but was focused on Sawoniuk. The court was not interested in the thousands of dead Jews of Domachevo, but in the 21 Jews who were mentioned in the indictment. The prosecution was only interested in the parts of Blustein's story that it wished to use to construct the case against Sawoniuk. It was not interested in Blustein's dreams and his fears and his demons. It was not interested in his philosophising, or his anger, or his last conversation with his mother.

Cross-examination is Primo Levi's nightmare come to life. An educated, intelligent, articulate person is paid by the state, in the interests of the Nazi killer, to act the part of the friend who refuses to hear.

The British court was making great efforts to appear disinterested and neutral; simply balancing the arguments. It appeared almost embarrassed by Blustein's Jewishness. When the jury had been sworn in at the beginning, they were told that if any of them had relations who had suffered in the Holocaust, they should excuse themselves from service. Probably, then, there were no Jews in the jury; Jews were considered unsuitable to serve on such a jury. Jews, as witnesses, or as jurors, were suspected of being unable to 'put aside their feelings', as the jury was asked to do both by the prosecution and the defence in summing up.

---

24 Levi, 1987.

It seemed to me that Blustein was one of those Israelis who feels that the only safe place for Jews is Israel, more particularly that Israel is the only safe place for him. Being a witness in this court, and undergoing cross-examination, must have been, and indeed appeared to be, an unpleasant and uncomfortable job for him.

Dan Stone writes about Holocaust memoir, and the ways in which many historians of the Holocaust have undervalued survivor testimony in relation to more 'solid' types of evidence such as documentation.[25] Jean-François Lyotard has argued that a part of the enormity of the crime of the Shoah was that it eradicated the witnesses and the evidence, making it impossible to reconstruct or represent the events exactly. Stone quotes Lyotard as follows:

> The 'perfect crime' does not consist in killing the victim or the witnesses ... but rather in obtaining the silence of the witnesses, the deafness of the judges, and the inconsistency (insanity) of the testimony.[26]

Stone adds that:

> In other words, it is the attempt to gain cognitive control over the events of the Holocaust, to master them by fitting them into existing narrative frameworks ... that really constitutes a 'wrong' [tort] to the victims. In attempting to counter this wrong, Lyotard puts forward the notion of the Holocaust as a sublime event, a 'sign of history' which must be 'felt' rather than known, because the magnitude of the event has rendered the usual instruments of measurement obsolete.[27]

Stone argues that survivor testimonies, full of both traumatic truth and factual inaccuracies, transcend traditional forms of writing histories, that:

> ... testimonies make more clear than other evidence why the excess of the Holocaust breaks the bounds of 'normal' philosophy of history ... and that this is the primary reason why historians tend to shy away from testimonies ...[28]

Many have been critical of attempts to capture the Holocaust, or elements of it, by means of representation.[29] Hence Theodor Adorno's proposition[30] that there can be no poetry after Auschwitz. Hence Lanzmann's refusal to use archive footage or reconstruction in his film *Shoah*,[31] and his outrage at Spielberg's Hollywood production.

The court required a different method of finding and understanding the truth. Different from Lyotard's 'feeling' of the event; different from survivor memoir; different from Lanzmann's cinematic presentation of carefully produced and edited memoir; different from Spielberg's representation; different from academic historical investigation.

Academic historical representation, and analysis of documentary evidence, was fine for briefing the jury on the background to Sawoniuk's crimes, and this task was carried out by Browning. But to convict the defendant, the court required direct witness testimony. This testimony, it is hoped, is rendered profoundly different from the memoirs of survivors by the process of cross-examination. Some documentary evidence, so valuable to historians, was

---

25 Stone, 2000, pp 219–34.
26 Stone, 2000, p 220.
27 Stone, 2000, p 220.
28 Stone, 2000, p 229.
29 See discussion in Bernard-Donals and Glejzer, 2001.
30 Adorno, 1973.
31 Lanzmann, 1985.

rendered inadmissible by the court in the absence of the testimony of the individual who created the document.

One document in particular, discovered in a German archive, later became the subject of much argument. It was a document that threw light on Sawoniuk's life in the period after his time as a policeman in Domachevo when he committed the crimes of which he was accused by the court. The document showed that he had retreated with the German forces when they were pushed out of the region by the Russian counter-offensive, and that he quickly became a member of a Belorussian unit of the SS (Schutzstaffel). The judge ruled that this document was inadmissible as evidence since its authenticity could not be verified by a direct eye witness; presumably the creator of the document was long dead.

This document did not help us to know whether Sawoniuk was guilty of the four counts of murder in Domachevo. But it did tell us that he was, or became, a Nazi; and that he won sufficient trust from the SS while he was in Domachevo for them to recruit him as a member. Moreover, this unit of the SS was later involved in perpetrating atrocities in the Warsaw region; and it was subsequently moved to France to conduct the war against the partisans, a job that Sawoniuk had been learning in Domachevo. It was in France that Sawoniuk joined the Free Polish army, telling them that he had been a member of the SS. We know this from another document, his Polish army record, which was also inadmissible. We also know that this unit of the SS suffered from many desertions in France at this time.[32]

These two documents on their own might be enough for an observer who was persuaded that they were genuine to come to the decision that Sawoniuk was, at least, a Nazi, and almost certainly a mass killer. The jury was allowed to know none of this. I do not know, either, how many other incriminating but inadmissible documents were turned up by the police investigation. The prosecution, in fact, managed to leak some of this information to the jury during its cross-examination of Sawoniuk, but technically this evidence was inadmissible and the jury was instructed to ignore it by the judge in his summing up.[33] For this court, the available documentary evidence was not considered sufficiently safe evidence on which to base a conviction. Eye witness testimony was required, given in specific and controlled circumstances. It was necessary for the evidence to be immediate, given in person, and available for cross-examination.

---

32 According to the *Report of the War Crimes Inquiry*, 1989, it was common practice for men who had been in auxiliary police or militia units in the occupied territories to be recruited into the Waffen SS, rather than the *Wehrmacht*, when the Germans retreated (p 90, para 9.2). 'Some ... fighting units were designated SS units, but were used simply as part of an army.' (p 3, para 1.13.) It is only possible to imagine what connotations the words 'Waffen SS' had for the jury, especially when it became clear that they were not really supposed to have heard them.

33 'Anglo-American adversary procedure organises the trial as a battle of wits between the prosecution and defence, with the judge acting as their referee, constantly deciding what line of questioning and what material should be allowed to enter the minds of the jury. Yet the judge's authority in this respect may be more official than real: a skilful lawyer will be able to make his point before his adversary can open his mouth to object. The resulting wrangling on admissibility and the judge's ritual exhortation in summing up what points to disregard – for example, the political loyalties of the defendant in an espionage trial – only make the forbidden fruit more tempting to the jury than all the rest.' Kirchheimer, 1969, p 342.

In the appearance of Blustein as a witness, we can see the difference between the memoir and oral testimony of a survivor-hero, and the admissible legal evidence required by a court of law. Blustein gave evidence in Hebrew through an interpreter who stood next to him. He was two years younger than Sawoniuk, and had known him as a child. He told the court how he remembered playing with Sawoniuk and his pigeons as a child. 'I never let no one play with *my* pigeons,' retorted Sawoniuk later, under cross-examination, denying ever having met Blustein, or anyone else who claimed to know him in Domachevo during his childhood.

Blustein recalled the general atmosphere of fear in the Jewish community before the German invasion of 1941. Occupied Poland was, literally, a stone's throw away across the river. He told how he remembered the invasion. He told how the Germans, immediately after they arrived, killed the Rabbi of Lubatov, who used to spend his summers in Domachevo, along with 40 of his followers; they killed a few other leading Jews as well. Blustein told of the creation of the local police force, and how Sawoniuk joined at the outset. He told of the establishment of the ghetto in Domachevo three weeks after the invasion; how it was fenced in with barbed wire, and how the police station was moved to a building at the gate of the ghetto; how Jews were forced to wear yellow stars, and not allowed out of the ghetto; how the morale of the Jews of Domachevo decayed with hunger and disease until 'the living envied the dead'.

Blustein told how, on the Friday before Yom Kippur 1942, Jews were ordered to obtain shovels and present themselves. And how they were then ordered to dig mass graves 'in which to bury large numbers of prisoners'. And that shortly afterwards the ghetto was surrounded by Ukrainians and Germans who had arrived from out of town. And how his mother was 'almost certain' that the Jews were going to be killed, and so they hid in a previously prepared hiding place in the cellar of their house in the ghetto instead of reporting for 'parade' as ordered on Yom Kippur. I reproduce my notes from the trial:

Nutting: What did you hear?

Blustein: At this stage of my testimony is the most difficult time of my life. I dream about it. Think about it every day. I had a dilemma whether to come to this trial. It is difficult to talk …

N: [*to interpreter*] We would be grateful to have his testimony.

[*Blustein still talking about his difficulties, dreams, and so on. Clegg shakes his head sadly as if to say that this display of emotion must stop.*]

Judge: [*politely, gently*] Answer the questions directly.

B: We heard lots of shooting. Shots and cries. We understood what was happening there.

Judge: Answer the question only; what you heard.

N: That evening, after the shooting stopped, did you hear anything to indicate that those who had left that morning had returned to their homes?

B: No.

N: What did you decide to do?

B: Where could we go? If they'd done this here they'd have done it everywhere.

[*He explains that the family decided (led by the mother) to commit suicide.*]

N: Your stepfather had access to drugs at the clinic?

B: He had a bottle of morphine and some powder. We took leave of one another. My father swallowed the morphine and we swallowed the drug. My stepfather was the only one who died. We remained in hiding for the next eight days. Mother decided to cut our veins. Or could we burn down the ghetto at least? We came out to burn down our house but then realised there were others alive in hiding …

N: [*interrupting*] What did you do?

B: My mother said to me don't kill yourself. Maybe you can live. I said Mummy how can I leave you? She ordered me to leave. I departed from my mother and the children. I left the hiding place and fell down and fainted, I don't know for how long. I went up to the attic. This took me some time. I was very weak. I remained there for two days.

N: What did you see through the tiles?

B: I saw the Ukrainian police take out a Jew, 80 years old, named Shaya Idel. This happened 20 metres away. He was wearing his prayer shawl and tefillin. He was carrying a book, I imagine the Talmud. His prayer shawl was red with blood. The police were following him, stabbing him with their bayonets. They set fire to his beard and sidelocks. He didn't cry out.

N: Did you recognise anyone who took part?

B: Andrusha … and many others. They dragged him away.[34]

The court listened in silence. Blustein was emotional, and tired. The mediation of the interpreter made everything slower and more difficult. This was Blustein's Holocaust memoir. Undoubtedly he had told the story many times before. Blustein wanted to tell *his* story and the story of *his* family and of the Jews of Domachevo. All the emotion made the court, the legal process, uncomfortable. The two lawyers and the judge were constantly having to encourage Blustein to answer the questions, to allow the court and its rules to take the lead, to be in charge. Blustein wanted to tell his story, but the court wanted to hear 'evidence'.

Only after many hours of testimony did Blustein mention Andrusha, in passing. Sawoniuk was not charged with killing Shaya Idel. Yet Blustein, with one remark, had clearly implicated him in this murder. Did Blustein really remember Andrusha's presence at that particular incident, 57 years on, after having hidden in a cellar for nine days without food or drink, after having taken drugs to kill himself and then spending two days semi-unconscious? Now, at this trial, Sawoniuk was central; but at the time, for Blustein, it was Shaya Idel who was central, and Andrusha was no more important than any other policeman or soldier present. Can we be sure that he accurately remembered Andrusha's presence? The jury was being presented with 'inadmissible' evidence as to Andrusha's guilt in a murder of which he was not accused. No one can doubt that Idel was taken off and killed. Yet there was no evidence.

Later in the trial, Clegg was to argue for the judge to throw out the whole case against Sawoniuk for reasons such as this. There were other murders in which Sawoniuk was implicated by witnesses but not charged. This evidence was therefore inadmissible and, argued Clegg, highly prejudicial. And when, in the end, the jury came to consider Sawoniuk's guilt or innocence for the two remaining charges, they must have been influenced by evidence such as this.

---

34 24 February 1999.

They were able to say to themselves: 'We know Sawoniuk is a killer and a torturer; we must therefore take the opportunity of convicting him on the two charges, whether we are convinced of those two particular charges or not.' In normal life, we put together many disparate pieces of 'doubtful' evidence to make a whole. We add them up. In court, doubtful evidence detracted from, rather than added to, the clarity of the truth.

A German truck had entered the ghetto while Blustein was watching and wondering what to do. It had a number of Jews on the back, who jumped off the truck and went to collect some personal belongings, bedding and such like from their houses. They had been saved by the Germans to use as slave labour. Blustein was able to join the group and thereby secure work for the German mounted police unit, looking after their horses.

While Blustein was working at the base, he saw a Jewish friend of his, Mir Barlas, after he had been captured and interrogated. The murder of Mir Barlas constituted count four of the indictment against Sawoniuk:

Nutting: In what condition was he?

Blustein: Very bad. I saw him after a German interrogation. The Germans gave him to the Ukrainian police.

N: Whose custody?

B: A number of policemen. Amongst them was Andrusha Sawoniuk.

[*Blustein explains that he had a conversation with Andrusha a few days later.*]

N: What did Andrusha tell you?

B: I understand that he killed him. He told me that Barlas was very courageous. He said that we will soon meet again in the next world.

N: Did you ever see Mir Barlas again?

B: No.

N: Did you have any other conversations with Andrusha?

B: I was looking after the horses at night. Andrusha entered for warmth. He said: 'Don't think you'll live for ever. When the Germans leave they'll hand you over to us. We'll massacre you as we've massacred many.'[35]

Blustein's evidence was entirely credible. No one, usually, would either wish or dare to question a word of it. But it was Clegg's job to do so, and he managed to create some doubt as to Blustein's accuracy and even as to his honesty. Blustein was cross-examined for two days. It was a fascinating confrontation; cruel, dramatic, informative, thought-provoking and sometimes funny. Blustein was determined not to give an inch: he was stubborn, intelligent, defensive and sometimes ironic. When he was in danger, when Clegg was having success with some small point that he was pursuing, Blustein's characteristic response was 'it doesn't matter to me!' or 'I was not interested in such things'. Blustein was interested in the killing of the Jews and of his family. The court was interested in Sawoniuk, the four counts, and various details that may have been important. All of the witnesses, for example, were asked many detailed questions about the uniforms of the local police force. Probably Clegg was trying to construct an argument relating to uniforms but was, in the end, unable to do so on the evidence:

---

35 24 February 1999.

Clegg: Can you tell me about the police uniforms. Did they have uniforms in the first few days after the German invasion. Wasn't it later?

Blustein: This thing didn't interest me and I didn't know about it. I still think they had uniforms very soon after the invasion.

C: Do you remember giving evidence last year in the magistrates' court?

B: Yes.

C: What did you say about police uniforms?

B: I don't know.

C: You said 'They eventually had a uniform'. Remember?

B: No.

C: Do you accept that's what you said?

B: Yes. But it makes no difference.

C: That's not what you said yesterday.

B: It is not my duty to know about uniforms.

...

C: Early on, 50 or so people, mainly Jews, were killed?

B: I'm only talking about Jews.

C: Some gentiles were also killed?

B: Maybe. I don't know who.

C: Communists maybe?

B: It didn't interest me.[36]

And then an ideological disagreement:

C: The Germans didn't confine their murder to Jews?

B: They also killed the mayor and his son and another policeman.

C: Yes. So the Germans killed Jew and Gentile?

B: The Jews they killed because they were Jews. Others they killed because they feared they were against them.

C: They killed communists because they were communists?

B: [*No answer.*][37]

There were three measures that Clegg possessed with which he could test Blustein's story. One was his client's story. This wasn't very useful to him, since he must have been well aware that his client was lying about almost everything. The second was to test Blustein's evidence against its own internal consistency. The third was to test Blustein's evidence in this court against previous versions of his own testimony.

It must be one of the unique features of this case that the witness was confronted with a statement he had made in 1944, two years after the offence, but 55 years before the trial. The prosecution was in possession of a signed statement Blustein had made to the People's Commissariat for Internal Affairs (NKVD), forerunner of the KGB, after the Russians had driven out the German

---

36 24 February 1999.
37 24 February 1999.

forces. The story that Blustein had told the NKVD was significantly different from the story that he told in court 55 years later. Much of the difference was easily explainable: Blustein admitted that he lied to the NKVD because he was afraid of them. Yet much of his story in the NKVD statement was different. He had told them that he and his family had hidden in the woods, not in the cellar, that they had hidden for three days, not for nine, and that his mother had been caught and shot. Why was his story so different?

Clegg: Can you confirm that is what you said in 1944?

Blustein: Mostly.

C: Let's go through it sentence by sentence. [*He does so, at length.*] Did you give a wholly different account to the Russians in 1944 from what you say today?

B: Not completely.

C: You would have had a motive for lying about your work as a telephone engineer under German occupation before the massacre, so that you couldn't be accused of collaboration. You would have had no motive for lying about where you hid?

B: The NKVD official wrote what he wanted. I was waiting for him to finish and let me go.

C: You read and signed it?

B: I can't remember. I would have signed anything.

C: Why did you lie about hiding in the woods rather than the ghetto?

B: I didn't want to get into an argument with him. Maybe he was drunk. Who knows?

C: Was he unsteady on his feet?

B: I don't know. He was sitting down.

C: Were his eyes glazed? Was his speech slurred?

B: I can't remember.

C: You have no motive for giving a different account to the Russians?

B: My evidence was the same as I've said here. What he wrote was up to him. I wanted him to finish so I could leave. It didn't make any difference to me what he wrote.[38]

Blustein's strategy was to be entirely indifferent. He was not used to being asked such impertinent questions. His answers seem to be those that would satisfy a group listening to the story of a survivor-hero. Maybe the Russian was drunk? Of course! Everyone knows that Russians are always drunk. But in the court, it is different. Blustein's story is that he told the NKVD man his correct version, the man wrote whatever he wished to write, and Blustein signed it in order to get away from the NKVD quickly and unscathed. It is perfectly plausible. But why would the NKVD man have changed three days to nine? And why would he have changed the cellar into the wood? And Blustein's reply is, of course, 'who cares?'. He is not interested in that; he is interested in telling the world that everyone he knew was killed on Yom Kippur 1942, and that Sawoniuk was involved.

Blustein claimed too much. He claimed that his evidence was infallible in every respect. He used the word 'holy' to describe it. He did not trust the court

38 25 February 1999.

to assess his evidence fairly, to use its judgment in interpreting his honesty. So he claimed that every single word was exactly true. Clegg had little difficulty in comparing his words at the Old Bailey with his words the year before in the magistrates' court, his original statement to the British police, his testimony to Yad Vashem, his book and his NKVD statement, and discovering small but definite differences in each account.

This was the cross-examination that related directly to the killing of Mir Barlas, count four:

Clegg: Turning to Mir Barlas. You couldn't see which way they went on the Borisy Road, could you?

Blustein: They turned right. They could have gone to the forest or to Domachevo.

C: You don't know where he went, or when or where he was killed, do you?

B: How could I know?

C: The conversation you say you had with Andrusha about Mir Barlas. Did Andrusha say to you that he had killed Mir Barlas?

B: Yes.

C: Not that Mir Barlas had been killed by somebody?

B: No.

C: He said 'I killed him'?

B: He said: 'He was very courageous before I killed him. We will see each other in the world to come.' No, that's wrong. He said 'before I liquidated him'.

C: At the magistrates' court you said that Andrusha did not say 'I killed him'. You said the opposite.

B: What did I say?

[*Clegg reads it out again: there is no direct confession.*]

B: Even if he did not say to me 'I liquidated him' this was the biggest proof that he did it.

C: But before, you said that he had said 'I liquidated him'.

B: Yes, he said that.

C: You decided that Mir Barlas had been killed by Andrusha. That is different from a confession … In your evidence to Yad Vashem, transcribed from a tape machine, you didn't mention the incident with Mir Barlas at all. Can you confirm this?

B: I don't remember.

C: In your book *One of the Sheep* …

B: I didn't write it. I told it to a woman from Yad Vashem. She wrote it.

C: Not one word about Mir Barlas?

B: It may be so.

[*Clegg refers to Blustein's May 1995 statement to the British police.*]

C: Not one mention about Mir Barlas or Andrusha confessing to his murder?

B: They asked me to remember names of policemen. I remembered Andrusha.

C: Is it true that you made no mention of Mir Barlas?

B: I don't remember.

C: Will you accept it from me?

B: It could be.

C: You described other people's fate. Nothing about Mir Barlas. You were asked: 'What can you tell me about Andrusha?' Why didn't you tell them about his confession?

B: I told them about tens or hundreds that he killed. For me it held no special meaning. I could even now give you more names of people he killed that I haven't mentioned …[39]

It seems likely that the truth was that Sawoniuk had said something to Blustein along the lines that he gave in his first examination by Nutting, something like 'Mir Barlas was very courageous before he was shot'. This was the story Blustein had given to the British police, to the magistrates' court and to Nutting. In this cross-examination he changed his story, claiming that Andrusha had used the words 'I liquidated him'. Blustein was trying to make sure Sawoniuk was convicted by claiming that he had said those particular words. And Blustein also claimed that he remembered the phrase exactly, word for word.

Judge Potts accepted Clegg's argument. He judged that, since Blustein had given a different story in his evidence-in-chief and in his cross-examination concerning Sawoniuk's confession, this evidence could not be relied on to make a safe conviction. It is interesting that in his many accounts of events in Domachevo, Blustein had never mentioned the fact that Andrusha had confessed to the murder of Mir Barlas. Is it possible that Blustein invented this incident after he knew who the defendant was? That was Clegg's implication in cross-examination. And Blustein's answer: who cares? 'I could even now give you more names of people he killed that I haven't mentioned.' The jury, in a murder trial, heard this accusation. It was entirely 'inadmissible', entirely 'prejudicial', and probably also entirely true.

The evidence of the local witnesses

The court moved on to hear the evidence of the non-Jewish Belorussians who had travelled from the region of Domachevo to give evidence. They had all been to Britain before, for the magistrates' hearing. Apart from these trips to London, I do not think any of them had travelled very far from Domachevo during their entire lives. It must have been exciting to be picked out of the crowd, to be made to feel important, to be flown off to London and put up at a nice hotel.

Nutting began his examination of Gallina Pushkina full of self-consciously absurd Englishness: 'May I be so ungallant as to ask your date of birth?', he asked. Speaking Polish, she replied, through an interpreter, that she was 68 years old. She had lived in Domachevo during the war and was 11 years old in 1942. She offered a great deal of coherent and cohesive background evidence about Domachevo and the setting up of the police force following the invasion: she remembered Sawoniuk and told how he had joined the police force. 'Judging from the way he behaved afterwards, I believe he joined voluntarily.'

She gave evidence about the day of the main massacre. It was a Sunday:

Nutting: What happened when you arrived at church?

---

39 25 February 1999.

Pushkina: We heard a fairly loud noise come from the ghetto.

N: What sort of sounds?

P: Lots of people crying and shouting.

N: Did you see what happened?

P: No. We heard it. I did see the people who were crying.

N: Could you tell me why they were crying and shouting?

P: Of course I do, they were all being taken to their death.

N: Who was taking them?

P: The local police and the Germans.

N: How many Jews were there?

P: Lots. Absolutely lots. Around 2,000. This was right at the beginning. We were taken out of the church by a German who had a translator with him and told to watch. We were standing outside the church on the top of the hill looking down into the ghetto.

N: That was the first time you *saw* people being escorted?

P: We immediately saw that a large group of people were taken away.

N: 2,000?

P: No, much less.

N: How many, roughly?

P: It's difficult to say, 100, 150, 200.

N: Were they all Jews?

P: Yes.

N: How could you tell?

P: They all had yellow sewn-on badges.

N: Male or female?

P: All of them.

N: Both sexes?

P: Yes.

N: Children?

P: And children.

N: What sort of ages were they?

P: All sorts of ages from the very old to very young children.

N: What happened?

P: They were undressed before us.

N: Where did they put their clothes?

P: I can't tell you.

N: Where were they taken?

P: They went leftward towards the forest.

N: Towards the place marked in the plan as 'massacre site'?

P: Yes.

N: Were Germans and Ukrainians participating all the time?

[*Clegg objects.*]

Judge: Rephrase.

N: What were the escort doing?

P: Beating them along.

N: Who were the escort?

P: German soldiers and police.

N: German police or local police?

P: Our local police. I can't really remember anybody else.

N: Did the group remain in your view?

P: They were herded away into the pine forest.

N: Were the Germans who had ordered you out of the church still there?

P: Yes.

N: Did you see one group or more than one group of Jews?

P: I remember three groups.

N: The second group: was it the same size?

P: I find it difficult to say. We were afraid ourselves.

N: Were they also told to undress?

P: Yes.

N: Then escorted in the same direction as the first group?

P: Yes.

N: The third group. The same story?

P: Yes.

N: They were told to undress?

P: Yes.

N: Then led away?

P: Yes.

N: Were the escorts armed?

P: Yes.

N: Did you hear shooting?

P: After they took the first group away I heard the sound of machine gun fire.[40]

A German official was sent to the Catholic church with a translator on the day of the killing of the Jews of Domachevo. His job was to interrupt the Sunday church service and bring the congregation outside the church, which stood on some high ground above the ghetto. The Catholic men, women and children were made to watch the final solution to the Jewish problem of Domachevo as though it was a theatrical performance. Why? I can think of two different reasons. It may have simply been to spread terror. The Catholics were being shown what sort of a regime was in charge; it was one that ruled by means of terror. They were being shown how cheap life was, and they were being shown the fate that could await them also. Alternatively, it may have been

---

40 2 March 1999.

intended to make the Catholics of Domachevo feel some complicity in the killing. They were being told: 'This is what you have always wanted; for the Jews to disappear, for the Jews to be punished; but you were too weak to do it; we Nazis are doing it *for you*.' The killing of the Jews was not a secret. It was not supposed to be a secret. It was not a crime committed on the quiet or in the shadows. It was done in front of an audience. In Lublin, the concentration camp was on the outskirts of the town and the railway station in the centre of the town; Jews were marched from the railway station to the camp, past the local population. The Nazis had a taste for the dramatic; for a public drama of death.

Pushkina had little more to say about Sawoniuk himself. She did not see him kill or mistreat anybody, but she was aware of his reputation as a man of power, a man to be afraid of.

All the other prosecution witnesses spoke Belorussian, and were from Borisy, a tiny hamlet near Domachevo. They were small farmers and their religion was Russian Orthodox.

The first was Mrs Fedora Yakimuk, aged 73. She was the most 'peasant-like' of all the witnesses, small, wrinkled, old, tough and stubborn. Clegg entirely broke her down under cross-examination and made her admit that all her evidence against Sawoniuk was gleaned from village gossip. Yet, strangely, this did not affect her credibility. Clegg made her look ridiculous in cross-examination primarily because she was uneducated, unintelligent, and in a wholly foreign country and setting; but not necessarily because she was a liar. The godmother of Yakimuk's nephew, her sister's baby, was Sawoniuk's first wife, Anna Maslova.

Yakimuk told the following dramatic story:

Nutting: Did you used to use a sickle when you worked in the fields?

Yakimuk: Yes.

N: Did you injure yourself?

Y: Yes. I cut my shoulder one day.

N: How did you treat the cut?

Y: My mother bound it up. She put iodine on it. The iodine came through the bandage on my arm as a yellow stain. Andrusha saw me and shouted '*Jude, Jude*' to make me stop. Andrusha and some Germans dragged me away to be shot. I was crying, begging, kissing their feet. I was on my knees explaining I was not a Jew and pleading for my life. Andrusha knew me very well but he didn't protect me. The German pulled off the bandage and saw the wound. He let me go. This was one week after the massacre.[41]

It is a great story, and the press loved it. The headline in *The Times* was 'Sawoniuk stood by as I begged for life'.[42] Undoubtedly it could be true, and for this reason it is a powerful story. Yet it is just as possible that it was only partly true. Maybe it did really happen to her, but Sawoniuk wasn't actually there? Maybe it really happened, but to somebody else, and Yakimuk was telling it because it was true in a sense, and she wanted to be involved, she wanted the trips to London, and she wanted the bad guy Sawoniuk put behind

41 2 March 1999.
42 Jones, 1998.

bars. Fifty-seven years is a long time. Mrs Yakimuk did not do well under cross-examination:

Clegg: You never saw Andrusha commit any act of violence against anyone, did you?

Yakimuk: His behaviour to everyone was violent.

C: Yes or no?

Y: Yes, but we weren't allowed to see it. People did see acts of violence but we weren't allowed to go there.

C: Look at your statement of 12 February 1997 … Is it a copy of your statement to Scotland Yard?

Y: Yes.

C: Turn to page five. 'I never personally witnessed any acts of violence during the German occupation.' Did you say that?

Y: I did not say that.

C: [*Repeats the quote.*] Today you've told us you saw Sawoniuk beat people. You didn't say that to the police, did you?

Y: I did see him herd people towards the sand hills but I couldn't be close.

C: You are changing your evidence to fit in with other people's stories.

Y: I'm telling you what I saw.

C: You have twice travelled here to give evidence in the company of other people from Domachevo … People in Domachevo are talking about this trial …

Y: Yes.

C: Everybody's talking about Andrusha?

Y: Yes.

C: It is in the papers?

Y: Yes.

C: And on the TV?

Y: Yes.

C: Everyone is saying what Andrusha did in the war. But the truth is you never saw anything in the war, isn't it?

Y: We weren't allowed to go there.

C: It's untrue that you saw him beat people, isn't it?

Y: People weren't allowed to see.

C: You said 10 minutes ago that you saw him beat people. You've just been caught out saying something that you never saw, haven't you? Why did you tell us that you saw Andrusha beat people?

Y: I didn't say that.

C: You said it a few minutes ago. You're coming here and repeating a lot of gossip, aren't you?

Y: I did see people being driven towards the sand hills.

C: I suggest you're repeating gossip.

Y: I would see people being led away while I was queuing for bread.

C: When you said that you saw acts of violence, that's what others have told you?

Y: Yes. I saw them led away but I was too afraid to go myself.

C: What you were telling me earlier was what others had told you.

Y: I repeat, I saw people led away and I heard shots.

C: When you saw the British police you knew they were investigating Andrusha?

Y: Yes.

C: You told them everything you knew about Andrusha?

Y: Yes.

C: Your story about the bandage is not mentioned in your statement. Nothing about anyone or Andrusha herding anyone anywhere … Not a word about anyone being beaten by anybody.

Y: I did see him leading people away to be shot while I was queuing for bread.

C: Mrs Yakimuk, that is something that everyone is talking about?

Y: Yes.

C: But the first time you've said you witnessed it is today.

Y: I said he drove people to the sand hills. I wasn't allowed to go there myself.

C: [*with a slightly bullying tone*] You didn't say that in the police statement because he didn't do it.

Y: Every morning I went to buy bread …

C: Every morning throughout the war you saw Andrusha herding people to their deaths?

Y: Yes. I saw this many times.

C: Do you remember giving evidence in the magistrates' court?

Y: I can't remember.

C: Do you not remember coming to England last year?

Y: Yes.

C: Mr Nutting asked you some questions?

Y: Sorry, they all look the same. [*Nutting is tall and thin, and Clegg is shorter and a little round. Everyone laughs.*] You could be brothers! [*Yakimuk enjoys the laugh that she is getting.*]

C: [*After having enjoyed the joke with everyone else, suddenly turns serious again.*] Andrusha is on trial for murder … You were given every opportunity to say what you wanted in the magistrates' court?

Y: Yes.

C: Why didn't you say you'd seen Andrusha herd any people to their death?

Y: I think I answered all the questions put to me.

C: You knew the purpose of coming here was to give evidence against Andrusha? If it is true that every time you went to buy bread you saw Andrusha herding people to their deaths why didn't you tell us?

Y: I think I did.

C: All you told us was that you could hear shots, but no suggestion of Andrusha being present. If it was true you would have told the court last year?

Y: Yes.

C: You didn't tell the court, did you?

Y: I don't know …

C: You were read every word in the Russian?

Y: Yes.

C: Today is the first time ever you have told this story about Andrusha?

Y: Yes.

C: Because you want to tell the same story as everyone else?

Y: Yes.

C: You said last year that you were frightened to go to Domachevo during the war?

Y: Yes.

C: The truth is that you're just saying things other people have told you, aren't you?

Y: I'm telling the truth.

C: You never saw Andrusha herding anybody towards the sand pits, did you? He wasn't present when any German officer tore off the bandage?

Y: Yes the German officer was there. Andrusha knew me very well. I was frightened.

…

Nutting: What age were you in 1942?

Yakimuk: 14, 15, I don't know.

N: [*Works it out slowly.*] You were 16.

Y: I'm illiterate. I don't know.[43]

The next witness was Ivan Baglay. He was also from Borisy, and he gave the same general background information as the other witnesses. He knew Andrusha; everyone, he said, knew Andrusha. He described the day of the main massacre: 'The sound was like a full-blown war.' He described having seen the pits where the Jews were buried: 'I saw blood seeping through the sand and lots of flies.' He told of an incident a few days later when he saw Sawoniuk, armed, escorting a woman and her child to the police station:

Baglay: Sawoniuk carried a carbine and a pole, about two metres long made of birch. The woman and the child were frightened. Sawoniuk took hold of the pole with both hands and gave her a heavy blow to the right shoulder.

Nutting: Could you detect any reason why he should have hit her?

B: In order to appeal himself to the *Gendarmerie*. He wanted to show that he had discovered more Jews.

N: What happened to the woman?

B: She fell to the ground. The child was screaming in a hoarse voice. Andrusha then put the pole back on his shoulder. He started dragging the woman, shouting 'Schnell, Schnell'. When the woman rose, one shoulder was lower than the other and her hand was immobile. So she took the girl instead by her left hand.[44]

Ivan Baglay also told how he saw Sawoniuk escorting the Biumen family, for whom his mother had sometimes worked:

Baglay: I saw Biumen turning to Andrusha imploring that he save the life of this family.

---

43 2 March 1999.
44 3 March 1999.

Nutting: Was Mrs Biumen present?

B: Yes. She was walking in front of them.

N: Were their daughters there?

B: They were with their mother, holding her hands.

N: How old were the daughters?

B: They were about seven and five.

N: What did Andrusha's reaction appear to be?

B: He didn't even want to listen. He merely forced them onwards. They continued walking in the direction of the sand hills.

N: Did you ever see Mr Biumen or any of his family again?

B: No.[45]

In the cross-examination, Clegg pursued Baglay, but not very far, and in the end was satisfied to make it clear to the jury that these two stories did not relate to any charges against Sawoniuk.

Ivan Baglay's brother, Alexander, gave evidence. It was the father of the Baglay brothers, a carpenter, who carried out the work when Sawoniuk stole a house from the ghetto and had it moved and rebuilt elsewhere in the town. Baglay told the story that related to count one of the indictment. Of the four counts, it was by far the strongest. Baglay had witnessed Sawoniuk kill three people; he had known Sawoniuk; and he had been close to him as the murder was committed:

Nutting: Why did you go to the ghetto?

Baglay: We wanted to find something for ourselves ... shoes or clothes.

N: What happened?

B: We were caught by the local police.

N: What did they do to you?

B: They took us to the police station and then towards the sands.

N: Was the police station opposite the ghetto gates?

B: Yes.

N: Who took you to the sand hills?

B: Andrusha. We thought that we were going to be shot. When we came out of the police station we saw three Jews. We realised that we would not be shot but would be burying them. It was about two o'clock. We went directly to the sand hills. The Jewish people had been discovered in a cellar in the ghetto.

N: Was Andrusha the only policeman?

B: No, there were two others.

N: Did Andrusha have a weapon?

B: Yes.

N: What sort?

B: A pistol.

N: Were you carrying anything?

---

45 3 March 1999.

B: No.

N: Where did you first see the Jews?

B: They were standing by a hole that had been dug out. There were three Jews, two men and one woman. Andrusha ordered them to undress. The men were about 40. They undressed. The woman, about 28, was reluctant to take her pants off. Andrusha insisted. Andrusha threatened her with a beating. The Jews were emaciated and unshaven. Andrusha shot the Jews in the back of the head.

[*Baglay explains that he and his friend were told to bury the bodies, and told that they could take the clothes.*]

N: Who shot the Jews?

B: Andrusha.

N: With what?

B: With the pistol, in the back of the head.

N: Did they fall into the pit?

B: Yes. One after the other.

N: Where was Andrusha?

B: Standing behind each.[46]

The next witness was Ivan Stepaniuk. Stepaniuk told of the death of Shlemko, which related to count two of the indictment. Stepaniuk had known Shlemko before the war when he had worked for him in his team on the railway. Stepaniuk had seen Shlemko being taken away by Andrusha towards the massacre site a few days after the main massacre. Andrusha was beating Shlemko:

Nutting: What was Shlemko's reaction?

Stepaniuk: He was picked up, beaten again, picked up again ... The other policeman held his right arm.

N: For how long did they remain in your sight?

S: Two to five minutes. No more.

N: Where were they going to?

S: Towards the woods.

N: You said he was killed. What happened after you lost sight of them? Did you hear anything?

S: I heard the sound of gunfire.

N: When he was being hit was he doing anything to protect himself?

S: No.

N: How did he appear?

S: I can't describe him. How can I describe him?

N: What sort of spirits did he appear to be in?

S: How should he feel when he was being led away to his death? He was quite insensitive.

N: Can you explain?

---

46 5 March 1999.

S: He appeared to be without feeling. He was picked up, dragged on, fell down again.

N: How many times did he fall when you were watching?

S: About four times.

N: Did you see the face of Andrusha?

S: Yes, I did. Every time he picked up the Jew Shlemko he would turn round so I could see his face.

N: Had you seen anything like that before?

S: No.

N: Did you see Andrusha again that day?

S: I saw him return from the woods where the shooting was.

N: Did he still have the carbine?

S: Yes. The carbine and the spade.

N: Was Shlemko with them?

S: No.

N: The other policeman?

S: Yes.[47]

However, under cross-examination, Stepaniuk made the following admission:

Clegg: On that day when you saw Shlemko and the two policemen, *then* you didn't know the name of either, did you?

Stepaniuk: Yes. I didn't know him then. But I was told after it was him.

C: By another policeman you described as Andrusha's brother?

S: Yes.

C: A couple of months later?

S: No, a couple of days.

C: The man you call Andrusha wasn't present at the conversation, was he?[48]

Later, the judge felt unable to allow this count to go to the jury because of the unsafe identification of Sawoniuk. In his re-examination, Stepaniuk had told how he had seen Andrusha often in Domachevo after the Shlemko incident; but under his first examination, it had appeared that his identification of Shlemko was completely based on the hearsay of the man Stepaniuk knew as Sawoniuk's brother.

The next witness that Nutting called was Detective Sergeant Griffiths from the War Crimes Unit at New Scotland Yard. On 21 March 1996 they had decided that they had enough evidence against Sawoniuk to interview him. They went to his flat at 31 Cadbury Way, London SE16. He lived alone there. He answered the door to the police and they introduced themselves. They had a search warrant, and they searched his premises. They found two documents that they took away, a travel document and a photograph of Sawoniuk in a Polish army uniform.

47 8 March 1999.
48 8 March 1999.

Sawoniuk attended Southwark police station on 1 April 1996 for an interview. It was recorded by video and audio. He was represented by solicitors. The police told him that they were investigating charges of murder and manslaughter in the German occupied territories during the period 1939–45.

What followed in court was a bizarre piece of theatre. Nutting wanted to get the police interview before the jury and into the record. Nutting and the policeman, Griffiths, 'performed' the interview, Griffiths playing himself and Nutting playing Sawoniuk. Nutting speaks very much the 'Queen's English'. He speaks slowly, deliberately, and in a self-assured way. Now, Nutting was reading Sawoniuk's words from the police interview transcript. Sawoniuk is clearly not educated and is not a master of language. He has learnt his English in Bermondsey. The words from the transcript seem like a foreigner who has learnt to speak bad cockney. Nutting says the words in his usual voice, but of course they sound ridiculous. At the time this evidence was given, it was not clear yet whether Sawoniuk was going to testify. So this reading of the transcript might have been Nutting's only opportunity to allow the jury to hear Sawoniuk's own words.

The next morning one of the jurors had been taken ill. Her doctor reported that she would be in hospital for a week. The judge decided to let her go and carry on with 11 jurors. Clegg asked that there should be no contact between the 11 jurors and the one in hospital:

Clegg: It'd be the most natural thing in the world if they were to send her flowers, but I must ask that there be no contact.

Judge: Very well Mr Clegg. Would you like to ask me in front of the jurors for them to have no contact?

Clegg: I'd rather that my Lord appeared to take the responsibility lest I appear unchivalrous.

[*Miss Evans, the jury's usher, agrees to send flowers on behalf of the jury and the court if Mr Clegg will pay.*][49]

As so often in this trial, the English gentility of the language and sentiments contrasted greatly with the substance of the case.

Proceedings continued with the last witness for the prosecution, Fedor Zan. Zan testified that he had seen his uncle and cousins escorted to their deaths by local policemen including Sawoniuk in the spring of 1943. This, however, did not constitute a crime under the War Crimes Act 1991, since it was part of the 'war' against the partisans, and not against the Jews. It might, however, be used by the defence to show that Zan had a motive to hate Sawoniuk, and therefore, possibly to lie in order to secure his conviction. On the other hand, it was further evidence to the jury of the fact that Sawoniuk was a Nazi killer.

Zan told of the incident that related to count three of the indictment. He had visited his sister in Kobelka, a nearby village, on his way home from work. He was making his way there from the train station, through the woods, when he heard crying and shouting. He saw a group of about 15 Jewish women undressing on the instructions of Sawoniuk. He lined them up next to a pit, and shot them with a machine gun. While in Domachevo, Zan had taken the court to the spot where he had hidden and he showed the jury the spot where

---

49 15 March 1999.

he says he saw Sawoniuk shooting the women. The defence and the prosecution agreed that the distance was 127 or 128 paces. The jury had to decide whether an identification at that distance was safe. In the end they decided that it was, and found Sawoniuk guilty on this count. By the time the jury considered this count, they had reason enough to want to find Sawoniuk guilty; but an identification at such a distance and such a length of time after the event must, surely, be open to some reasonable doubt.

Sawoniuk under cross-examination

After the presentation of the case for the prosecution, things were going fairly well for Sawoniuk. Clegg had just succeeded in having two of the four counts thrown out by the judge. It was not certain that the jury would find that the Crown had proved the remaining two counts. It is absolutely clear that Sawoniuk must have been advised by his lawyers not to testify. It was his arrogance, his feeling that he knew better, that he was cleverer than the lawyers, the judge and the jury, that made him testify. Perhaps it was his arrogance that in the end caused him to be convicted as much as the fact of his guilt.

Under cross-examination Sawoniuk was, simply, absurd. He routinely denied everything. He denied things that he didn't need to deny; things that every witness had agreed upon; and things that were clearly established historical fact.

For example, he began by denying the existence of the ghetto in Domachevo. So Nutting asked him whether there was a ghetto in Tomashevska, which he denied, or in Brest, which he also denied. He denied that there was barbed wire round the ghetto. He denied that he had ever seen Jews wearing yellow stars. He denied that there were any greater restrictions on Jews than on anyone else. He claimed that the police station was moved to a building just opposite the gate of the ghetto by coincidence.

Sawoniuk claimed that during the main massacre he was visiting a friend in another village. Nutting asked him why, when he found out about the massacre, he had not decided to leave the police. His answer was:

> I wasn't ready for that. I decided a year later. I brought myself up. I used my brain. Nobody told me nuttin'.[50]

This was, perhaps, an echo of an argument he had had long ago with his brother about leaving the police. He was his own man. He wasn't going to be told by anyone else what was right and wrong. He would make his own decisions:

Sawoniuk: I wasn't ready.

Nutting: You knew you could leave at any time?

S: Yes.

N: Some did leave?

S: I wouldn't know.

N: Didn't your brother leave?

S: He left soon after he joined.

---

50 22 March 1999.

N: Because he realised what the whole racket smelt of?

S: Yes.

N: I used the language that a witness used.

S: My brother never discussed anything with me why he left.

N: Did he leave because he was ill?

S: His health wasn't good.

N: Was his health an excuse?

S: Yes.

N: But the real reason was he didn't like what he had to do?

S: He didn't want to do things like hitting people or killing people.

N: What went wrong for the Jews in the six months after your brother joined to make him think that?

S: He never told me. I do know he didn't like the idea that the Jews didn't have their freedom.

Judge: His answer was voluntary.

N: [*Reads out the remark about hitting and killing people.*] Those were your words? [*Repeats quote.*]

S: Correct.

N: Tell the jury what it was in autumn 1941 that your brother didn't like?

S: Nothing whatsoever. The police were friendly. We never interfered.

Judge: This was your answer: 'He did not like it what was going on in Domachevo with the Jewish.' What did you mean by it? [*Repeats quote.*] What did you mean by that?

S: Jew people never had their freedom.

N: When did this restriction occur?

S: Never. We were never told Jewish mustn't go here, go there. My brother left because the Jews never had freedom. In the German occupation they couldn't do what they wanted.

N: What were the restrictions?

S: They mustn't go far from where they lived.

N: You told me this morning there were no restrictions.

S: The Germans never had respect for us. We protect Domachevo from the partisans. They wasn't friendly with us.

N: What were the other restrictions on the Jews?

S: There were no restrictions.

N: Was there any ill treatment of the Jews?

S: How should I know if they were ill. I'm not a doctor.

N: [*Quotes.*] 'Yes he, one of those persons same as myself. He didn't want to do it. Hitting people. Killing people.' What alerted you and your brother to this?

S: [*loudly*] Lie.

N: But I'm repeating your own answer. What was it that caused your brother to fear that he might have to kill Jews?

S: If he'd been ordered to kill Jews he'd have done it else he'd be dead. He never discussed with me anything. He was only a half brother. We didn't have good relations.

N: What you have done is to lift a corner of the truth. I suggest that what you have told us about your brother leaving the police, that your brother didn't like having to kill Jews, was true.[51]

Sometimes Sawoniuk's testimony was so bizarre and incoherent that it was not even incriminating. The one issue that made him really lose his temper was the accusation that he had been a member of the SS after he left Domachevo. He told a long and certainly fictional story about how he travelled from Domachevo to France to join the Free Polish army. In fact he had travelled from Domachevo to France with the German army as a member of the Belorussian section of the SS. Nutting was able to confront him with his Polish army document but it was only of use to the prosecution if Sawoniuk could be enticed into authenticating it himself.

Nutting: Were you serving in the German army?

Sawoniuk: I never ever joined the German army.

N: We've had that document translated. What it says is '1 August to 11 November 1944, German army according to his own statement'.

S: [*angry*] Prove it me in black and white. Rubbish.

N: Why does it say so?

S: You are lying in front of the jury, everybody. I hope the jury doesn't believe you.

N: Look at exhibit seven. Did you ever join the Waffen Border Regiment of the SS number 76, 1st Battalion?

S: [*very angry*] You call me liar twice. I call you liar.

Judge: Yes, but did you or didn't you?

S: Never. Don't talk to me about German army. I won't answer no more questions about German army.

N: Were you transferred from Warsaw to France in that regiment?

S: No.

N: Does the document give your surname, Sawoniuk? Is that you? ... Does it give your date of birth?

S: Yes. 7 March 1921. That's correct.

N: Place of birth, Domachevo?

S: Yes sir.

N: Against the German for place of birth does it say Domachevo?

S: I was born in Domachevo, yes.

N: Does the document say that?

S: Yes. I see it.

N: That is German isn't it?

S: What you putting German for?

---

51 22 March 1999.

N: Does it say 'Rank: Corporal of Schuman Schukmanshaft'? Were you a Corporal of Schukmanshaft?

S: [*very angry, shouting*] I've listened to lies. I'm not going to listen no more.

[*Clegg interrupts, pleading for a break on behalf of his client.*]

Judge: Mr Nutting has the right to cross-examine.

S: I don't want break.

N: Could I have the document back.

S: [*shouting*] Don't show me it no more. I won't accept that.

[*He withdraws from the witness box as if he is about to leave.*]

Judge: [*sternly*] Listen to me. Please understand that if you are asked an improper question I will stop Mr Nutting. So far it is not improper. Will you listen to Mr Nutting's questions?

S: I'm not prepare to answer on German army. I never been in it. I hate Germans and I hate Russians.

N: Just have this document back.

S: No.

[*Judge asks nicely.*]

N: The usher will point to the next bit I want you to look at. Does the German word mean 'married to' in German?

S: I don't speak German.

N: Does the word after that say Nina S?

S: I don't know what S stands for.

N: What was Nina's last name?

S: I don't know. She was Russian.

N: Would Nina S refer to Nina Sawoniuk by any chance?

S: [*No answer.*]

N: How is it that a German SS document contains your name, date of birth, place of birth and the word Nina S?

S: [*shouting, pointing at Griffiths and the other policeman at the back of the court*] He printed it!

N: This is a Scotland Yard conspiracy?

S: Yes. Probably.

N: All part of the KGB conspiracy?

S: They work together innit?

N: Are you tired, Mr Sawoniuk?

S: I'm tired enough of you!

Judge: We'll have a break now.[52]

Sawoniuk lied about almost everything under cross-examination, but nearly all of the things he lied about were not centrally important to the counts with which he was charged. Did he kill the 16 women in the forest as Zan said, and did he kill the three Jews and force Baglay to bury the bodies? These were the

---

52 22 March 1999.

only crucial questions. Perhaps if Sawoniuk had been charged with the crime of genocide, or crimes against humanity, the court would have been more easily able to take into account the whole story that emerged about his conduct during the war. It would not have been necessary to focus exclusively on the two murders, and it would have been possible to take into consideration other evidence that added to the picture of Sawoniuk as a Nazi killer. And perhaps, even if it had proved impossible to convict him of the two specific murders, it might still have been possible to convict him of being part of the common plan or criminal conspiracy to kill the Jews of Europe. But in this trial, the charge was simply murder, and so the two particular counts were all-important.

Clegg's closing speech was interesting and, given that by this time Sawoniuk seemed to have very little case left, surprisingly compelling. He noticed that all the important witnesses, all the witnesses who testified to having seen Sawoniuk committing atrocities, came from Borisy. The witnesses who came from Domachevo itself, while providing background information, did not tell of having seen Sawoniuk actually commit any crimes. But every single person from Borisy who was alive during the war, said Clegg, and who is still alive today, gave evidence of particular crimes carried out by Andrusha.[53] Clegg argued that this was too much of a coincidence. Therefore, there must have been either some sort of conspiracy in Borisy, or some sort of communal action that was based on the Borisy collective memory, or gossip, of wartime and of Andrusha's involvement.

Clegg went on to give a reason why Sawoniuk would be particularly hated in Borisy, a hamlet consisting of no more than 30 houses. Borisy was a partisan village, and Sawoniuk freely admitted to having killed partisans. He even recalled the incident where Zan's uncle, aunt and cousins were killed. Also, Clegg pointed out, Yakimuk, Melaniuk, and Alexander Baglay had not mentioned important parts of the stories they told about Andrusha in court at the time of the first British police interviews, so they gave new and important information only when they knew who the suspect was. And further still, there was much media interest in Domachevo concerning Sawoniuk, and much talk about Sawoniuk's guilt. Zan had given interviews to both British and Russian television journalists about Sawoniuk. It is certainly possible that by the time of the trial it was 'well known' in Borisy, as well as Domachevo, that Sawoniuk was guilty, and that it was important for him to be found guilty.

It might be the case, however, that the jury had already tacitly agreed upon their verdicts before Clegg's closing address but after Nutting's, since it was at this lunchtime that most of them were seen for the first time in the pub across the road from the Old Bailey enjoying alcoholic refreshment.

The jury were certainly convinced of the general guilt of Andrei Sawoniuk, and the two counts, based on the evidence of Alexander Baglay and Fedor Zan, enabled them to convict him, which they did. Since he was found guilty of murder, he was sentenced – the judge having no discretion – to life imprisonment.

The trial of Sawoniuk was, at least partly, a cosmopolitan trial. It dealt with events in Belorus, organised by German Nazis as part of their attempt to kill the Jews and take over the world. Perhaps, then, it would have been most appropriate to have held the trial in an international criminal court, and for the

---

53 This, Clegg admitted at Sawoniuk's appeal, was a little – but not much – of an exaggeration.

defendant to have been charged with crimes against humanity. In the absence of the existence of such a court, the trial was held in London under English law and so took a transitional form between national and cosmopolitan.

The court dealt with evidence that was 56 years old and that had been compromised by fading memories, by the telling and retelling of stories, by the cross-contamination of evidence, and by the reconfiguration of old enmities. The particular form of evidence that was demanded by English law was quite specific, that of immediate oral testimony, subjected to cross-examination. Other forms that might have shed light on the case, such as documentary evidence, were excluded. Evidence offered in the form of Holocaust memoir and of nationalistic narrative was aggressively transformed by the processes of the court into its preferred forms. The court acted to legitimate survivor testimony by locating it in the sacred space of law, but simultaneously to de-legitimate it by trying to remove control of the narrative from the hands of witnesses and by contesting the value of much of the testimony.

A complex picture of Andrei Sawoniuk emerged from the process. The contrast of ordinariness and extraordinariness in his story was striking. Sawoniuk would surely not have become a killer if he had not found himself in a situation where killing was expected and sanctioned by authority; yet neither was he forced into it. Some aspects of Sawoniuk's transformation into a mass killer are in tune with Bauman's framework, but others are in contradiction to it. It is true that, believing the Nazis were destined to win the war, his strategy of becoming a policeman and behaving in such a way as to be trusted and promoted by the occupying power had a certain logic from the point of view of his own narrow self-interest. It gave him a job, a living, power and the possibility of promotion.

It is stretching the facts, however, to suggest that Sawoniuk's decision to become a *génocidaire* was simply an example of rational decision making. First, since his brother chose to leave the police force, and is still living quite happily just across the river from Domachevo, it is clear that Sawoniuk could have made the same choice if he had wanted to. He chose a different course, and it was a free and conscious decision. He had an argument with his brother; he chose to kill Jews and his brother chose to take his chances outside the police force. Secondly, a decision such as whether or not to become a mass killer must involve factors other than rational choice. It is only possible to speculate about Sawoniuk's early life and what kind of person he was when he chose to become a killer. It is clear enough that he was not brought up in a loving family and that he was poor. It also seems that he suffered as a child from some bullying. None of this, of course, can explain how a person becomes a brutal mass murderer, but it is not irrelevant that he was an excluded, alienated, unloved young man. He found a way to improve his social prospects and also, perhaps, an outlet for his anger. But Sawoniuk was in no way a Weberian bureaucrat who just obeyed orders and carried out professional duties. He chose to become a killer and he chose to kill and beat with more brutality than the efficient pursuit of a bureaucratic goal could possibly require.

When they gave evidence, both Blustein and Sawoniuk had attempted to wrest control of their stories from the court. Blustein was mistrustful of the court and its rules; he did not trust the court to hear his evidence fairly or to believe him. He wanted to be in control of the story he told, to tell what he wanted to tell, rather than be confined and guided by the adversarial system.

He did not want to play the game of cross-examination; rather he wanted to be believed. He did not mind if the court was unhappy with one true story; he could tell another true story. It didn't matter to him. Sawoniuk felt that he was cleverer than the court, and cleverer than his own lawyers; if only he could have a chance to tell his story to the jury, they would believe him. He thought that he could talk his way out of the Old Bailey, as he had, presumably, talked his way out of many a tight spot before.

Both of the men, the one who as a young man had seen everybody he knew killed, and the one who as a young man had taken part in that killing, felt that they could circumvent the rules and norms of the court. They both wanted to talk straight to the jury and they did find ways of doing so. They might have done better if they had trusted the court more, if they had attempted to use the rules of the court in their favour rather than attempting to rise above those rules. Blustein might have avoided having the count that was based on his testimony thrown out if he had trusted the court to believe his original evidence of an indirect confession; it was because he did not trust the court to do so that he embellished it with his claim that Sawoniuk made a direct confession. Sawoniuk would have avoided showing himself so clearly to be a liar. On more than one occasion during his cross-examination, Nutting was happy to allow Sawoniuk to speak directly to the jury without intervention. Sawoniuk would have had more chance of success by exercising the right to silence, which was offered to him by the law, than by following his strategy of trying to communicate in an unmediated way with the jury.

On the other hand, it might be that the jury was swayed as much by evidence that was inadmissible or prejudicial as it was by the evidence upon which it was supposed to come to a decision. The witnesses found ways to talk to the jury that were non-legal, outside the formal rules of the court. Blustein presented the jury with his emotional and moving Holocaust memoir. He challenged them to accept it in spite of Clegg's smart cross-examination and the judge's earnest directions. The existence of the jury and the privacy of the jury's discussions are also within the rules and norms of the criminal trial, not outside them. Evidence is given in the presence of the jury so that they can assess non-verbal messages from witnesses. They must be able to see the witnesses giving evidence, and enduring the pressure of cross-examination, in order to come to a judgment as to their truthfulness. The rules and norms of law insist that the jury make its judgment not only from the words spoken by the witnesses but also from the ways in which they are spoken. Embedded within the norms and rules of the criminal trial are the mechanisms by which the rules and norms of evidence may be subverted. The extraordinariness of the events with which this trial was concerned accentuated the difficulties that the trial process has with abstracting and shaping events in the world so that they can be judged in the courtroom.

Chapter Seven
Irving v Lipstadt and the legal construction of authoritative cosmopolitan narrative

The *Irving v Lipstadt* libel trial was a different kind of trial from the criminal trials examined so far. It was centrally concerned with assessing the parameters, rules and norms of academic historiographical methodology. It was asked to decide whether the work of David Irving, which questions and denies central facts about the Holocaust, fell within or without those parameters; or, at least, whether someone who says that Irving is a Holocaust denier rather than a historian should be stopped by the law from publishing. Inevitably, this decision necessitated some investigation into the actual events in question as well as into the accuracy, limits and legitimacy of the historiography that has mapped them. Thus, the trial was judging the events of a particular set of crimes against humanity in a different way from a criminal trial. Instead of asking whether a particular defendant shared a legal responsibility for them, it was asked to make a judgment about the two different forms of narrative that claimed to chart them: the academic form of Deborah Lipstadt and the 'revisionist' form of David Irving. The court was being asked to produce a form of narrative of its own.

Two forms of narrative, then, were given to the court as inputs: an academic form and a 'revisionist' form. The court had to produce a cosmopolitan and legally authoritative output by working on those inputs according to its own procedures, rules and norms. Even though the court was a national one, its task was to give an impartial, that is, not nationally particular, verdict regarding a profoundly supra-national event. The judgment consisted of a 349-page document that sketched the central events and facts of the Holocaust, and showed how Irving's writing could not be rightly understood as even an eccentric or dissident attempt at honest historiography.[1]

The judgment was a cosmopolitan narrative. The second half of this chapter discusses the significance of this kind of legal production of cosmopolitan narrative. It draws on other cases from this book and elsewhere. I argue that cosmopolitan trials are in a particularly strong position to produce authoritative descriptions of highly contested sets of events; events that are the subject of shaping and reshaping by competing mythologies of nationalism. Cosmopolitan courts contain mechanisms that aim to free their judgments of national particularity. They require evidence to be scrutinised in rigorous ways; they can hear different forms of evidence, evidence from different countries and different points of view. The narratives produced by cosmopolitan courts are produced with the authority of an established body of international humanitarian and human rights law.

---

1   *Irving v Lipstadt* judgment.

Irving v Lipstadt

I was in the queue outside the courtroom where the case was being heard. A man behind me was explaining the issues very loudly to his companion. 'Why doesn't Irving have the balls to tell the truth?' he asked:

> He knows as well as we do that no Jews were ever killed, there were no gas chambers. So why does he admit that *some* existed but not others? He's just trying to please the judge. But we all know that he's made his mind up already. All they have to do is go to Auschwitz, dig up the rubble, and find that there's no holes in the roof.[2] Then they'd know there were no gas chambers. But they won't do it. Because then the whole game would be up ...

I turn round to watch and listen, not knowing what to do. Should I attack him? Argue with him? I just continue to watch and listen, keeping eye contact with him. He enjoys the attention. His self-righteous little monologue puffs up, becoming louder and more confident. He is aware that he has an audience to shock. He covers many important issues, the flood of asylum seekers, the weakness and hypocrisy of the Labour government: 'If "they" continue to come over here, then perhaps I'll leave the country.' I, and those near me in the queue, listen for about five minutes, until the courtroom is opened and we are allowed to file in, making every effort not to have to sit next to the Nazi for the entire morning.[3]

The *Irving* case was in some ways more unpleasant and shocking to observe than the crimes against humanity trials. There was always a sprinkling of Nazis in the audience, ready to laugh at Irving's witticisms and marvel at his cleverness. Irving himself was not being asked to answer for any Nazi crimes in court. On the contrary, his performance in court actually constituted his political activity. We were not observing the consequences of his activity, but the activity itself, that of a racist intellectual who had made it his business to defend Hitler and to ridicule Holocaust survivors.

Deborah Lipstadt first published her book, *Denying the Holocaust: The Growing Assault on Truth and Memory,* in 1993. It was an academic study that sought to expose the methods, strategies and political agendas of those who deny the Holocaust. It mentioned David Irving 16 times. She called Irving 'one of the most dangerous spokespersons for Holocaust denial'. 'Familiar with historical evidence,' she wrote, 'he bends it until it conforms with his ideological leanings and political agenda'.[4]

Irving sued Lipstadt and Penguin Books for libel but he presented himself as a victim. In court he was alone, representing himself. On the other side of the room was barrister Richard Rampton and the late Princess Diana's divorce lawyer, Anthony Julius, accompanied by a team of about 10 busy, scurrying young lawyers; they were able to elicit the testimony of five eminent academics, backed up by long reports prepared with the help of their research assistants; they had the financial backing of the Penguin corporation. Outside the courtroom was the entire world Jewish conspiracy trying to silence Irving. But the truth, sometimes overlooked by the commentators on the trial, was

---

2   The holes he meant were the ones through which the gas was introduced.
3   Kate Taylor says: 'On most days, assembled at the back of the courtroom were a motley crew of Irving supporters. At least three were known members of the BNP, Bob Gertner, Arthur Flinders and Ron Smith.' Taylor, 2000, p 30. I don't know if this Nazi was one of these.
4   Lipstadt, 1994, p 181.

that it was Irving who was trying to silence Lipstadt; it was he who instigated the trial; it was she who was forced to spend five years of her life defending her right to publish. It was David Irving who had nothing to lose.

At the beginning of the trial it was agreed by both sides, and Judge Charles Gray, that there would be no jury. Anthony Julius explained later[5] that the Lipstadt side's motivation for agreeing to this was that it would simplify and shorten the trial. He denied that they would have been more worried about the outcome of the case had it been tried by a jury. He also argued, with hindsight, that the greatest benefit of having no jury was that the judge produced a large, comprehensive and closely argued written judgment that vindicated Lipstadt in detail, and that also concluded that Irving was a liar motivated by racism. A jury would only have been able to produce a guilty or not guilty verdict.

Julius also explained why they never called eye witnesses of the Holocaust to give evidence against Irving. Some survivors had been unhappy at this decision, arguing that they spoke with a unique authority, and felt marginalised because they were not allowed to be central in rebutting Irving's case themselves. Julius argued that the Lipstadt legal team had a moral objection: they did not want to expose survivors to days of cross-examination by the 'belligerent anti-Semite'. They also had a forensic objection: they wanted to run the case as if it was their case, to take the initiative in the trial. They wanted to show that Irving was corrupt; that his 'history' was full of lies and distortions. The best way to do this, they decided, was to call historians to speak for the historical documents. They wanted to put Irving on the defensive, to 'run the case like a history seminar with Irving as a rather bad student'.[6] Lipstadt, too, did not give evidence. Her team felt that her evidence was in her book. They wanted to focus the case on Irving and his books, not on Lipstadt.

In the case, Irving denied three central things: that Jews were killed in gas chambers at Auschwitz; that Hitler directly ordered their slaughter; and that there was any systematic plan to destroy European Jewry. Irving claimed that the well known pictures of bodies taken in concentration camps were victims of typhus, of death by 'natural causes'. Why were they all so thin, he asks, if Jews were taken straight off the trains and killed? He boasted that Auschwitz was the 'flagship' of the Holocaust legend; if that were sunk, as it would be within six weeks, the whole legend would crumble. In this case Auschwitz became a substitute for the whole genocide; and the gas chamber Birkenau II became a substitute for Auschwitz.

The first expert witness for Lipstadt was, therefore, Robert Jan van Pelt, an architectural historian who has done some of the most interesting and authoritative research on Auschwitz.[7] He had spent a number of years in the archives there, reconstructing the architectural history of the camp and particularly of the gas chambers. Van Pelt's report said that the overwhelming evidence showed that a million Jews were murdered at Auschwitz. He said that the convergence of testimony made it a 'moral certainty' that the gas chambers were the main instrument of murder between summer 1942 and 1944. Van Pelt cited eye witness evidence that had been given by prisoners

---

5   Julius, 2000.
6   Julius, 2000.
7   van Pelt and Dwork, 1996.

including Stanislaw Jankowski, Shlomo Dragon and Henryk Tauber on gassings in the five crematoria. Others had given evidence of how the gas chambers were demolished in late 1944 and early 1945 to destroy evidence. Van Pelt also cited confessions by Nazis, including SS (Schutzstaffel) officers Pery Broad, Rudolf Höss, Adolf Eichmann and others.

Irving's position was that eye witness accounts by Jewish witnesses are in need of 'psychiatric evaluation', or are concocted by the world Jewish conspiracy, or are accounts of other accounts, or are infected by other well known accounts. German eye witness accounts that admit the existence of gas chambers, he alleges, were extracted by Allied torture after the war. Eye witness accounts that come from Irving's own post-war interviews with some of Hitler's loyal followers, such as Julius Schaub, on the other hand, are readily believed.[8]

One of Irving's 'theories' was that the gas chambers were in fact air raid shelters for the SS. Van Pelt showed that the gas chambers would have been very impractical air raid shelters; they were one and a half miles from the SS barrack. He showed his slides in the court: he pointed out the undressing room, the Zyklon B insertion columns, the dissection room, and the chimneys of the crematorium. He explained how some of the buildings, originally built as real, honest crematoria, were adapted and redesigned into gas chambers; he showed plans that detailed the modifications that were necessary, stage by stage, to convert innocent crematoria into gas chambers. He showed enlarged wartime negatives of the gas chambers that had been taken by Allied bombers; Irving examined the photographs closely, and said he could see no holes in the roof. Van Pelt had already obtained scientific evidence from photographic experts showing that the dots on the pictures could well be holes in the roof. Irving argued that there were no holes, and that therefore no gas could have been introduced into the chambers. '[I]f you were to go to Auschwitz the day after tomorrow ... and find a reinforced concrete hole where we anticipate it would be from your drawings ... I would happily abandon my action immediately'[9] was Irving's hollow boast. But van Pelt had already given the answer: 'I have authored a report already in 1993 for the Poles in which I actually argued that they needed very, very strict preservation standards, and the last thing I would ever have done is start scraping away at the roof without any general plan or archaeological investigations.'[10]

Irving had first publicly supported the cause of Holocaust denial in early 1991 when he went to Canada to help in the defence of Ernst Zundel, who was on trial for the crime of Holocaust denial. The defence commissioned Fred Leuchter to write an 'expert' report on the gas chambers at Auschwitz. Leuchter was a designer of execution equipment in the USA. Even though he was no expert, he went to Auschwitz, secretly chiselled holes in the remains of some of the gas chambers, and submitted the samples for chemical analysis.

---

8   'I discovered plenty of evidence in the archives indicating that Julius Schaub was one of Hitler's most loyal followers. He had joined the Nazi Party in the early 1920s, taken part in the failed *Putsch* of 1923 ... and been decorated with various prestigious Nazi awards ... After the war he did his best to exonerate Hitler from responsibility for the crimes of Nazism, claiming he had cursed the war and "was always for peace". He was not a very trustworthy witness, therefore.' Evans, 2002, pp 62–63.

9   Guttenplan, 2002, p 181.

10 Guttenplan, 2002, p 181.

He said that they recorded only very small traces of cyanide in the gas chamber remains and relatively large traces in the delousing chamber remains; therefore the gas chambers were never in fact gas chambers.[11] 'The report was flawed rubbish,' said Rampton, Lipstadt's barrister. 'It was pioneering work, even though it has been superseded. Leuchter was barking up the right tree,' said Irving. Van Pelt said that the residues were different in the different types of gas chamber due to differences of heat and humidity levels when gassing people and clothing. The Leuchter report was, indeed, an amateurish report produced by a man with no expertise, either historical or forensic.[12] Irving admitted that it was fatally flawed, but he insisted that Leuchter was nevertheless right in his conclusions.

In his cross-examination, Irving grilled van Pelt on one document in particular, questioning its authenticity. He rattled off questions: about a serial number out of sequence, an incorrect rank for the signing officer, the initials of the typist (which Irving said existed on no other document), even the precise location of the margin. All these discrepancies, bragged Irving, suggested a forgery. 'This is where Irving is happiest, rolling around in swastika-embossed paper. He knows their mannerisms. On this terrain, Irving can be frighteningly convincing.'[13] In fact, after two days' research, van Pelt was able to authenticate the document, and to give satisfactory explanations for Irving's anomalies.

One of the strategies of the defence was to present documents deliberately ignored by Irving that showed things that he wished to deny. Irving responded either by calling them forgeries, or by claiming that he had never seen them and therefore could not be guilty of distorting them. This was not fundamentally a trial about the truth of the historical account of the Holocaust; it was a trial about David Irving's distortion. Thus Irving had to deny having read books that he owned, and even ones that he had commented upon in public, if they contained evidence that he claimed never to have known about.

The other expert reports produced by the defence were written by Christopher Browning, by Peter Longerich, whose account detailed evidence concerning the Holocaust outside Auschwitz, by Jaho Funke, whose report examined Irving's contemporary links with neo-Nazis in Germany, and by Richard Evans, whose report examined Irving's historiographical methodology.

Browning said that the total number of Jewish victims in the Holocaust was between five and six million. A good approximation could be made for the numbers from Poland and westwards, but there is more uncertainty about the figure in the Soviet Union, since records, both Russian prewar records and Nazi records during the war, were not as accurate as in Europe. Irving spent much time in cross-examination of Browning trying to dispute these figures. He tried to suggest to Browning that the Madagascar plan (to send all the Jews

---

11 Shapiro, 1990.
12 Leuchter 'had taken great chunks out of the wall instead of scrapings off the surface, thus greatly diluting whatever residues were to be found there. Even more crass, he had also ignored the fact that the concentration of cyanide gas needed to kill humans was far lower than that needed to kill lice in clothing, and so failed to understand that, far from disproving the existence of the gas chamber as an instrument of murder, his findings actually tended to confirm it'. Evans, 2002, p 133.
13 Freedland, 2000.

from the Reich to Madagascar) might have been a good one. Browning argued that it could have been attempted only if the British had been defeated, so that the Nazis could use shipping safely. Anyway, argued Browning, it was only ever a bizarre fantasy; the results would have been disastrous, and a large percentage of the people would have perished in an SS-run state. Irving replied: 'I think the Jews are a very sturdy people.' Irving argued that there had been no explicit reference to killing at the Wannsee conference; Browning argued that there were a number of passages whose meaning was viewed by most people as 'transparent'.

Richard Evans was not a Holocaust specialist, but a specialist in German political history and in historiographical methodology. Evans claims that he began the investigation into Irving's work with an open mind; he was paid by the hour, he said, and not for his conclusions.[14] Irving based his books on primary sources; he is proud not to rely on the work of other historians. On a first reading, said Evans, Irving's books appear entirely plausible. However, he and his research students had carried out a most detailed and painstaking investigation into Irving's sources. They followed up each reference, found the documents to which they referred, and checked them. Evans found that every piece of Irving's work that they examined in this way, not just those that referred to the Holocaust but others that they examined as a control, turned out to be a 'tissue of small manipulations' rendering his entire output 'absolutely worthless'. An example Evans gave was drawn from Irving's account of the main trial at Nuremberg. Irving claimed that Biddle, a judge at Nuremberg, had commented about a witness in his diary, 'all this I do not believe'. So in Irving's work all the testimony of this witness was invalidated. When the reference was checked by Evans, he found that the truth was that Biddle had in fact said 'this I do not believe', clearly referring to a particular piece of the witness's testimony, and emphatically not to the rest, which he certainly did believe. Irving had inserted the word 'all' and changed the entire meaning of the original.

Another example of Irving's distortion of the historical record was his treatment of a document known as the 'Schlegelberger memorandum'. Irving used it in the 1991 edition of *Hitler's War* to show that Hitler could not have ordered a policy of genocide against the Jews.[15] The document included the apparently startling information that 'the *Führer* had repeatedly explained … that he wanted the solution of the Jewish Question put back until after the war'.[16] This undated and unsigned document was found in a file that had been put together from Ministry of Justice papers after the war. Evans showed how the accepted explanation for this document amongst historians was that it was part of a discussion being held after the Wannsee Conference about the fate of 'half-Jews' and Jews in 'mixed marriages'. This explanation fits well with other documents from the same file, and with a meeting between Franz Schlegelberger and Hans Heinrich Lammers which took place on 10 April 1942. It may, on the other hand, argued Evans, date from the summer of 1941, when no fixed plan had yet been made for the 'final solution' and when the end of the war was thought to be only weeks away. Irving was pretending to

---

14 Evans, 2002.
15 As discussed in Evans, 2002, p 89.
16 Evans, 2002, p 89.

his readers that this document proved Hitler's lack of culpability for the genocide, while he knew full well that it had in fact 'long been regarded by professional historians as [proving] nothing of the kind'.[17]

After the trial, Evans presented an interesting point of view in relation to the often repeated argument in the press that a courtroom is no place to be discussing and judging academic debate. Evans said that the rules and facilities of the courtroom were, in fact, very helpful. In court, time was unlimited. If Evans wanted to dispute the meaning of the precise placing of a full stop in a document with Irving, for example, then he could do it; and he could do it for hours, until he had made his point. This, Evans, remarked, was not always possible in an academic seminar. Also, he said, the transcripting process in the court was invaluable. It created an accurate record of what had been said. If someone claimed they had not said something that they had in fact said, if they changed their story subtly, then this could easily be shown in the transcript. The court had resources of time, people and money that are not usually available to academics.

Evans concluded that Irving's methodology is informed by the fact that Irving thinks that he already knows the real truth; given this fact, the documents may be manipulated a little in order that they should show this true picture. Irving's work could not be regarded as history because it consistently asserted things that the documents did not allow as possibilities. There is vast space for debate and disagreement within the parameters of what the historical evidence allows as possibilities; but Irving was not at all constrained by the documents that he knew so well.

The defence spent some time showing Irving's motivation. Evans, Browning and van Pelt had shown how he consistently lied about the historical evidence; the defence now showed that the reason he did this was that he was a racist, and was motivated by a wish to exculpate the Nazi regime and specifically Adolf Hitler. His political project was to deny that the Nazis carried out the genocide, and to show that, in any case, Hitler had not ordered one. This is the first step in the rehabilitation of the *Führer* and his ideas. The defence found many examples of Irving's racism. One of the most striking perhaps was from a passage in Irving's diary in which he says that he sang a rhyme to his nine-month-old baby daughter Jessica when 'half-breed' children were wheeled past them in their prams:

I am a baby Aryan
Not Jewish or sectarian
I have no plans to marry an
Ape or Rastafarian.

Another example of Irving's racism was gleaned from a transcript of a speech that he had made to his friends in the 'Clarendon Club'. He regretted that newsreaders at the BBC no longer wore dinner jackets when they read the news. He suggested that on the BBC, in future, a newsreader in a dinner jacket should read the serious news, then a lady should read the less important news, the gossip about showbusiness and so on, and then Trevor McDonald[18] should present the latest news about muggings and drug busts. 'I wish I could go to Heathrow and get on a plane and land back in England as it was when I was

---

17 Evans, 2002, p 94.
18 Trevor McDonald is a well known black newsreader.

born in 1938,' he mused in a speech. He feels 'queasy' because there are black cricketers in the England team:

> I was speaking about what a pity it is we have to have blacks on the team and they are better than our whites. I say it's a pity because I am English … I call it patriotism … patriotism is pride in a country that has been handed to you by your fathers. I don't think there is anything despicable or disreputable about patriotism …

The defence spent two days at the trial cross-examining Irving over his racist speeches and writings. Irving laughed it all off as fun, or as patriotism.

One of the most telling pieces of evidence against Irving was a video recording of a speech that he made in Tampa, Florida, in October 1995. It was organised by the National Alliance, an American Nazi group. Jaho Funke testified that Irving had spoken at eight of their events between 1990 and 1998. Irving denied knowing who had organised the meeting, even though there was a very large National Alliance symbol visible close to him, and the meeting had been introduced by a man who welcomed the audience to the National Alliance event. The speech contained many unpleasant examples of Holocaust denial, racism and antisemitism. But the recording of the speech also showed, quite clearly, that David Irving considers himself to be part of the movement. He uses the word 'we' often. *We* are making progress; *we* are beginning to cast doubt on the Holocaust legend; *we* are engaged in a heroic struggle for truth. Irving was speaking to his comrades.

Funke, a political scientist from the Free University of Berlin, wrote a 140-page report for the defence about Irving's links with neo-Nazis in Germany. Using video clips of footage of Irving speaking in German at far right events, Funke identified an assortment of leading extremists and neo-Nazis who had also been present. Skinheads in boots were shown marching to a rally in Halle in 1991, where Irving was one of the speakers. When he spoke they were heard to shout '*Sieg Heil*'. 'Did you see me put my hand up to tell them to stop?' Irving queried. He went on to suggest that he had been 'shocked' by some of his audience. 'Did you get the impression that I was overjoyed? Was I happy?' he asked. Funke retorted that Irving had known the character of the event.

Funke's report said that Irving had strong and consistent connections with many German neo-Nazi organisations between 1990 and 1993. Some groups were subsequently banned for inciting racial hatred. 'How could I have anticipated … that they would be banned?' asked Irving. 'As an intelligent man who knows German, you could have known,' replied Funke.

Funke told the court that Irving had said at a press conference in Berlin that 'it is a defamation of the German people if one talks of extermination camps or death camps'. Irving said he was misquoted. Funke said that 'Mr Irving committed himself wholeheartedly to the cause of revisionism, and thus neo-Nazism, in Germany'. For 10 years, until he was banned from Germany in 1993, he was in a political alliance with the German People's Union, an antisemitic party, and its leader Gerhard Frey.

Irving denied joining a toast to a 'certain statesman' to mark what would have been his 101st birthday at a 1990 Munich dinner. 'I had no glass as I don't drink. If one has no glass and one doesn't drink, how can one toast?' A characteristic example of the arrogance of Irving; he uses this childish logical trick and assumes that everyone is forced, against their will, to the conclusion that nothing can be proved against him.

Irving claimed in the case that many Jews died while working and were not murdered; he asked why there were doctors and hospitals at Auschwitz if it was an extermination camp. Peter Longerich replied that the policy of 'extermination through work' was illustrated by the 'death audits' maintained by the camp authorities. The duty of Nazi doctors was not to keep inmates alive but to keep their effectiveness as a workforce as high as possible.

Speaking later,[19] Anthony Julius downplayed the importance of the *Irving* case; no new knowledge or insight came out of it; his side had not wanted the case to happen at all; it was important only to Irving's side. Therefore the case would have been very important if Irving had won it. Julius also argued that the written judgment, a 334-page document, gave the case some importance because of its clarity, detail and authority. From his point of view, something good came out of the case in the end. What he felt had been achieved was this newly authoritative narrative that gave the truth of the events of the Holocaust, and of David Irving's distortions, to the world and to future generations.[20]

The legal construction of cosmopolitan social memory

If the cosmopolitan project is to have successes, some of the mythology that underpins the ideologies of nationalism must be undercut. These mythologies of nationalism are produced and reproduced through the telling and retelling of particular national narratives, and through the suppression of others. English nationalists, for example, are much happier telling themselves stories about surviving Viking and Norman invasions and victory in two world wars than they are about the racist exploitation of the inhabitants of their former colonies. Some stories are distorted into glorious myth, while others are quietly forgotten.

One institution of the nation state that plays a part in producing and reproducing myths of nationhood is the legal system. Every trial is a drama, a story; each has a *dénouement* where the judge pronounces the verdict, the judgment, the truth. The truth that the judge pronounces is a national truth.

---

19 Julius, 2000.
20 There was a strange parallel to the *Lipstadt v Irving* case being heard in the same building at the same time. Independent Television News (ITN) was suing the magazine *Living Marxism* for libel. *Living Marxism* had published an article about the breaking of the story of Omarska and Trnopolje in the Western news media. ITN journalist Penny Marshall and her cameraman, Jeremy Irvin, accompanied by Channel 4 journalist Ian Williams and Ed Vulliamy from *The Guardian*, had been the first journalists to see and report on the camps. The journalists had shot some videotape on 5 August 1992 from which was reproduced a well known picture showing an emaciated Muslim prisoner at Trnopolje, called Fikret Alic, behind a barbed wire fence. The media made much of this picture because of its obvious similarities to images of emaciated prisoners from Nazi concentration camps. 'The barbed wire in the picture is not around the Bosnian Muslims; it is around the cameraman and the journalists,' wrote Thomas Deichmann in *Living Marxism*. The article went on to argue that the picture and the account of the camps had been invented by the journalists in order to propagate the myth of Serbian concentration camps in Bosnia. This case of left wing 'denial' of the Serbian campaign of ethnic cleansing and terror was shorter and simpler than the *Irving* case, and received much less publicity. ITN and the journalists wanted to defend their reputations, and to defend the truth of their 'scoop'. Their story, indeed, had been a profoundly important one for the public understanding of the war and for public pressure on the UN. The case was heard before a jury and was won by the journalists. The damages that were awarded bankrupted *Living Marxism*.

The citizens must be protected from this dangerous criminal; the publication of that official document is not in the national interest; this strike is unconstitutional; that publication is obscene. Courts themselves play a significant role in the production of narratives that define the nation. The narratives that they produce are official narratives; they carry extra weight because they have at their disposal certain state resources and powers. So what kind of narratives do cosmopolitan courts produce and reproduce? An important part of their function must be to produce cosmopolitan narratives; narratives of the type that can play their part in undercutting myths of nationhood. There are, of course, many other sources of cosmopolitan narrative, as there are other sources of national myths; yet cosmopolitan courts also speak with a particular authority. It is an authority that is derived from their foundations in the discourse of human rights and in internationally agreed legal rules and norms. Cosmopolitan courts have a role in mediating between the claims of competing nationalisms that renders them well suited to the production of authoritative cosmopolitan narratives.

Nationalism, as Ernest Gellner[21] has argued, is a doctrine that holds the nation state to be the natural unit of political and social organisation. The term 'nation state' is notoriously difficult to define. It is based on the idea that people are naturally divided into nations, and that these nations achieve self-determination, self-rule, through their own sets of political structures, their own states. There have been many attempts to define the nation in terms of sets of criteria, for example Joseph Stalin's 1912 definition:

> A nation is a historically evolved, stable community of language, territory, economic life and psychological makeup manifested in a community of culture.[22]

Yet these criteria are 'fuzzy, shifting and ambiguous',[23] and it is easy to think of examples of 'nations' that lack one or more of these criteria. This difficulty of defining the objective existence of the referent of the world 'nation' focuses attention back onto nationalism as an ideology, and onto the nation state.

There is agreement in the sociological writing on nationalism that nations and nation states are modern phenomena, no more than one or two centuries old; this finding is, of course, starkly at odds with the claim of all nationalisms to be age-old communities that stretch back into the mists of time. Moreover, 'nations' are more the creation of 'states' than the other way round; the emergence of groups of people who feel a national belonging with each other was in fact the result of, not the cause of, the development of the modern state.

Benedict Anderson's[24] anthropological approach to the question emphasises the fact that the nation state is bound together by the telling and retelling of myth. The use of the term 'myth' in this context highlights the sacred or pseudo-sacred nature of the narratives. They are narratives that social actors, consciously and unconsciously, have succeeded in imbuing with that sacred quality. Nations are imagined communities, first because they are based on myths of foundation and of common history, and secondly because they are so large that the relationship of one citizen with others can only be mediated by ritual, by printed communication and through the mass media. A nation

---

21 Gellner, 1983.
22 Cited in Hobsbawm, 1995, p 5.
23 Hobsbawm, 1995, p 6.
24 Anderson, 1995.

forges an identity through telling itself stories. Stories give a sense of direction and continuity, and therefore identity and community.

Kevin Foster uses the term 'myth':

> ... to describe a chain of associated concepts, usually rendered as a narrative, by which individuals and communities mediate their personal and collective anxieties and through which they are able to understand, express and communicate to themselves and others a sense of their identity as members of specific social, cultural and national groups.[25]

Foster discusses the forging of myth in relation to the Falklands War and British identity. He argues that accounts of the war assumed a classically mythic form, in Roland Barthes' terms, by making 'a historical intention a natural justification, and [making] contingency appear eternal'. The decision to go to war and the conduct of the war were presented as an expression of the essential character of the British nation: there had been no other possibilities. The Britain that turned defeat into victory at Dunkirk and that developed the Blitz spirit could only have gone to war in the Falklands, and could only have emerged victorious. The image of the heroic, modest but invincible British soldier is not only derived from myths of Britishness but also bolsters those myths. Foster focuses on the Falklands War as a struggle for ideological rather than physical terrain.[26]

Given that nation states are the ubiquitous form of political community in our time, and that nationalism relies heavily on the creation of myths of nationhood, then much of the writing about social memory focuses on its nationalistic character. Narratives of nationhood are one of the pillars upon which nation states are built and maintained. While the narratives speak of timeless community, stretching back into the mists of history, the narratives themselves, like the nations they constitute, are much more flexible than they appear. Which narratives are to be told, which are to be heard, which are to be accepted as national truth; these are questions of the utmost political importance. There is always political controversy about how history and religion are taught in schools; how are narratives of nationhood to be taught to the next generation?

Norman Cigar[27] argues that the processes of narrative creation occurred very quickly in the former Yugoslavia at the end of the 1980s. It was the conscious strategy of the nationalists to create and recreate ancient myths of nationhood, to rewrite and retell the glorious history of Serbia or of Croatia. Cigar argues that, contrary to the widely accepted myths that so quickly came to be regarded as common sense in the late 1980s, 'Islamic-Christian co-existence, not genocide against the Serbs, was the rule during the 500 years of Ottoman presence'.[28] In the 1980s, the Serbian nationalists brought the myth of heroic Serbian martyrdom to the fore; Serbia had been the victim of many centuries of Islamic domination. The idea of a Greater Serbia, as the only way for Serbs to avoid this continuing domination, had been a core idea of the Serbian nationalists since the 19th century. Now, the Serbian nationalists were on the rise, and an important part of their work was to imbue Serbs with a

---

25 Foster, 1999, p 2.
26 Foster, 1999.
27 Cigar, 1995.
28 Cigar, 1995, p 12.

particular narrative of their past. In 1986, the Serbian Academy of Arts and Sciences, an organisation of Serbia's leading intellectuals, produced the 'Serbian memorandum', which argued that the Serbian people had been denied their destiny of a Greater Serbia following the Second World War by the communists; Greater Serbia was a democratic right, and was the only political programme for freedom. The Serbian nationalists wove narratives of ancient victories and defeats, of Ottoman, and therefore Turkish, Muslim, domination.

In 1989, Milosevic went to Kosovo, and with much rhetoric concerning the battle of Kosovo of 1389, 500 years earlier, he proclaimed the end of Kosovar domination over the Serbs. Similarly, the nationalists focused on remembrance of the pro-Nazi Croatian Ustasa atrocities during the Second World War. The wars in the former Yugoslavia have often been presented in the Western media as the result of age-old conflict in the Balkans. Yet, as Cigar shows, it was in fact a conscious reconfiguration and repopularisation of the narratives of age-old conflict in the late 1980s by the nationalists that helped to energise the people for the wars of conquest and ethnic cleansing. Timeless myth can be changed very quickly by purposive political action. The project of imbuing particular social memories with a sacred and eternal quality is central to the political work of nationalists.

Crimes against humanity, ethnic cleansing and genocide are inevitably preceded by this political work of creating and consolidating timeless narratives. How can these genocidal and mythical social memories be replaced, fought against, or superseded?

In this book I have been surveying a facet of the tentative emergence of cosmopolitan law. There is emerging a body of law and a set of institutions that is developing the ability to try those responsible for violations of international humanitarian law, crimes against humanity, ethnic cleansing and genocide. Such trials are important in themselves, in order to hold to account those who commit such crimes, and to deter others from committing them. But in order to do this, a trial has first to establish a true picture of the events under investigation. This function of finding truth is a particularly important one in the field of crimes against humanity. One of the central purposes of the Nuremberg tribunals was, particularly within Germany, to publicise the truth about what the Nazis had done;[29] similarly the International Criminal Tribunal for the former Yugoslavia (ICTY) aims to show clearly what the nature of the genocide and the ethnic cleansing was. The *Tadic* judgment is a long and closely argued document showing how the war started in Bosnia, how the politics of the communities evolved, how ethnic cleansing and genocide was possible, how it was carried out, and who was responsible. The trial was about

---

29 '[At Nuremberg] Justice was served, but, above everything else, in a strange way, in a dark poetic way, it was memory that was confronted and celebrated at Nuremberg. When hundreds and hundreds of witnesses emerged to piece together a story – a story that we all must remember, although our memory and our mind and our soul are too small to comprehend it, to take it all in. Our sanity was at stake. If we remembered everything, we would lose our minds. But then, if we don't remember everything, we also lose our minds. Nuremberg, therefore, was the repository of testimony. Hundreds, thousands, hundreds of thousands of documents were introduced in evidence in Nuremberg. Thus, it was an important and meaningful event. For the first time, I think, it gave memory such an exposure. Now we know that if there is one word among others that also symbolised the dark years of that tragedy that has no pertinent name, it is *Memory*.' Elie Wiesel, Inaugural Raoul Wallenberg Lecture: Cotler, 1995, pp 15–16.

more than Tadic. It was about producing a version of the truth of what happened; a version that claims authority because it is produced by an impartial cosmopolitan court according to the rules, methods and traditions of international law.

Legal processes of finding truth claim a particular authority since they have the right to impose sanctions on those who are found guilty. Their decisions are implemented by the use or threat of legitimated violence. The process that we can see happening in the emergence of cosmopolitan law is also in part a process of the development of a cosmopolitan social collective memory. Courts receive particular and contradictory testimony; they act upon this according to their own rules, and produce a single narrative. Cosmopolitan courts receive nationally particularistic narratives as testimony that they transform into an authoritative cosmopolitan social memory.

The Sawoniuk trial demonstrates this process very clearly. The narratives that the witnesses brought to the court were all heavily influenced by their own national social memories. The subject matter that was under investigation by the court, the Holocaust and the Second World War, is centrally important to the national myths of Israel, Belorus, Poland, Britain, Germany, the USSR and Russia. All the nation states involved in the trial have different tellings of the story of the war and the Holocaust, and these tellings are central to the ways in which they produce and reproduce their national identities. To have an identity is to have a story; a story that gives a sense of direction and a sense of continuity. The way in which a nation involved in these events understands its role in the Second World War and the Holocaust is one of the most crucial determinants of its national identity. These stories were told and developed for 56 years before the trial; and then the witnesses, imbued with their own national versions of the big picture, came to court to give evidence on matters intimately connected to central myths of their own nationhood.

When Ben-Zion Blustein tells his personal story, he is also telling the founding myth of the state of Israel. His childhood was spent in an uneasy co-existence with the majority community, which tolerated him but which was always liable to intolerance; his family, and almost every Jew he knew, was murdered by the invaders with the complicity of that majority community; by a combination of great toughness, good luck, bravery, stubbornness, guile and intelligence he managed to survive the genocide. After the genocide, Blustein was one of those pioneers who built the homeland; a land where Jews could be genuinely free, where they could make the desert bloom …

Sawoniuk was born in poor but proud Poland. During his childhood it was invaded first by the USSR; they closed down all private businesses and shops; they caused Sawoniuk, and Poland, increased hardship and hunger; and in place of food and prosperity they provided party men and propaganda. The Germans invaded briefly in 1939, only to withdraw from that part of Poland and allow the Russians to reoccupy. They invaded again after two years of terrible poverty and terror under Stalinist rule. Poland was a plaything in the hands of the Great Powers across its borders. Sawoniuk joined the police in order to protect his town and his country from communist and Jewish enemies who wanted to kill, exploit and enslave ordinary people like himself; enemies who in fact killed his first wife in a raid on the police station. Sawoniuk's story was prevented from becoming central to the official collective memory of Poland because of the military defeat of the Nazis; it was prevented partly by the Nuremberg tribunals themselves, and also by the successor trials, the latest of which was the one in London.

Belorus is a small nation that emerged out of the old USSR. It has a history of occupation by Russia, Poland and Germany. During the last German occupation there was a proud and heroic resistance that fought against the brutal occupiers; Sawoniuk was a collaborator with those occupiers, implementing their indiscriminate and bloody suppression of the popular partisan movement. Fedor Zan's uncle, aunt and cousins were murdered in a raid in which Sawoniuk participated. Borisy, where the Belorussian witnesses came from, was a partisan village. This spirit of Belorussian patriotism was subsumed under Soviet domination until 1989, when the independent nation re-emerged, one which was finding a voice of its own in the international community.

Perhaps an additional nationalist mythology that impacted on the Sawoniuk trial was a British one. The wood-panelled courtroom; the wigs of the court officials; the impeccable manners of John Nutting and William Clegg; the history of the 'Old Bailey': these all told of British fair play, understatedness and reasonableness. English law allowed only charges of murder 'against the common law'; nothing continental or ideological like crimes against humanity or genocide. Britain did not allow itself to be invaded during the war; and it was central in the defeat of Nazi Germany. However, notwithstanding the heroic role that it played, Britain is not a place for show trials …

Another form of narrative presented to the court was that given by Chris Browning; a narrative created by the norms and rules of academic historiography. This tradition aims to take all the available evidence, documents, eye witness testimony, trial transcripts, other historiography, and, carefully, methodically and disinterestedly, to build up the best picture of the truth that the evidence allows.

It was the task of the court to hear testimony that was necessarily informed by these differing narratives, to process it and work on it according to its own legal rules and norms, and to produce a judgment that was free of these contradictory nationalist influences. It is as if a cosmopolitan court is a machine whose inputs are national narratives, but whose output is a single cosmopolitan one. The hardware of the machine is a set of developing cosmopolitan institutions; the software is the developing body of cosmopolitan law and the increasingly clear and precise body of rules, procedures and precedents that are being produced by the institutions.

Crimes against humanity are exactly the kinds of events which national social memories make, and of which they are made. In order for them to occur in the first place, there are inevitably sophisticated and widely held narratives that tell why the other group needs to be disposed of. The Jews have, through the ages, been the cause of Germany's defeats and problems; the Muslims in Bosnia have, through the ages, been collaborators with the invaders against the Serbs; the Tutsi in Rwanda have been, through the ages, the oppressors of the Hutu. This is one of the central reasons why international courts are necessary. It is necessary to create institutions to deal with these crimes that have some chance of raising themselves out of myths of nationhood and ethnic superiority. When a group or a nation has survived such severe disasters as genocide and ethnic cleansing, it weaves the narratives of these disasters into its own tapestry of identity. When a court comes to address these events, it is forced to attempt to abstract the story of what happened from its powerful embeddedness in narratives that are central to conflicting national identities.

A central task of the ICTY is to carry out this work. It hears evidence wrapped up in Croatian, Bosniak and Serbian narratives; it also hears academic evidence. It is also able to hear evidence from organisations that are self-consciously trying to be cosmopolitan, to differing extents, such as NGOs and UN peacekeeping forces. The rules and norms by which it constructs a cosmopolitan narrative are those of cosmopolitan law. The ICTY is engaged in the task of creating and building those rules and norms. It is borrowing principles and procedures from different legal traditions and binding them into a body of law and precedent. It produces judgments that are, literally, in the form of narratives.

The *Kristic* judgment,[30] for example, finding Kristic guilty of genocide in Srebrenica, is another remarkable document. In a little over 100 pages of text, it contains 1,519 footnotes. Every assertion is backed up by evidence from the trial or other sources. It outlines the origins of the war in Bosnia; it tells the story of the siege and the cleansing of the town; it focuses on the Drina corps, of which Kristic was Chief of Staff, and its role in the genocide; it focuses on Kristic himself, and his role in the corps. A court is not a bad place to produce an authoritative narrative. It has time, and is relatively well resourced; it has the expertise of defence and prosecution lawyers and investigators, a panel of judges, translators and transcriptors; and it has the power to call witnesses and experts.

The judgment in the *Irving* case could also be seen as a remarkable cosmopolitan narrative. Irving often attempted to present himself as an English nationalist rather than a neo-Nazi, but the narrative of Englishness that he attempted to present was an unusual one. In court, and also in a television interview with Jeremy Paxman on the night of the verdict, he presented his racism as nothing more than a genuine expression of English patriotism:

Paxman: You said in your diary that you recited [the verse 'I am a baby Aryan'] as you passed a half-breed.

Irving: Yes indeed.

P: What is a half-breed?

I: It's something that didn't exist in England at the time that I was born here, shall we say?

P: A half-breed, you would accept, is a term of racial categorisation?

I: I think you're absolutely right.

P: As is Aryan?

I: You're absolutely right.

P: And you're seriously trying to maintain that there's nothing racist about this verse?

I: It's a vestige of English patriotism in me and of my Englishness, not of racism. I think you'll find that 95% of English people of my generation hold exactly the same attitude.

---

30 *Prosecutor v Kristic.*

P: I have never heard 95% of people of your generation reciting racist verse like that.

I: You've got to be able to write good verse, yes.[31]

Irving portrays his version of English nationalism as 'genuine', the view of the silent 95%, rather than the 'official' post-Second World War version of the 'traitors' like Lord Hailsham, whose treachery consisted in advising the British cabinet in 1958 not to bring in immigration controls. The official version is the multiculturalist one that emerged after the (mistaken) war against Hitler (who, incidentally, knew nothing about the final solution). Events during that war, such as the mass campaign of aerial bombing of German cities, were presented by the official narrative of Englishness as heroic military victories. This made it necessary for Irving's 'genuine' history of the bombing of Dresden to be written, which showed that when England was run by the 'traitors' it committed atrocities far greater than those committed by England's genuine friends. It only requires David Irving to show the 95% of honest English racists the true history of the Second World War for them to see through the official nonsense and revert to their instinctual racism. Thus, if only Irving could explain the truth clearly enough, everything would revert to its natural state. He told Paxman:

> [T]hose who were in the courtroom will remember today that at the end of the trial I said to the judge that I have to apologise for the fact that I have failed to express myself with sufficiently articulate language so that you have understood the historical problems with which you are confronted in this case.[32]

To what extent Irving believes in his alternative version of English nationalism, rather than in some sort of German nationalism or supra-national Nazism, is not clear. In Irving's narrative, there is a convergence between English and German nationalisms; his rewriting of history was also a rewriting of German history and of Germany's historical relationship with England. Its logic is that there should have been no war between racial brothers.

In court, Irving's strange narrative of English and German nationalism, and of the nationalism of the white race, was being judged against an academic historiographical narrative; one that the Nazis might have called a Jewish cosmopolitan narrative.

It could be argued that the court was not a cosmopolitan one, but rather one that represented the official history of Englishness against Irving's dissident version. But it was the nature of the subject matter and the nature of the evidence presented by the Lipstadt legal team that pushed the British court onto a cosmopolitan terrain. The crimes of the Nazi regime were committed throughout Europe; they had already been the subject of the Nuremberg tribunals; the claims of the Holocaust deniers are not bounded by any national boundaries; Irving's commentary was daily put on his website and accessed globally; and trials similar to this had occurred in other jurisdictions, such as criminal trials for the crime of Holocaust denial in Germany or the *Zundel* case in Canada. Lipstadt is an American whose book had been published all over the world. She had been sued in England because that was where Irving thought he had the greatest chance of success. The expert witnesses were

---

31 *Newsnight*, BBC 2, 12 April 2000.
32 *Newsnight*, BBC 2, 12 April 2000.

American, Dutch, English and German. Many factors, therefore, contributed to the British court taking on some of the characteristics of a supra-national one.

But we are left with a paradox. Is not legal discourse itself, and the narratives that it produces, equally susceptible to deconstruction? In this book we have already examined examples of the insensitivity and the arbitrariness of legal discourse. In the *Sawoniuk* case much relevant evidence, including some survivor testimony and some documents, was ruled inadmissible by the judge who closed the ears of the jury to it. At the ICTY the judges, to an extent, self-consciously create the rules as they go along. In the *Irving* case, Irving was alone while Lipstadt had the backing of a large corporation, an extensive legal team, five leading academics and their research assistants. The charge is that the legal discourse, and the rules that govern trials, create only a different method of producing narrative, not necessarily a better one.

Law is not outside or above society, even if its own rhetoric requires that it appear to be so. Legal language, argues Peter Goodrich, 'like any other language usage, is a social practice and … its texts will necessarily bear the imprint of such practice or organisational background'. He goes on to say that we should treat legal discourse as an 'accessible and answerable discourse, as a discourse that is inevitably responsible for its place and role within the ethical, political and sexual commitments of its times'.[33] Certainly the narratives produced by cosmopolitan courts are not, in some absolute sense, 'the truth'. But neither, in fact, do they claim to be. They claim to be 'judgments'.

There are many ways of producing truth: law, fiction, journalism, art, memoir, historiography, religion, science, astrology. All have their own rules, methods and norms, but also their own claims and purposes. If we understand these different approaches to truth-finding as social processes, then we do not have to judge that one is authentic and the others fake; but nor do we have to judge that they are all equally valid. While they overlap, they all have distinct objectives and ways of operating.

Reiko Tachibana makes use of Michel Foucault's concept of 'counter-memory', which Foucault puts forward as an alternative to '[t]he traditional devices for constructing a comprehensive view of history and for retracing the past as a patient and continuous development', a view that 'must be systematically dismantled'.[34] Tachibana focuses on the work of post-war German and Japanese authors who write 'counter-memory': who do not seek to create all-embracing historical narratives, but who instead write de-centred and incomplete accounts that 'emphasise the subjectivity and selective nature of any record of events'. Such writing, continues Tachibana, 'seeks a liberation of the reader from a dogmatic perspective on, or blindness towards, the legacies of the Second World War, aiming instead at provocation towards an active participation in history'.[35] Tachibana is interested in the ways in which authors such as Günter Grass and Ôe Kenzaburô have produced work that seeks to tell truths of histories of mass brutality in micro rather than macro voices. Tachibana tells how, in a letter Grass wrote to Ôe in 1995, he recollects the fact that 20,000 deserters from Hitler's armies were executed during the

---

33 Goodrich, 1987, p 2.
34 Foucault cited in Tachibana, 1998, p 1.
35 Tachibana, 1998, p 2.

war. They were hanged from trees with boards around their necks reading 'I am a coward'. These men, for Grass, should be remembered as the truly courageous heroes of Germany.[36] Ôe praised the Japanese writers who had been producing 'counter-memory' in the post-war period:

> In the history of modern Japanese literature, the writers most sincere in their awareness of a mission were the 'post-war school' of writers who came onto the literary scene deeply wounded by the catastrophe of war yet full of hope for a rebirth. They tried with great pain to make up for the atrocities committed by Japanese military forces in Asia, as well as to bridge the profound gaps that existed not only between the developed nations of the West and Japan but also between African and Latin American countries and Japan. Only by doing so did they think that they could seek with some humility reconciliation with the rest of the world.[37]

Memoir, fiction and historiography are three irreplaceable methods of telling truthful stories about totalitarianism. Cosmopolitan law is another. Law does not produce *the* truth, it produces *a* truth; it is not the antidote to totalitarianism, but is one method of fighting against it. If you want to know what happened at Srebrenica, and how many Muslim men were murdered when the town fell, then a good way of finding out is by reading the *Kristic* judgment;[38] if you want to know how many people were killed during the Holocaust, read the *Irving* judgment.[39] Different forms of representation have different strengths and tell different kinds of stories. Primo Levi[40] and Elie Wiesel[41] can communicate with an immediacy that gives us an idea of what it was like for them to be taken from their homes to Auschwitz. Claude Lanzmann's film, *Shoah*, which begins by showing Simon Srebnik revisiting Chelmno, where he was forced to sing folk songs to Nazis as a young boy, as well as burn the remains of those gassed in their vans, communicates with a different sort of immediacy.[42] None of these can show definitive truth, but they show different aspects of the whole. All such forms of representation demand to be read critically, with a focus on what they are, where they come from and what kind of truth they aim to tell.

During the Sawoniuk trial, Ben-Zion Blustein wanted to give his testimony. He wanted to tell what it was like when nearly everyone he knew was killed one day; he wanted to tell what it was like to see his family try to commit suicide; he wanted to tell us that we must believe that such things really happened. The court had a different aim: it needed to judge, beyond reasonable doubt, whether Sawoniuk was guilty of particular crimes. Blustein certainly knows better than any of us what it was like for him. The strength of the legal process is that it aims to bring together different forms of evidence for a particular purpose: to guard against the danger of convicting an innocent person. Because the legal process has such severe safeguards built in, it produces, as a by-product, its distinctive form of authoritative narrative.

36 Tachibana, 1998, p 6.
37 Ôe Kenzaburô in his Nobel Prize acceptance speech in Stockholm in 1994: quoted in Tachibana, 1998, p 250.
38 *Prosecutor v Kristic*.
39 *Irving v Lipstadt* judgment.
40 Levi, 1987.
41 Wiesel, 1981.
42 Lanzmann, 1985.

Lawrence Douglas[43] is critical of Hannah Arendt[44] for arguing that the main business of the Eichmann trial – the weighing of charges brought against the accused, the rendering of judgment and the meting out of due punishment – was in danger of being undermined by the court's wish to accomplish other purposes as well, such as education, the writing of history and the creation of a forum to host survivor testimony.[45] Douglas argues that Holocaust trials have rightly been concerned with these broader issues as well as focusing on the particular guilt or innocence of the accused. This dispute is apparently about the weight that the two writers assign to the different functions of the trials. But Arendt, in fact, certainly did appreciate the Eichmann trial as a forum for setting out an authoritative narrative of the events of the final solution: most of her book on the trial is taken up with a repeated presentation of the evidence presented in Jerusalem of the detailed picture of the genocide across Europe. And Douglas certainly does admit that 'the primary responsibility of a criminal trial is to resolve questions of guilt in a procedurally fair manner'.[46] For Arendt, it is the foundation of the fair procedure, designed to resolve questions of guilt, upon which the value of the narrative produced is based. For Douglas, the aim of doing justice to the defendant seems to be parallel to the other aims, rather than one upon which the subsidiary functions rest. 'The Eichmann trial,' he says, 'even more explicitly than Nuremberg, was staged to teach history and shape collective memory … This mindfulness of the past was meant, in turn, to support the Zionist politics of the present'.[47]

The question becomes not whether it is a legitimate function for a trial to have a role in shaping collective memory, but what kind of collective memory it shapes. Arendt's disquiet about the Eichmann trial was not about whether or not it had a function in educating people about the Holocaust. Rather it was about the tension that ran throughout the trial due to the court's constitution as a hybrid or transitional form between national and cosmopolitan. She defends Israel's right to kidnap and try Eichmann because a trial based on more cosmopolitan principles and institutions was not on the agenda. She criticises the prosecutor, Gideon Hausner, and the Prime Minister, David Ben Gurion, for trying to build the trial into the foundation of the nationalist collective memory of the state of Israel. She praises the judges for standing against that project and for limiting the court to the task of trying Adolf Eichmann. The methods that cosmopolitan trials use to come to their judgments are ones that seek to produce a narrative free from national particularity. But the Eichmann trial was also a national trial, dealing with a subject matter that was central to Israeli national identity. Arendt was not critical of the trial's function of producing authoritative narrative of the Holocaust; she was critical when Hausner tried to use it to tell an Israeli nationalist narrative about the foundation of the state.

By 1987, the Israeli legal system was ready to subordinate entirely the requirements of a fair trial to the requirements of restaging national drama. John Demjanjuk was accused of being 'Ivan the Terrible', a gas chamber operator at Treblinka. The trial 'turned into a drama of collective unburdening,

---

43 Douglas, 2001, p 2.
44 Arendt, 1994a.
45 This discussion of the Eichmann trial is indebted to Robert Fine's conference paper: Fine, 2002b.
46 Douglas, 2001, p 2.
47 Douglas, 2001, p 3.

a public rehashing of both the history of the Holocaust and the horrific tales of the survivors'.[48] But they had the wrong man. Demjanjuk was accused on the basis of a questionable identity card[49] that allegedly linked him to Sobibor; it was Treblinka survivors, however, who identified him as 'Ivan' on the basis of photospread identification procedures in which his photograph was about twice as large as the others and significantly clearer.[50]

Willem Wagenaar, a Dutch psychologist who had previously testified as an expert witness on the subject of memory at 40 trials, gave evidence for the defence, telling the court that the photospreads conducted in the *Demjanjuk* case lacked any evidential value.[51] Later he wrote that he knows of 'no other case in which so many deviations from procedures internationally accepted as desirable occurred'.[52] The court allowed spectators in the theatre where the trial was held to shout abuse at the defence lawyers and the defendant. Demjanjuk was convicted and sentenced to hang, but on appeal the conviction was overturned. Evidence from the crumbling Eastern Bloc, which the US Justice Department's Office of Special Investigations had known about at the time of the trial, showed that 'Ivan the Terrible' was, indeed, another man. The production of authoritative narrative is a by-product of procedurally and substantially fair trials; if the production of narrative is the central goal of a trial and justice is subordinated to it, then there can be no authoritative narrative.

There are two cosmopolitan tribunals, for Yugoslavia and Rwanda; the International Criminal Court is facing substantial opposition from the United States. In contrast, national legal systems are well developed across the world. There can be no question of waiting until some notional point in the future at which cosmopolitan courts become institutionally mature before proceeding with the business of conducting cosmopolitan trials. In this book I have discussed a number of examples of cosmopolitan trials being organised under national legal systems: the cases of *Irving*, *Sawoniuk*, *Eichmann* and *Demjanjuk*. Many other significant cosmopolitan cases[53] have also been tried in national courts. If Osama Bin Laden was captured, there would be no reason to oppose in principle a trial in the United States for crimes committed in New York and Washington DC. The key aspect of cosmopolitan trials is not the particular institutional shape that they take but the fact that they happen and they happen fairly, that they actualise the principles of cosmopolitan law. In the *Eichmann* case, the court successfully resisted pressure to bend towards the needs of Israeli nationalism; in the *Demjanjuk* case it did not. A supra-national cosmopolitan court is necessary to try cases where national legal systems are unable or unwilling to hold fair trials.

Whether actualised within the framework of a national or an international court, cosmopolitan law has the particular advantage of containing within

---

48 Douglas, 2001, p 98.

49 'The judges ignored the clearest evidence that the crucial documents (delivered to Israel from the Kremlin by the corrupt Dr Armand Hammer) ... were forgeries.' Robertson, 1999, p 223.

50 Sheftel, 1998.

51 Sheftel, 1998, p 164.

52 Wagenaar, 1988, p ix.

53 Such as the trial of Klaus Barbie in France; the trial of Ernst Zundel for Holocaust denial in Canada; the attempts to force General Pinochet to stand trial; and the whole host of national Nuremberg successor trials in Germany, Poland and other countries which had been occupied during the Second World War.

itself mechanisms that aim to rid judgments of national particularity; it also has a particularly concrete connection to the discourse of human rights. It contains mechanisms that aim to make it more reliable for its purposes than raw witness testimony or memoir. None of these mechanisms are perfect, none produce a result that can be regarded as absolute. But we do not expect law to be able to produce some sort of extrasocial absolute. The narratives that it does produce are imbued with a certain further social power; and perhaps they contain enough of the sacred to shake the certainty of eternal myths of nationhood and ethnic superiority.

Chapter Eight
Conclusion

Costas Douzinas tells how Spanish soldiers, in response to the Napoleonic invasion, unfurled banners that read 'Down With Freedom'. He suggests that the oppressed may soon be ready to raise the slogan 'Down With Human Rights'.[1] He understands the current supremacy of the rhetoric of universal rights to signify their weakness as a means by which ordinary people can seek to limit the power of state sovereignty. For Douzinas, the concept of human rights is at its strongest when it is understood as a contemporary form of natural law, sharing a 'common tradition of resistance and dissent from exploitation and degradation and a concern with a political and ethical utopia, the epiphany of which will never occur but whose principle can stand in judgment of the present law'.[2] He connects the triumph of human rights to the post-Cold War idea of the 'end of history'[3] that posits pragmatism as the only legitimate political framework and rejects ideology or utopia as naïve, dangerous and discredited. 'The end of human rights comes when they lose their utopian end.'[4]

Human rights may be useful for fighting tyranny and for conceiving of a better world, but for Douzinas those positives are greatly outweighed by the negative and destructive forces that are mobilised under their banner. The post-Second World War codification and institutionalisation of human rights in tribunals and charters is opposed by Douzinas to the self-organisation of those whose lives have been blighted by oppression or exploitation. He proposes to leave the UN and their diplomats to 'their standard setting and their lunches and return to the state or the community, the only territory where human rights are violated or protected'.[5] He follows Arendt in focusing on the plight of refugees who are denied even the right to have rights by virtue of their expulsion from their particular communities and the refusal of other communities to allow them to join. He re-emphasises the centrality of state sovereignty as the centrally important terrain for the battle over rights in a globalised world.

Douzinas does see clearly that the problem of exclusion is at the heart of the concept and the history of national communities and of a polity based on the rights of citizenship.[6] Yet he is unwilling to embrace a project of anchoring human rights, which do not have a foundation in the exclusion of non-citizens,

---

1 Douzinas, 2002.
2 Douzinas, 2000, p 380. Also: 'Human rights are the necessary and impossible claim of law to justice.' (Also from p 380.)
3 Fukuyama, 1992.
4 Douzinas, 2000, p 380.
5 Douzinas, 2000, p 145.
6 '... the modern subject reaches her humanity by acquiring political rights which guarantee her admission to the universal human nature, by excluding from that status those who do not have such rights. It is the law of the nation state which defines the alien as alien and the refugee as refugee. The alien is not a citizen. She does not have rights because she is not part of the state and she is a lesser human being because she is not a citizen ... To have citizens we must have aliens, to have a home or a home country others must not share it ...' Douzinas, 2000, p 142.

in supra-national institutions which have some power to enforce them. The more that human right gains an institutional and worldly existence, the less he likes it, since in that case it moves away from its utopian form as a measure of the existing world and into the compromised terrain of actuality.

Just as Arendt told us that the Rights of Man was compromised from its inception, due to its necessary realisation as the right of the citizen, so Douzinas tells us that human rights were always compromised by precisely the same link, that of rights with national sovereignty. The major powers, in the period of the post-war codification of human rights, he tells us, 'unanimously agreed that these rights could not be used to pierce the shield of national sovereignty'. The new body of human rights and humanitarian law, and the possibility of its institutional actualisation, was a promise made by the victorious powers not to replicate the crimes of the Nazis. It was a statement that they accepted that there was at least a basic minimum of human community. They needed to make that promise for purposes of legitimation, to draw a line under the old regime. Again, after 1989, the major powers renewed their commitment to the rhetoric of human rights in order to legitimate their victory over 'communism'. Douzinas says:

> The contradictory principles of human rights and national sovereignty, schizophrenically both paramount in post-war international law, served two separate agendas for the great powers: the need to legitimate the new order through its commitment to rights, without exposing the victorious states to scrutiny and criticism about their own flagrant violations ... Once again human rights were a main way for underpinning the power of states.[7]

For Douzinas, the use to which the great powers put the concept of human rights expresses the central truth of human rights. Their existence as cover for the ambitions of the powerful carries more weight than any other; their existence as an updated form of natural law against which we can measure the actual world is important, but only to the extent that it is kept clean, out of the compromised actuality of international law.

The thesis I have been arguing in this book is rather different. It is that the great powers, for purposes of legitimation, have allowed cosmopolitan law to emerge and have allowed it a certain institutional existence; they have always attempted to keep control of it and prevent it from attaining an independent existence; they will not always succeed in thus controlling it because that to which they are forced to agree for purposes of legitimation is precisely that which makes it possible for cosmopolitan law and its institutions to gain a life of their own.

The concept of crimes against humanity is powerful. Its acceptance by the major powers as a central part of international humanitarian law constitutes an acceptance that such crimes are the business of humanity as a whole. It is a recognition that there is no sovereign right to commit such crimes and that the claim made by cosmopolitan law, that it has jurisdiction within all sovereign states in relation to such crimes, is legitimate. The actuality of international tribunals competent to prosecute crimes against humanity underlines the validity and legitimacy of the concept.

The reason that cosmopolitan law cannot simply be wheeled out for purposes of legitimation and then pushed back when it interferes with the business of government is that it attains an independent existence from the

---

7   Douzinas, 2000, pp 118–19.

powers that allow it to develop. The need for legitimation is enduring; legitimation is not a project that is achieved, but one that is continually in need of renewal. Douzinas is right to say that the principles of human rights and sovereignty are contradictory; he is also right to say that they are both paramount in post-war international law and that they are intertwined principles that develop together. Yet his conclusion suggests that one is somehow more real, more enduring, more powerful than the other. He is not right to suggest that sovereign power is real while human rights exist only as epiphenomena, as tools that have the function of entrenching it. Legitimation is not just a trick; people are not so easily fooled.

The Rights of Man developed alongside the national state, which excluded non-citizens from rights; human rights developed alongside the principle of national sovereignty, which allowed states to ignore them. These are not questions of form and content or of phenomena and epiphenomena but of the dialectic that runs, in many different forms, throughout the heart of modernity. Both have a real and embattled existence. Cosmopolitan criminal law and human rights cannot be reduced to state power and sovereignty since they have emergent properties. They have the possibility to emerge as structures in a social reality with a certain independence of their own. There is a struggle between the powerful states, who have an interest in allowing them a limited but controllable independence, and the immense power that is immanent within the concept and actuality of cosmopolitan law.

This book has focused on an apparently institutional antidote to totalitarianism. It is concerned with the development of official structures and institutions that aim to deter or punish the biggest crimes known to humanity. If, however, social life is understood as a whole, without particular explanatory emphasis placed on one sphere or another, then it can be seen that the dichotomy between people-based strategies and institutionally based strategies begins to break down. A cosmopolitan politics that informs the struggles of people against totalitarianism is not counterposed to a cosmopolitan law that aims to create official structures that struggle against totalitarianism. Popular movements can be powerfully reinforced when global institutions add legitimacy to their claims over locally based tyranny. Arguments to the 'national interest' which aim to silence local opposition may be counteracted by the authority of cosmopolitan law. Supra-national responses may be called into existence, and made practicable, by local struggles. It is not necessary to choose between the local and the global, or between the official and the unofficial; but it is necessary to choose between cosmopolitan principles, those that are based on the fundamental equality of worth of all human beings, and particularist principles, those that assert the primacy of the claims of one group over another.

Douzinas argues that universal morality and cultural identity express different aspects of human experience,[8] and that the elevation of one over the other would result in a dangerous essentialism either of the universal or of the particular. 'Both principles, when they become absolute essences and define the meaning and value of culture without remainder or exception, can find everything that resists them expendable.'[9] The illustration he offers is the

8   Douzinas, 2000, p 138.
9   Douzinas, 2000, p 136.

futility of choosing between the Serbian massacres of Kosovars in the name of community and the Allied bombing of Serbia in the name of humanity. Douzinas says that he is not against external intervention to prevent genocide in principle, but he lays down a list of stringent conditions that such an intervention must meet in order to win his support.[10] 'None of these conditions exists today,' he admits, and 'it would be pious to expect that they will develop soon'. In the meantime, he will continue to watch genocides live on CNN, oppose military action to stop them, and yearn for the long distant future when the world has been radically remade; only then will he support external military intervention to save people from genocide.

Humanitarian intervention and cosmopolitan trials are two aspects of the same process: intervention is necessary if it is still possible to prevent or stop a crime against humanity, whereas a trial is necessary if that process has already failed and such a crime has actually taken place. The central legal claim is the same: an outside force claims the right to override the national sovereignty of the state where the crime takes place. For intervention this takes the form of sending in forces. For trials it takes the form of sending in investigators, and perhaps a force able to arrest suspects; the external court, anyway, claims jurisdiction within the state where the crime took place.

Douzinas is in favour of the concept of human rights but is against its actualisation. For him human rights are at their strongest when they are utopian and at their weakest when they are tied to institutions or actions in the existing world. The actualisation of a universal necessarily involves its particularisation. It becomes tied to particular interests and to particular projects. Appeals to universal values have often accompanied the greatest abuses of human rights. But each particularisation of a universal is distinct. The horrors of colonialism and Stalinism have been perpetrated in the name of universal values. American interventions into Vietnam, into Kosovo, into Afghanistan and into Iraq have been based on similar claims. International tribunals and human rights instruments are posited in the name of universal values. It is necessary to interrogate these claims closely rather than simply to disqualify all of them on the basis of the disqualification of some.

It is possible to defend a cosmopolitan approach to politics, one which is based on a fundamental human equality of right, without elevating that universal principle to an essential absolute which finds everything that resists it expendable. If we accept one claim to universality it does not bind us to accepting all claims to universality. The fact that the North Atlantic Treaty Organisation (NATO) intervention into Kosovo was done in the name of humanity and the Serbian campaign of ethnic cleansing against the Kosovars in the name of community does not make it impossible to make distinctions

---

10 'There must be a new international framework which will organise intervention independently of the interests of the powerful states; the role of governments and governmental organisations such as NATO should be minimised; non-governmental organisations should be actively involved in decision making; the aims and methods of the intervention should be removed from the power games of presidents, prime ministers and generals and focus on protecting individuals; the military should be in close contact with local democratic organisations and observers and should aim to enable them to protect civilians and help them overthrow the murderous regime; a clear set of guidelines should regulate the conduct of war and minimise casualties on all sides; such a war should aim to rescue the victims and prevent putting more people at risk and not to engage another government.' Douzinas, 2000, pp 140–41.

between the two. And the Kosovo intervention was not the Vietnam War, was not the Gulf War, was not the Second World War: it was itself.

Milosevic's claim that the campaign against the Kosovars was carried out for the protection of the community in Kosovo is currently being tested in court. It is a false claim; as is Douzinas' apparent claim that the conflict was more appropriately characterised as an equal fight between two fratricidal nationalisms[11] than as a campaign of ethnic cleansing by a Serbian state machine which had previously carried out other such campaigns and which had been brutally running Kosovo as a colony for 10 years.[12] And NATO's claim that the intervention was carried out for humanitarian reasons is in part credible. Undoubtedly, it was also motivated by a number of interests; an interest in stability; in preventing a huge 'refugee crisis' spilling over borders and destabilising neighbouring states; in thwarting Greater Serbian expansion; in developing, testing and showing off military power and technology; in diverting domestic electorates from domestic politics. NATO's strategy was also influenced by interests; centrally, the interest in not seeing NATO body bags arriving back home. In its decision to intervene, there was a component of self-interest and a component of political will to prevent a repetition of Bosnia and Srebrenica. It is necessary to judge each claim. Universals are necessarily particularised.

This book has considered exactly that process which compromises universal values: their actualisation in the world as it exists plunges them into arenas of competing powers and interests that often overwhelm them. This book is not a general defence of universal values but an effort to trace one set of their particularisations. I have argued that in cosmopolitan criminal law it is possible for universal values to find a worldly existence that is not wholly subverted by power and interest.

It is not enough to set out a list of conditions for humanitarian intervention or for humanitarian law which can never be met but which would, in an imaginary world, allow us to support such interventions. It is necessary to find ways of intervening to prevent genocide and ethnic cleansing in the world as it exists and not in the world as we would like it to exist. It is necessary to find ways of holding criminals like Milosevic to account in this world and not in the next. It is also necessary to find ways of holding to account individuals like Saddam and Sharon, Putin and Kissinger, Xiang Zemin and Pinochet. But principled opposition to all existing possibilities is not a serious way to relate to actual developments. We cannot stand aside from the world as it is in order to keep ourselves and our ideas pure:

> To recognise reason as the rose in the cross of the present and thereby to delight in the present – this rational insight is the reconciliation with actuality which philosophy grants to those who have received the inner call to comprehend ...[13]

This book is about tracing the trajectory of the development of cosmopolitan criminal law as it exists. Cosmopolitan law is hypocritical and unfair; it is saturated with *realpolitik* and the fear of the great powers; it is compromised by its partiality; it is crippled by its lack of money, resources, publicity and

---

11 Douzinas, 2000, p 137.
12 Demjaha, 2000, p 33.
13 Hegel, 1991, p 22.

political support. I do not want to reheat the old brew of cynical critique, nor do I want to weave utopian dreams of a world made safe by good policemen and judges; I have focused on existing developments, and searched for the rose in the cross of the present. There is a seed within the compromised present that is as radical and exciting as the dreams of the utopians; there are also trends, potentialities and events that are as dark and terrifying as the nightmares of the cynics.

The strongest critique of the existing cosmopolitan courts is that the process that decides who will be tried is entirely problematic. It is a critique not of the universalist values of the process but of the aspect in which it fails to be universal. The International Criminal Tribunal for the former Yugoslavia (ICTY) is possible because it does not threaten the interests of any of the great powers. There have been no trials of Americans for the Vietnam War, no trials of Russians for Chechnya, no trials of Chinese for Tibet. Is it possible for cosmopolitan courts to have any genuine independence from the great powers?

At the moment, there is not much independence, but there is some. The great powers, with their vetoes in the Security Council, are in control of where and when ad hoc tribunals are set up, and under the International Criminal Court (ICC) treaty they will be in control of where and when the ICC prosecutors will be allowed to investigate. However, that control is never absolute or guaranteed by the powers. Social institutions have emergent properties; they are never absolutely closed. Bourgeois domination of social life, in contrast to totalitarian domination, allows space and relative freedom for social institutions to change, develop and live. Even if human rights and due process were only rhetoric, the rhetoric itself would grant some space and autonomy to the institutions that are based upon it. It is clear that the judges and the prosecutors have a certain independence of action and decision. The judges are not told how to find. The chief prosecutor showed herself able to indict Milosevic at a moment during the Kosovo conflict when it might have been inconvenient for NATO. As Otto Kirchheimer[14] argues in relation to Nuremberg, one method available to the great powers of reacting to genocide is due process. The great powers allowed the ad hoc tribunals to administer a small part of their power by prosecuting some of those responsible for crimes against humanity. An event can be both a manifestation of power and a legal trial at the same time. It may be a means of asserting power, but not arbitrary power.

Can it be rightly argued that cosmopolitan law is nothing more than a means for pushing 'Western' values onto the rest of the world? It is particularly hard to make this criticism stick when discussing crimes against humanity. As far as I am aware, there is no one who argues that genocide is traditional in a particular 'culture', and that therefore the imperialist West has no right to march in and thrust its own values onto those for whom genocide is an age-old and legitimate way of life. If human rights mean anything, they mean that there is universal agreement that a social formation, a group of people, must not be allowed to murder entire populations. The argument that human rights are just the values of the rich does not fare much better with less extreme examples of threats than genocide, since human rights abuses are

14 Kirchheimer, 1969.

perpetrated by the powerful against the powerless. And the argument that human rights abuses are traditional within particular cultures, and should therefore not be criticised, leaves the voices for freedom within those 'cultures' isolated and unsupported. Such an argument is often, anyway, a misrepresentation of the actual 'traditions' of the 'culture' in question. It may be true that human rights are more likely to be enforced when they have powerful backers; it may also be true that many atrocities have been committed in the name of human rights; but these facts do not strip human rights of their legitimacy, nor do they show that human rights cannot act as powerful mobilising principles for the powerless.

Would people in imminent danger of genocide be better off relying on their own self-organisation than on the international community and cosmopolitan law? Would someone being mugged on the street be better off attempting to defend themselves, or waiting for the police or a criminal trial for their assailant? Certainly, there is a right to self-defence, and self-defence, if it is possible, must be legitimate. Crimes, however, are committed against people or groups who are unable to defend themselves, who are unable to stop the crimes being committed. If self-defence were always possible then law would be redundant. Conversely, if law were always effective, then self-defence would rarely be needed. There is no necessary conflict between international intervention from above and self-defence from below; a conflict is possible, but not inevitable.

There was a conflict in Bosnia between outside help and self-defence. For example, in Srebrenica the UN forces actively persuaded the Muslims to stay in their homes, and brokered an agreement of which it was a condition that the Muslims should disarm if they were to receive outside help. Similarly in Kosovo, those at risk of genocide were forced to disarm and give up their claims to statehood before international help was forthcoming. At the time of the war in Bosnia, there was some disagreement between the Americans, who leaned towards a policy of arming the Bosniaks so that they themselves would not need to intervene, and the Europeans, who wanted to keep the arms embargo in force as a price for their own 'help', thus disempowering the Muslims in particular, since the Serb forces were already well armed. Thus, it is not an argument that suggests that the international community should refrain from intervention on behalf of those at risk from the greatest imaginable crime, for fear that it might inhibit the efforts of the victims to defend themselves; neither is it an argument that suggests that when self-defence has been unsuccessful, the perpetrators of the crime should not be brought to justice. This experience warns people at risk to be mistrustful of those who suggest that they should sacrifice self-defence in order to encourage outside help. And it means that in some situations, such as that in Bosnia, the international community must be clearer about who is attacking whom and who is at risk of genocide from whom.

A policy of neutrality between criminal and victim will not do; neither will one that seeks to prevent unarmed victims from arming themselves in self-defence. At the same time, it is true that self-defence against a perceived threat of genocide will often take the form of nationalism, and that the most dangerous, exclusive and ethnic nationalisms always present themselves as being at a special and imminent risk of eradication from outside; aggression is often presented as self-defence. These points do not bolster an argument against cosmopolitan law. The best situation is one in which outside intervention and local self-defence bolster and reinforce each other; where legal proceedings against perpetrators strengthen and give confidence to indigenous movements, and those local campaigns and forces demand and thereby add strength and legitimacy to international help. When a group is in imminent danger of genocide they are, by definition, unable to defend themselves. Then, the world is faced with a choice: intervene or watch.

Is it possible for cosmopolitan trials to be fair trials? The jurisdiction that is organising the trial may not have state power where the offence was committed; witnesses may be hostile or intimidated; forensic evidence may be difficult to collect; there may be language barriers and a conflict of national cultures; judges may be biased, particularly in the absence of juries; witnesses may be politically motivated; rules of evidence may have to be looser than in national trials; media coverage can warp and infect testimony; witnesses can be provided by governments hostile to the defendant; the great powers can require certain politically useful verdicts. The best way I can answer this question is to say that the trials I have observed and reported in this book have been, more or less, as far as I can judge, fair trials; the courts have developed strategies to overcome these difficulties. The evidence presented here shows that it is harder to organise a fair trial under these circumstances, but it is possible. The judges I have observed, particularly in the *Sawoniuk*, *Tadic*, *Blaskic* and *Irving* cases, have appeared to be thoughtful and fair.

Are individuals scapegoated for crimes for which there is, in fact, much wider responsibility? The Lockerbie trial was held in the Netherlands, under Scottish law, to try two defendants who had been handed over by the Libyan state for the bombing of an American airliner. This trial seems to have exemplified some of the possible shortcomings of cosmopolitan law. It was, like the *Sawoniuk* and *Irving* cases, a hybrid of national and cosmopolitan justice. It seems, however, to have been more compromised by the requirements of *realpolitik* than the crimes against humanity trials that I have been discussing. One defendant was found guilty on shaky circumstantial evidence; the Libyan state, and its secret service, seem to have been offered some sort of *de facto* immunity in return for handing over the suspects; Britain and the USA want to appear to have secured justice in order to relieve the pressure put on them by the families of the victims. Now 'normal' relations between Britain and the USA and Libya can be resumed.[15]

The trials that I have reported in this book are not compromised in the same way as the Lockerbie trial. The conviction of Sawoniuk did not thereby exonerate Hitler; the conviction of Tadic did not exonerate Milosevic; the conviction of Blaskic did not exonerate Tudjman. While these three are certainly unlucky to have been brought to justice, given that the vast majority of their comrades have escaped, their sentences were not unjust. They were not scapegoats. The failure to try Hitler or Tudjman, while serious, does not make the trial of less central figures meaningless.

---

15 '[The UK Foreign Secretary] had earlier announced that he would support the suspension of international sanctions placed on Libya by the United Nations as soon as the [suspects] were handed over for trial. Colonel Gaddafi would have sought assurances ... that sanctions would not be reimposed at a later date, even if any testimony was offered during the trial suggesting a direct link between the bombing of Pan Am Flight 103 and the Libyan regime.' Wallis, 2001.

Against those who argue that international relations are only determined by power, I have argued that processes of decision making that rely on the authority and due process of law can also have influence.

Against those who argue that the only legitimate sovereign is the national state, I have argued that crimes against humanity have been recognised as the business of all human beings and therefore global institutions may develop that have jurisdiction within all states to prosecute such crimes.

Against those who argue that individual criminal responsibility for these crimes is just a legal fiction, I have argued that those who perpetrate crimes against humanity have had alternatives and that, while their alternatives may have been severely constrained, they still made free choices.

Against those who argue that cosmopolitan law is utopian, I have shown that in the ICTY and the ICTR, as well as in national courts, it is coming into being.

Against those who argue that the practical difficulties of organising fair trials for such crimes are insurmountable, I have presented evidence that fair trials are indeed being held.

Against those who argue that cosmopolitanism cannot hope to pull people away from their own sacred myths of nationhood, I have shown one mechanism by which a cosmopolitan social memory is being forged.

In the introduction to this book I asked whether there were sparks and flashes of cosmopolitanism in the darkness of totalitarianism; if they exist, what do they illuminate, and what is their significance? I have argued that in cosmopolitan criminal law, we can see coming into being one new way of challenging totalitarian horror. Rather than a smooth and institutional process of civilisation, I have argued that it is more appropriate to understand these trials as shards of light in the darkness. We do not know how things will develop; whether processes such as the Nuremberg tribunals, the ICTY and the International Criminal Tribunal for Rwanda will appear to history as the beginning of the coming of age of a new form of human regulation, or as compromised, isolated sparks in the darkness. But even if they do remain nothing more than historically isolated examples of flawed cosmopolitanism, their existence will still have been remarkable and profound, even if the sparks were unable to ignite a more enduring flame.

Bibliography

Adorno, TW, *Negative Dialectics*, 1973, London: Routledge and Kegan Paul

Allot, P, *Eunomia: New Order for a New World*, 2001, Oxford: OUP

Anderson, B, *Imagined Communities*, 1995, London: Verso

Anderson, DL, *Facing My Lai – Moving Beyond the Massacre*, 1998, Kansas: University Press of Kansas

Archibugi, D and Held, D (eds), *Cosmopolitan Democracy: An Agenda for a New World Order*, 1995, Cambridge: Polity

Arendt, H, *Eichmann in Jerusalem: A Report on the Banality of Evil*, 1994a, Harmondsworth: Penguin

Arendt, H, 'Understanding and politics', in *Essays in Understanding*, 1994b, New York: Harcourt Brace

Arendt, H, *The Life of the Mind*, 1978, New York: Harcourt Brace Jovanovich

Arendt, H, *The Origins of Totalitarianism*, 1975, San Diego: Harvest

Arendt, H and Jaspers, K, *Correspondence 1926–1969*, 1992, New York: Harcourt Brace Jovanovich

Asch, RG, *The Thirty Years War: The Holy Roman Empire and Europe, 1618–1648*, 1997, Basingstoke: Macmillan

Baldwin, J, 'Research on the criminal courts', in Kin, RD and Wincup, E (eds), *Doing Research on Crime and Justice*, 2000, Oxford: OUP

Bass, GJ, *Stay the Hand of Vengeance*, 2000, Princeton: Princeton UP

Bassiouni, MC, *Crimes against Humanity in International Criminal Law*, 1999, The Hague: Kluwer Law International

Bauman, Z, *Postmodern Ethics*, 1996, Oxford: Blackwell

Bauman, Z, *Modernity and the Holocaust*, 1993, Cambridge: Polity

Beck, U, *What is Globalization?*, 1999, Cambridge: Polity

Berk-Seligson, S, *The Bilingual Courtroom*, 1990, Chicago: Chicago UP

Bernard-Donals, M and Glejzer, R, *Between Witness and Testimony: The Holocaust and the Limits of Representation*, 2001, Albany: State University of New York Press

Bilton, M and Sim, K, *Four Hours in My Lai*, 1992, London: Penguin

Bland, MA, 'An analysis of the United Nations international tribunal to adjudicate war crimes committed in the former Yugoslavia: parallels, problems, prospects' (1994) 2(1) Indiana Journal of Global Studies 1

Bohman, J and Lutz-Bachmann, M (eds), *Perpetual Peace: Essays on Kant's Cosmopolitan Ideal*, 1997, Cambridge, Mass: MIT Press

Browning, C, *Ordinary Men*, 1993, New York: HarperCollins

Bullock, A, *Hitler: A Study in Tyranny*, 1983, Harmondsworth: Penguin

Burgess, RG, *In the Field: An Introduction to Field Research*, 1993, London: Routledge

Cargas, HJ, *In Conversation with Elie Wiesel*, 1976, New York: Paulist

Chalk, F, 'Redefining genocide', in Andreopoulos, GJ (ed), *Genocide*, 1994, Philadelphia: University of Pennsylvania Press

Chandler, D, *From Kosovo to Kabul*, 2002, London: Pluto

Charny, IW, 'Toward a generic definition of genocide', in Andreopoulos, GJ (ed), *Genocide*, 1994, Philadelphia: University of Pennsylvania Press

Chomsky, N, *The New Military Humanism: Lessons from Kosovo*, 1999, London: Pluto

Cigar, N, *Genocide in Bosnia: The Policy of 'Ethnic Cleansing'*, 1995, College Station: Texas A & M UP

Clark, RS, 'Crimes against humanity at Nuremberg', in Ginsburgs, G and Kudriavtsev, VN (eds), *The Nuremberg Trial and International Law*, 1990, Dordrecht: Martinus Nijhoff

Coates, K (ed), *Ethical Imperialism: The War after the War*, 1999, Nottingham: Bertrand Russell Peace Foundation

Cohen, S, *States of Denial: Knowing about Atrocities and Suffering*, 2001, Cambridge: Polity

Cotic, D, 'Introduction' (1994) 5(2–3) Criminal Law Forum 223

Cotler, I (ed), *Nuremberg Forty Years Later: The Struggle against Injustice in Our Time*, 1995, Montreal: McGill-Queen's UP

David Irving v Penguin Books and Professor Deborah Lipstadt, The Irving Judgement, 2000, London: Penguin

Demjaha, A, 'The Kosovo conflict: a perspective from inside', in Schnabel, A and Thakur, R (eds), *Kosovo and the Challenge of Humanitarian Intervention*, 2000, Tokyo: United Nations UP

Destexhe, A, *Rwanda and Genocide in the Twentieth Century*, 1995, London: Pluto

Douglas, L, *The Memory of Judgment: Making Law and History in the Trials of the Holocaust*, 2001, New Haven: Yale UP

Douzinas, C, *The End of Human Rights*, 2000, Oxford: Hart

Evans, RJ, *Telling Lies about Hitler*, 2002, London: Verso

Fein, H, *Genocide: A Sociological Perspective*, 1993, London: Sage

Fine, R, 'Cosmopolitanism and social theory' (2002a) European Journal of Social Theory, forthcoming publication

Fine, R, *Political Investigations: Hegel, Marx, Arendt*, 2001, London: Routledge

Fine, R, 'Crimes against humanity: Hannah Arendt and the Nuremberg debates' (2000) 3(3) European Journal of Social Theory 293

Fine, R, 'The "new nationalism" and democracy: a critique of *pro patria*' (1994) 1(3) Democratisation 423

Fine, R, *Democracy and the Rule of Law*, 1984, London: Pluto

Fine, R and Hirsh, D, 'The decision to commit a crime against humanity', in Archer, M and Tritter, J (eds), *Rational Choice Theory: Resisting Colonization*, 2000, London: Routledge

Finkelstein, N, *The Holocaust Industry*, 2000, London: Verso

Finkielkraut, A, *Remembering in Vain: The Klaus Barbie Trial and Crimes against Humanity*, 1992, New York: Columbia UP

Forsythe, DP, 'Politics and the international tribunal for the former Yugoslavia' (1994) 5(2–3) Criminal Law Forum 401

Foster, K, *Fighting Fictions: War, Narrative and National Identity*, 1999, London: Pluto

Foucault, M, *Discipline and Punish*, 1991, Harmondsworth: Penguin

Freeman, M, 'The theory and prevention of genocide' (1991) 6(2) Holocaust and Genocide Studies 185

Fukuyama, F, *The End of History and the Last Man*, 1992, Harmondsworth: Penguin

Fuller, LL, *The Morality of Law*, 1969, New Haven: Yale UP

Gellner, E, *Conditions of Liberty*, 1994, London: Hamish Hamilton

Gellner, E, *Nations and Nationalism*, 1983, Oxford: Blackwell

Gerth, HH and Mills, CW (eds), *Max Weber – Essays in Sociology*, 1991, London: Routledge

Giddens, A, *The Nation State and Violence*, 1985, Cambridge: Polity

Ginsburgs, G and Kudriavtsev, VN (eds), *The Nuremberg Trial and International Law*, 1990, Dordrecht: Martinus Nijhoff

Goldhagen, DJ, *Hitler's Willing Executioners*, 1996, London: Little, Brown

Goldstone, RJ, *For Humanity*, 2000, New Haven: Yale UP

Goodrich, P, *Legal Discourse*, 1987, London: Macmillan

Gutman, R, *A Witness to Genocide: The First Inside Account of the Horrors of 'Ethnic Cleansing' in Bosnia*, 1993, Shaftesbury, Dorset: Element

Guttenplan, DD, *The Holocaust on Trial*, 2002, London: Granta

Habermas, J, *The Postnational Constellation: Political Essays*, 2001, Cambridge: Polity

Habermas, J, 'Historical consciousness and post-traditional identity', in *The New Conservatism*, 1991, Cambridge: Polity

Habermas, J, *The Theory of Communicative Action, Vol 2: Critique of Functionalist Reason*, 1987, Cambridge: Polity

Havel, V, 'Anti-political politics', in Keane, J (ed), *Civil Society and the State*, 1993, London: Verso

Hegel, GWF, *Elements of the Philosophy of Right*, Wood, AW (ed), Nisbet, HB (trans), 1991, Cambridge: CUP

Held, D, 'Law of states, law of peoples: three models of sovereignty' (2002) 2 Legal Theory 1

Held, D, *Democracy and the Global Order*, 1995, Cambridge: Polity

Higgins, R, *Problems and Process: International Law and How We Use It*, 1999, Oxford: OUP

Hirsh, D, 'The trial of Andrei Sawoniuk: Holocaust testimony under cross-examination' (2001) 10(4) Social and Legal Studies 529

Hobsbawm, EJ, *Nations and Nationalism since 1780: Programme, Myth, Reality*, 1995, Cambridge: CUP

Hoffman, S, 'Foreword', in Bull, H, *The Anarchical Society*, 2nd edn, 1995, Basingstoke: Macmillan

Honig, JW and Both, N, *Srebrenica: Record of a War Crime*, 1996, Harmondsworth: Penguin

Hoog, G and Steinmetz, A, *International Conventions on Protection of Humanity and Environment*, 1993, Berlin: Walter de Gruyter

Hukanovic, R, *The Tenth Circle of Hell*, 1997, London: Little, Brown

Ignatieff, M, *Human Rights as Politics and Idolatry*, 2001, Princeton: Princeton UP

Irving, D, *Hitler's War*, 1977, 1st edn, New York: Viking; 2nd edn, 1991, London: Macmillan

Jackson, RH, *International Conference on Military Trials*, 1949, Washington DC: Department of State Publication 3080

Jaspers, K, *The Question of German Guilt*, 2000, Fordham: Fordham UP

Joyner, CC, 'Enforcing human rights standards in the former Yugoslavia: the case for an international war crimes tribunal' (1994) 22(2–3) Denver Journal of International Law and Policy 239

Kaldor, M, *New and Old Wars: Organized Violence in a Global Era*, 1999, London: Polity

Kant, I, 'Perpetual peace', in Reiss, H (ed), *Kant: Political Writings*, Nisbet, HB (trans), 1991, Cambridge: CUP

Katz, S, *Post-Holocaust Dialogues*, 1983, New York: New York UP

Kirchheimer, O, *Political Justice: The Use of Legal Procedure for Political Ends*, 1969, Princeton: Princeton UP

Kolodkin, RA, 'An ad hoc international tribunal for the prosecution of serious violations of international humanitarian law in the former Yugoslavia' (1994) 5(2–3) Criminal Law Forum 381

Kontou, N, *The Termination and Revision of Treaties in the Light of New Customary International Law*, 1994, Oxford: Clarendon

Koskenniemi, M, *The Gentle Civilizer of Nations: The Rise and Fall of International Law 1870–1960*, 2001, Cambridge: CUP

Kuper, L, *Genocide: Its Political Use in the Twentieth Century*, 1982, New Haven: Yale UP

Kushen, R and Harris, KJ, 'Surrender of fugitives by the United States to the war crimes tribunals for Yugoslavia and Rwanda' (1997) 90 American Journal of International Law 510

Lauterpacht, H, *International Law and Human Rights*, 1950, London: Stevens

LeBlanc, LJ, *The United States and the Genocide Convention*, 1991, Durham and London: Duke UP

Levi, P, *If This is a Man*, 1987, London: Abacus

Lipstadt, D, *Denying the Holocaust: The Growing Assault on Truth and Memory*, 1st edn, 1993, New York: Free Press; 2nd edn, 1994, Harmondsworth: Penguin

Lukashuk, II, 'Crimes against peace', in Ginsburgs, G and Kudriavtsev, VN (eds), *The Nuremberg Trial and International Law*, 1990, Dordrecht: Martinus Nijhoff

Markusen, E and Kopf, D, *The Holocaust and Strategic Bombing: Genocide and Total War in the Twentieth Century*, 1995, Boulder: Westview

Meron, T, 'International humanitarian law and human rights law', in Warner, D (ed), *Human Rights and Humanitarian Law: The Quest for Universality*, 1997, The Hague: Martinus Nijhoff

Meron, T, 'War crimes in Yugoslavia and the development of international law' (1994) 88(1) American Journal of International Law 78

Minow, M, *Between Vengeance and Forgiveness: Facing History after Genocide and Mass Violence*, 1998, Boston: Beacon Press

Murphy, JF, 'Crimes against peace at the Nuremberg trial', in Ginsburgs, G and Kudriavtsev, VN (eds), *The Nuremberg Trial and International Law*, 1990, Dordrecht: Martinus Nijhoff

Neff, SC, 'Rescue across state boundaries: international legal aspects of rescue', in Menlowe, MA and McCall Smith, A (eds), *The Duty to Rescue: The Jurisprudence of Aid*, 1993, Aldershot: Dartmouth

Neumann, F, *Behemoth: The Structure and Practice of National Socialism 1933–1944*, 1963, New York: Octagon

Nussbaum, N, 'Kant and cosmopolitanism', in Bohman, J and Lutz-Bachmann, M (eds), *Perpetual Peace: Essays on Kant's Cosmopolitan Ideal*, 1997, Cambridge, Mass: MIT Press

O'Shea, B, *Crisis at Bihac: Bosnia's Bloody Battlefield*, 1998, Stroud, Gloucestershire: Sutton

Piccigallo, PR, *The Japanese on Trial*, 1979, Austin: University of Texas Press

Pictet, J, *Development and Principles of International Humanitarian Law*, 1985, Dordrecht: Martinus Nijhoff

Pomorski, S, 'Conspiracy and criminal organization', in Ginsburgs, G and Kudriavtsev, VN (eds), *The Nuremberg Trial and International Law*, 1990, Dordrecht: Martinus Nijhoff

Provost, R, *International Human Rights and Humanitarian Law*, 2002, Cambridge: CUP

Reshetov, A, 'International law and crimes against the laws and customs of war', in Ginsburgs, G and Kudriavtsev, VN (eds), *The Nuremberg Trial and International Law*, 1990, Dordrecht: Martinus Nijhoff

Robertson, G, *Crimes against Humanity*, 1999, London: Penguin

Rosenberg, A and Silverman, E, 'The issue of the Holocaust as a unique event', in Dobkowski, M and Wallimann, I (eds), *Genocide in Our Time*, 1992, Ann Arbor: Pierian Press

Russell, B, *War Crimes in Vietnam*, 1967, London: Allen & Unwin

Salter, M, 'The visibility of the Holocaust: Franz Neumann and the Nuremberg trials', in Fine, R and Turner, C (eds), *Social Theory after the Holocaust*, 2000, Liverpool: Liverpool UP

Sartre, J-P, *War Crimes in Vietnam*, 1970, Nottingham: Bertrand Russell Peace Foundation

Scruton, R, *A Dictionary of Political Thought*, 1982, London: Macmillan

Shapiro, S (ed), *Truth Prevails: Demolishing Holocaust Denial: The End of 'The Leuchter Report'*, 1990, New York: Beate Klarsfeld Foundation and Holocaust Survivors & Friends in Pursuit of Justice

Sheftel, Y, *Show Trial: The Conspiracy to Convict John Demjanjuk as 'Ivan the Terrible'*, 1998, London: Gollancz

Smith, BF, *Reaching Judgement at Nuremberg*, 1977, London: André Deutsch

Stone, D, 'Holocaust testimony and the challenge to the philosophy of history', in Fine, R and Turner, C (eds), *Social Theory after the Holocaust*, 2000, Liverpool: Liverpool UP

Tachibana, R, *Narrative as Counter-Memory*, 1998, Albany: State University of New York Press

Taylor, K, 'Irving in denial: the trial', in Taylor, K (ed), *Holocaust Denial: The David Irving Trial and International Revisionism*, 2000, London: Searchlight Educational Trust

van Pelt, RJ and Dwork, D, *Auschwitz, 1270 to the Present*, 1996, New Haven: Yale UP

Vertovec, S and Cohen, R (eds), *Conceiving Cosmopolitanism*, 2002, Oxford: OUP

Vulliamy, E, *Seasons in Hell: Understanding Bosnia's War*, 1994, London: Simon & Schuster

Wagenaar, W, *Identifying Ivan: A Case Study in Legal Psychology*, 1988, London: Harvester Wheatsheaf

Wallis, R, *Lockerbie: The Story and the Lessons*, 2001, Westport, Connecticut: Praeger

Weisbord, RG, *Genocide? Birth Control and the Black American*, 1975, Westport, Connecticut: Greenwood Press

Wiesel, E, *Night*, 1981, Harmondsworth: Penguin

Zoller, E, 'International criminal responsibility of individuals for international crimes', in Ginsburgs, G and Kudriavtsev, VN (eds), *The Nuremberg Trial and International Law*, 1990, Dordrecht: Martinus Nijhoff

Conference papers and seminars

Buisman, C, 'Self-governed international criminal tribunals: are they in need of a constitutional court?', conference paper, Sociolegal Studies Association Conference, Bristol, 4–6 April 2001

Douzinas, C, 'Human rights: utopian or scientific', conference paper, Critical Legal Conference, London Metropolitan University, 6 September 2002

Evans, RJ, After the Trial, seminar organised by the Wiener Library at Birkbeck College, 25 June 2000

Fine, R, 'Holocaust trials and the origins of cosmopolitan law', conference paper, Critical Legal Conference, London Metropolitan University, 7 September 2002b

Geras, N, 'Singular question, singular crime', conference paper, Social Theory after the Holocaust, Warwick University, 5 February 1998

Julius, A, at After The Trial, seminar organised by the Wiener Library at Birkbeck College, 25 June 2000

Norrie, A, 'International justice as an emergent property', conference paper, Critical Legal Conference, London Metropolitan University, 7 September 2002

Human Rights Watch reports

Civilian Deaths in the NATO Air Campaign, 2000, Vol 12 No 1, New York: Human Rights Watch

Humanitarian Law Violations in Kosovo, 1999, New York: Human Rights Watch

Newspaper articles

Cesarini, D, 'At home with hatred' (1999) *The Sunday Times*, 4 April

Dodd, V, 'Deportation, not trial, for Nazi war crimes suspect' (2000) *The Guardian*, 4 January

Freedland, J, 'Court 73 – where history is on trial' (2000) *The Guardian*, 5 February

'Génocide rwandais: les quatre accusus reconnus coupables' (2001) *Le Monde*, 8 June

Hamilton, A, 'Jury's journey to a world between past and present' (1999) *The Times*, 2 April

Jones, T, 'Sawoniuk stood by as I begged for life' (1998) *The Times*, 3 March

Keller, A (ed), (2002) Nos 103–4, *The Other Israel*, July–August

'Message to Mladic' (1994) *The Times*, 2 November, p 15

'Prime mission of UN in Bosnia; Letter' (1994) *The Times*, 2 November, p 19

Traynor, I, 'War crimes trial finds Bosnian Serb guilty' (1997) *The Guardian*, 8 May

Film

Lanzmann, C, *Shoah*, Les Films Aleph, Paris, 1985

Television programmes

'A Bosnian betrayal', *Dispatches*, Channel 4, 1996

Newsnight, BBC2, 12 April 2000

'The killing of Kosovo', *Panorama*, BBC1, 28 April 1999

Official publications

Hansard, House of Commons Debates, Vol 127, 8 February 1988, London: HMSO

Hetherington, T (Sir), *Report of the War Crimes Inquiry*, 16 June 1989, London: HMSO

Index